BOOKS BY LOIS MARK STALVEY

The Education of an Ordinary Woman   1982
Getting Ready   1974
The Education of a W.A.S.P.   1970

The Education of an Ordinary Woman

Lois Mark Stalvey

THE
EDUCATION
OF AN
ORDINARY
WOMAN

NEW YORK

Atheneum

1982

LIBRARY OF CONGRESS CATALOGING IN PUBLICATION DATA

Stalvey, Lois Mark.
The education of an ordinary woman.

1. Stalvey, Lois Mark.   2. United States—Biography.
I. Title.

CT275.S657A33   1982   973.92'092'4 [B]   81-66039
ISBN 0-689-11143-6   AACR2

Published simultaneously in Canada by McClelland and Stewart Ltd.
Composition by American–Stratford Graphic Services, Inc., Brattleboro, Vermont
Manufactured by Fairfield Graphics, Fairfield, Pennsylvania
Designed by Mary Cregan
First Edition

This book is dedicated to my father.

Author to Reader

The people you will meet in this book are real. In order to write honestly and still protect their privacy, I have changed names and physical descriptions, including the names of my immediate family.

There are, however, many people who helped generously with my education and whom I would like to thank publicly. Among them are Conrad Stawski, the former Mildred Wulff, Richard Mayer, Josephine Lane, Joseph Deglman, Emmanuel Kroog, Evelyn Zysman, Bernard Miller, Edna Lee Smalls, Joan McGuinn Thurmon, Ann Vigilante Schoonmaker, John Howe, Perry Knight, Hal Libros, Trudi Mayer Dubis, and, most especially, Leo C. Freeman—and the Milwaukee Public Library system.

Thanks go too to my agent, Claire Smith, whose belief and realism sustained me; to my editor, Judith Kern, for her patience and perception; and to my friend Jean Gregg Milgram, whose tireless support made all the difference.

I want to thank my three children, who made being their mother the most challenging and satisfying education of all.

The Education of an Ordinary Woman

Chapter 1

I HAD NO SENSE of foreboding that day in 1928 as Mother and I prepared to cross in the middle of the busy Milwaukee street on which we lived. A three-year-old child can fail to perceive a parent's preoccupation.

Obediently, I held the side of my baby brother's carriage. Through the traffic I could glimpse the storefronts across the street. Inside were the friendly shopkeepers who had made being a little girl the best thing in the world. But mostly I could see only the muddy-green wicker side of the carriage, the gray curb, and the dark-brown cobblestones glazed with dirty snow.

We were crossing in front of the tire store that my father was trying to run successfully. Daddy had just helped us down the long, narrow stairway from the apartment above it, which was our home.

Mother tipped the carriage to ease it off the curb. I looked up at her for reassurance. Mother's face was the center of my world. Her blue eyes and light-brown hair meant food, comfort, safety. It was also an impassive face. If she felt anguish, confusion, or irresolvable conflicts that day, those feelings would not have shown.

Eager to reach the friendly butcher toward whom we were heading, I asked permission to run ahead. Mother nodded. I ran from the blind side of the carriage, feeling excited but secure.

The car that hit me had a shiny black fender. There was no

physical pain. My physical injuries, if any, were slight. But as I looked up at the circle of faces above me, my world shifted. At three, I had no words to express—even to myself—my loss of faith in the one person I had expected to protect me. There was only a vague but overwhelming sense of loneliness and loss.

I screamed for my father. In moments I was in his arms, and there I intended to stay. A doctor examined me on Daddy's lap.

For the next few weeks I followed my father everywhere. I attacked the barber when he brought a pair of scissors toward my father's head, biting his leg and climbing the chair to throw my arms protectively around Father. Father postponed the haircut.

He could not postpone what soon followed. Even a three-year-old senses a troubled marriage. Angry voices late at night woke me. So did nightmares—I screamed when hair from the barbershop filled the air to choke me, when my stuffed animals turned wild, attacking Mother, Daddy, and me.

Then one icy January night, Mother told me we were going to Grandfather's house "for a visit." But why were there so many suitcases, and why had Uncle Carl come to get us?

Daddy did not want us to go. Uncle Carl's voice got louder. I held my ears. When he hit Daddy, I hurled myself into the tangle of trousered legs, kicking Uncle Carl's. His push slid me across the linoleum and under a table. Daddy reached down and picked me up.

"Lois, honey, it'll be all right. I'll come to get you tomorrow."

No!

As I sobbed in Daddy's arms, I noticed that Mother, my baby brother, and the suitcases were already gone. Uncle Carl was now pulling at my arm. Father said, "Go now, darling. I *promise* I'll come get you tomorrow." Daddy always kept promises, but I was not leaving!

Then I was helplessly head down under Uncle Carl's arm, my kicking legs hitting the railing as he carried me downstairs. Someone held me down in the car. I could see only black floorboards with a gearshift protruding—then the snow and ashes of the steps to Grandfather's house and, inside, a brown oak door that my fists could not open.

Father did not come "tomorrow." That night he was lying, unconscious, on an icy road. He had collided with a truck on his way to enlist his brothers' help. He would be unconscious for three weeks and in the hospital for a year.

4

No one told me of the accident as I waited at the window for Daddy to come. I was told only, "Forget him. He doesn't love you." I stayed at the window.

Only Uncle Irv could occasionally persuade me to leave my vigil. In the dour German immigrant family Grandfather ruled, only my Catholic father and my Jewish Uncle Irv had ever laughed, teased, or cuddled me. Finally, as the weeks spun out to eternity, I left the window and transferred my love to Uncle Irv. Mother, Grandmother, and Irv's wife, Aunt May, were involved with May's pregnancy, but Uncle Irv had time for a little girl confused by adult events. For two glorious months I played in his store as I had played in my father's.

In 1929 pneumonia was an untreatable illness. Big, robust, twenty-seven-year-old Uncle Irv contracted it. No visits to his store, I was told. Uncle Irv had to stay in bed.

Then, on a cloudy March day, the black candlestick telephone at Grandfather's house rang. Grandmother answered it and then quickly called Grandfather's office, where Mother now worked. I stood at the edge of the living-room carpet, listening to Grandmother saying Uncle Irv was dead.

She began to phone others who needed to know. I remained at the edge of the carpet, sure that if I moved I would fall into some swirling black abyss. My brother cried upstairs. Grandmother pushed me aside to go to him. I was surprised that I had been moved and could still breathe.

But as I stood, allowing this new pain to join the others, my four-year-old's mind absorbed a single reality: that I was alone and responsible for my own survival.

In 1979, as my plane from Egypt approached New York, I grinned. I had just completed a list of goals set in my twenties: to go abroad, to publish a book, and to have a baby. Once, I had expected to complete the list in that order. Instead, I had reversed it—had three babies, published two books; and now, in my fifties, I was returning from a trip abroad to a new set of goals.

I hoped.

The 747 had been bucking and tilting for an hour and we were overdue for landing. A voice came over the speaker: "Severe storms along the east coast, but no reason to be alarmed." I wasn't. I had always felt safer on a plane than on a freeway.

Then: "All east coast airports are closed. But we have an hour's fuel and I'm going to try to make it to an inland airport."

I would have preferred a more positive word than *try*. But as I looked out at the dark-gray swirl around our plane, I felt an unexpected serenity. Planes did crash, and this one might, but in the dead silence that had now taken over the cabin, I thought of what I had told my now-grown children before I left.

Josh, twenty, had said, "Look, Mom, you'll be in a foreign country. Try not to stir up anything dangerous over there." Tige, twenty-two, had chuckled, "Tell Josh to let *Egypt* worry." Tina, nineteen, had said, "Planes *do* crash, Mom."

Cliché reassurances would not satisfy Tina; besides, there was something I wanted each of them to know. "If anything does ever happen to me," I said then, "I want you to know that I have had an absolutely wonderful life. Unfortunately, some people can't say that, but I can. I've come as close to having it all as anyone I know."

Now, put to the test, I knew I had not lied. I glanced at my watch. In about fifty minutes I planned to start fighting like hell to extend that life, but if this was the end, I had indeed had more than my money's worth.

The plane bucked again. There had been no more words from the pilot and twenty minutes had passed. But my inappropriate serenity persisted. Yes, I would miss knowing how my children's lives turned out, but my sons were capable and well on their way.

And then I thought about Tina.

Had I taught her enough about being a woman? She might have to struggle alone in a confusing world. Some people would tell her that man was the enemy—or the master; that being a woman was a handicap like being born lame. If she believed that, she could go through life fighting all the wrong battles.

I closed my eyes to visualize Tina's pretty and strong young face —and then I could smile. Tina would make it. Her childhood had been entirely different from mine, but she had been born a fighter. She would take detours as I had, make mistakes different from— and similar to—mine. But she would use her level little head and survive.

When the plane landed safely in Pittsburgh, however, I knew why I intended to write this book.

Even in the 1920s, child psychologists would have rushed to rescue me from the bleak block of Kinnickinnic Avenue in Milwaukee, Wisconsin, where I spent the first three years of my life.

Not a tree or a blade of grass was visible between the storefronts. I was the only child on the block. Other families had moved to "better surroundings in which to raise children." But from 1925 to 1928 I thought I was the luckiest child in the world.

My bedroom looked out on storefronts. Trolleys clanked by. At night, a blinking movie marquee lit my room with pretty colored lights, and, day or night, there were people to watch. If my teddy bear and I were too wide awake to sleep, I could tiptoe quietly to the windowsill. It was low, just right for my elbows. On warm nights I could hear people laugh.

During the day, the block was my playground, rich with sounds, sights, and smells. Mr. Brunner, the shoemaker, let me dab pungent glue on soles and whack his hammer on heels. The druggist, Mr. Foch, mixed beautiful liquids in bottles that he held up to the light. The ice-cream parlor was my favorite. I could smell chocolate bubbling in the kitchen and take deep breaths of the special sweetness of marble tables that had absorbed years of spills.

I knew I was something called a girl. Mother said, "Be a *good* little girl." Daddy hugged me and called me his "darling girl." Shopkeepers smiled and asked, "How's our girl today?" A girl, I decided, was the right thing to be. There were also creatures called boys. We had one—the result, I felt, of a huge adult mistake.

Mother had said, "We've ordered a present for you from the stork—a brand-new baby brother."

I had a fine relationship with Santa Claus and the Easter Bunny, but who was this stork? And why did anyone think I wanted a baby around? I had seen some when they passed through our block in carriages. They made strange noises and smelled.

It was apparently too late to cancel my "present." One day, after Mother had gotten terribly fat, Daddy drove us to Grandfather's house. Mother went upstairs to a bedroom, where I was not allowed to go. A woman in a white dress came through the living room where I had been told to stay. She patted the small satchel she carried and said, "I'm bringing a baby in here for you."

Later, a man with his own black satchel said the same thing. I was horrified. "No, thank you, I have one already." Daddy heard me, hugged me, and laughed.

That evening I was put in Grandfather's big, overstuffed chair and my "present" was put in my lap. This was Bobby, Grandma said, and how did I like my new brother? A circle of smiling faces

7

waited for my answer. It was naughty to lie. I looked at him closely.

"He's so little. He can't talk. He can't walk and he hasn't any teeth." Soon I would find another serious flaw in Bobby.

Back home in our apartment, I learned quickly that Bobby affected my daily life hardly at all. As I had expected, he did nothing but cry and create smelly diapers. Mother tended him while I continued my life on the block. Unlike Bobby, I could talk, walk, and use my little potty so that I did not smell. No wonder Daddy spent more time with me than with Bobby.

In Daddy's tire store downstairs, we were seldom interrupted by customers. In our low-income neighborhood and in 1928, Daddy was recklessly ahead of the times. He was right about the future of the automobile, but even Daddy, with his gregarious warmth, could not sell tires to people without cars. Folks met there to chat, but not to buy. I played in the black-rubber circles and watched Daddy make sad-faced people laugh. Sometimes when no one at all came in, Daddy would pull down the shade on the front door, pick me up in his arms, and take me to his car. From his lap I could see streets, trees, people, and, at last, the lake. I played in the sand of Lake Michigan while Daddy watched me and the waves.

Some days when lots of people were in the store, I went about my own business. Mr. Brunner sometimes had shoes for me to take to people on our block. Miss Ellen, who worked in the candy store, sent notes to Mr. Ted, the grocer. Mr. Ted paid me in apples, but the others gave me pennies. Heading for the candy store to spend them, I would look across the street at the new "charity" store. People in ragged clothes lined up with small wagons to get flour, canned goods, and peanut butter. Daddy told me these people were "poor" and that a church was helping them. Clutching my pennies, I knew I was "rich" and that being poor was actively to be avoided. The thought of sharing my candy with poor children posed no dilemma. I was not allowed to cross the street.

The street separating our block from the "charity store" was the northern boundary of my territory. The shoe store was my boundary to the south. On the way I could stop at Mr. Cohen's furniture store and play among the big boxes in his storeroom. At the shoe store, Mr. Corelli might hold me up to his new X-ray fitting machine while I watched him wiggle the bones in his feet.

Outside his store, I could look across to a block of houses with lawns, trees, and children who were also not allowed to cross the street between us. I felt sorrier for those children than the ones in the charity line. I had my street of shopkeeper playmates; they had no one but each other.

On Sundays when all my stores were closed, Father and I went to his church. Later in the day, I would go with Mother and Grandfather to *their* church while Grandma tended Bobby. Daddy's Catholic church was much more fun. There were vivid colors, the smell of incense, and rhythmic chants. A man in a pretty costume moved around a lot up front. So did Daddy and the people around us—kneeling, standing, sitting, and then kneeling again. Beads clicked in Daddy's hand and people made crisscross motions across their chests. At Grandfather's church there was a lot less going on.

After sitting as still as I could in Grandfather's church, we went to his house for dinner. Again, I was the only child among adults, but these adults were different. My aunts talked in one corner. Uncle Bernard, Uncle Carl, and Grandfather talked (mostly in German) in another. Only Daddy and Aunt May's husband, Uncle Irv, had time to play.

If I wandered into the kitchen, I was told to play in the yard but not to get my Sunday clothes dirty. There was no way to *get* dirty in Grandfather's yard. The flower beds had fences around them. The straight cement path to the back (locked) gate was swept clean of pretty leaves and funny twigs. A high green hedge kept me from seeing beyond the yard.

I would "get some fresh air" as I had been told to do, then return with relief to Daddy and Uncle Irv and their cigar smoke. On one of their laps I would fall asleep and wake up at home, where I wanted to be.

On Monday I was back to the happy bustle of my block, meeting the mailman at the end of his route, hiding in his big leather sack to be "delivered" to Daddy. "One hundred dollars, C.O.D.," Mr. Volkman would say. "Worth every penny," Daddy said with a laugh.

The day Mother said I could "help" her bathe Bobby, I politely agreed. On a high stool near his Bathinette, I sat ready to hand Mother the soap or the towel. But as she undressed him, I saw immediately that something was terribly wrong! I had expected his body to be as neatly made as mine. Instead, he had

9

strange growths between his little kicking legs, wrinkled bulging lumps and, attached to them, something that looked like a funny broken thumb.

I looked up at Mother. She must have noticed that something was wrong. When she helped me bathe, she could see I was properly made, my necessary little holes concealed and protected. What could be done for poor Bobby?

Then I remembered Aunt May talking to Mother about "circumcision." Maybe that was the cure. The doctor, Mother had said, was coming that day. When he did, Mother and the doctor took Bobby into the bedroom and closed the door. Bobby screamed extra-hard. At his next bath there was a bandage around his deformity.

But when the bandage finally came off, I knew the operation had been a failure. The growths were still there. Poor Bobby! He might have to live with those dangling parts for the rest of his life.

My concern for Bobby's plight ended abruptly on the day I crossed the street with Mother and was hit by the car. It receded further when I was torn away from my father

When Uncle Irv died, my aloneness was complete. Daddy had not come back to get me. Uncle Irv was gone. Life at Grandfather's house was going to be very different from my life on the block that I loved. I still watched from the window for Daddy. Sometimes when the light was right, I could see my reflection. At least she smiled back. I touched her face on the sun-warmed glass. Perhaps between the two of us, we would learn to survive.

Chapter 2

WHILE MOTHER RETURNED to work in Grandpa's office and Grandma tended Bobby, I was allowed to explore my new neighborhood, but not, of course, to cross the street. I stood on the deserted sidewalk, looking yearningly across to the grocery store on one corner and the drugstore on the other. Otherwise Grandfather's block had nothing but houses, dark-painted boxes that all looked alike. I had tried visiting one. A big, broad woman answered my knock. Wiping her hands on her apron, she looked down at me with a frown. I was not invited to come inside.

Three children lived on the street, but they were big and went to school. The boys, Buddy and Johnny, never came near me. Rosalie sometimes stopped by for a while, but she soon went home.

I tried to play with Bobby as soon as he could walk and talk. But he bit and hit my dolls. When I hit him back, Grandma hit me. And then Bobby got sick. Once again I heard the word *pneumonia*. If Bobby died like Uncle Irv, perhaps they would give me his room. I didn't like sleeping with Mother. She snored and rolled on me.

Dr. Jimmy came every day to see Bobby. Then he was taken away. "The hospital," Grandmother said, and she cried. But Bobby came back, better but terribly cross. From his bed he called to Grandma all day long, but if I took him his drink of water or his glass of milk, he screamed. When Mother came home from work and went straight to his room, he screamed if I followed her in. I sat outside the door while she read to him so that I could hear the stories too. "Sick," like "poor," was another thing I decided not to be.

While Bobby recovered, life on my new block improved. A family with four boys moved in. Jimmy and Jerry Maleski were older than I, but Jackie was near my age and Tommy could be Bobby's friend when he got well.

Grandfather had frowned. "Ach! Polacks and Catholics too!" But at last I had someone to play with, though not in my yard. "Rough boys trample the flowers," Grandmother said. The big, broad alley was our place to play. When Bobby was finally well enough to go outside, "rough boys," I was told, could also trample him. It was my job, Grandmother said, to be sure Bobby did not get hurt. I was a "big, strong girl" and he was "just a little boy."

Gradually, as the months passed, I began to see a rhythm in Grandfather's household. Things happened at certain unchangeable times. Six days a week, Mother and Grandfather marched down the sidewalk just as the trolley came up the street. In the evenings, right after the clock on the radio made six pings, the trolley brought them home. I watched from the window in winter, from the front steps in summer. Grandpa crossed the street as if no car would dare to hit him. Mother walked two steps behind.

Each morning at breakfast, I watched another unchangeable event. Grandfather took out a big black pen and a small piece of paper. Grandmother would always say, "Rheinhardt, don't make that check for a dollar. A dollar's not enough."

Grandfather's pen made thick black lines on the paper.

"Eggs are twenty-nine cents a dozen now and butter went up too." The items changed, but never Grandma's tone of voice.

Grandpa wrote on. His bushy eyebrows and thick black mustache did not even twitch.

"Pa, I can't feed this family on one dollar a day!"

He never looked up.

Grandmother's large hands folded the check and put it in the neck of her dress. Later, when I was old enough to cross the street, I would take the check with a note from Grandma to the grocery store. I would make, I knew, many trips each day for the things that Grandma burned, dropped, or simply forgot.

I did the best I could with Grandma. I had tried hugging her, but like Mother, she never stood still. If I crawled on her lap while she listened to radio stories, my body slid off.

I also tried very hard not to bleed. The first time I came home with a cut on my leg from a fall in the alley, Grandma put her apron over her head and sat down hard. Her usually loud voice was weak. "Blood makes me faint." Mother had felt the same way, so Daddy always fixed my cuts. Now I was on my own. I found a clean rag to try to push the blood back in. It seemed to work. The bleeding stopped. From then on, I never went home until it had.

It was best, I decided, to stay away from Grandma. If she *really* got angry, she looked like the witch in my fairy-tale books. Her long nose and sharp chin almost met as she said, again and again, "I raised four children. I didn't ask to raise *you*." Nor had I asked her to, but if "raising" children meant waiting while they grew, I would grow as fast as I could.

Conditions improved for me on evenings and weekends when Grandfather was home. After my happy life among the elderly shopkeepers, Grandfather seemed my most likely source of affection. He never spontaneously hugged or kissed me, but he did respond to my requests for hugs or piggyback rides. On Sundays, after church, he would open a small leather change purse and give me 5 cents for an ice-cream cone. He also ignored Grandmother's reports of my "misbehavior" as stoically as he ignored her pleas for more grocery money. During the day Grandma openly favored Bobby, but other times I was "Grandpa's little girl." Since Grandfather ruled the family, this worked out a shade to my benefit. Mother, neutralized between her parents, did not take sides.

One August, just after my fifth birthday, a lot of German was spoken in the house. This meant something I was not to know. Finally, Mother sat on the edge of our bed, looked at the bedspread, and said, "Lois, you are not to cry, but you have to start kindergarten next week."

Cry! I was too excited to sleep. I had heard about school from Rosalie, the ten-year-old girl down the street. In school you learned to read and write. Soon I would be able to read fairy tales to myself and write letters—maybe to Daddy. School was like a wonderful slide that would whoosh me into the marvelous world I suspected was out there.

Mother took the day off to enroll me in Fernwood Elementary School. I pulled at her hand all the way. Inside the big red-brick building, I breathed in its perfume—the fragrance of chalk, of pine-smelling soap. In a small room with bright-yellow walls, a black-haired woman with soft brown eyes sat on a chair as small as mine and talked to me. How wonderful to talk to an adult without looking way, way up!

Her name, she said, was Elsa Leiser, and she was the principal. Did I want to meet my teacher? I wanted to stay right there, talking to the nice lady with eyes the color of Hershey bars, but I had to learn to read. Best to get right to work.

Miss Leiser took my hand and, with Mother somewhere behind us, led me to a roomful of children. Another smiling woman, this one with red hair and freckles, bent down to ask my name and the name of Rosalie, who would be walking me home. Her own name, she said, was Miss Wasachek, but if I could not say that, "Miss Rosemary" would do as well. Since I had lived on Kinnickinnic Avenue, Wasachek was easy.

I plunged happily into the group, poked a finger in gray lumps of clay, strung a few beads, and looked at picture books. *Kindergarten,* Grandpa had said, meant "garden for children" in German. It felt that way. I was now planted—and would grow bigger and bigger. Grandmother would not have to "raise" me. I could raise myself.

When I remembered to say good-by to Mother, I found she had gone.

Kindergarten was only slightly disappointing. Miss Wasachek explained that *next year* I would learn to read. Meanwhile, I had other things to figure out—like how the piano worked and why the sky I painted logically at the top of the paper looked all wrong.

I was also giving some thought to why boys were treated less kindly than girls. Even sweet-tempered Miss Wasachek scolded them often. I noticed too that their clothes were of drab colors, whereas mine were pretty and bright. Well, boys did seem to get muddy a lot. Perhaps their mothers dressed them so that mud would not show. But even Miss Leiser spoke more sternly to the boys than to us. I felt sorry for them. Most of them were very nice. But I noticed too that, except for the janitor, there were no men in the school. Apparently, unlike in Grandfather's house, the outside world was run by women.

When I reached first grade, the real business of learning finally began. Mrs. Hughes explained that each letter had a sound. One day the process clicked. Mrs. Hughes held up a card. I put the sounds together: "Rr—ah-nn . . . ran?" I asked.

I had it right! I knew the trick! Soon I would be able to figure out millions of words. No more waiting until someone could read to me. I could read to myself—not only the books in school, but the books in the Llewellyn branch public library only eight blocks away!

Soon we were reading *Dick and Jane*. It was fun to read all by myself, but I had hoped for more interesting fairy tales. In *Dick and Jane,* a mother stayed home and a father returned each night. That was nice. But Cinderella's fairy godmother made a lot more happen.

By now I knew that all my classmates lived in homes like Dick's and Jane's. My three best friends, Jean, Jenny, and Martha, had never heard the word *divorce*. It was hard to explain. It meant, I said, that Father was gone for a while, but he would be back. On Father's Day, when we took our clay ashtrays home, I gave mine to Grandpa. At Christmas, I picked out my nicest present and told my friends it had come in the mail from my dad.

There were, I noticed, other differences between my classmates and me—some of them good. I was not fat and red-faced like Beverly, or thin and pale like Pat. I did not have Betty's doll-like coloring or her naturally curly hair, but I also did not have Oscar's gray skin and funny teeth. My hair was straight, but shining and blond. My eyes were blue, and none of my other features looked out of place. In fact, all the princesses in fairy tales had blue eyes like mine and the same blond hair, which had to be good. Added to that, I could answer the teacher's questions more quickly than most.

By second grade, learning had become more than a goal. It now seemed an urgent matter. One Sunday, Mother put Bobby and me on a bus to see a movie at the end of the line. I felt very grown-up when she gave me the money for the movie and for the bus fare back. But the woman in the glass cage took all the money! I looked up at the sign. This movie cost more than the one near home.

Bobby laughed happily during the show. I hardly saw the screen. The bus ride had been long and, without money, the walk home would be awful.

Outside the theater I took Bobby's hand. He was only five and would be frightened by our problem. I was a big girl of seven. No reason for us both to be scared. Bobby believed my lie that we were *supposed* to walk home. I looked longingly at friendly people, but I had been told not to talk to strangers. If I could recognize the streets the bus had passed, we could find our way. I *had* to remember.

After many, many blocks, Bobby began to cry. He did not *want* to walk so far. Neither did I, and I wanted to cry too. But not in front of Bobby. I had to take care of him, not scare him. We were passing a church.

"You rest here and don't you move. I'll be right back to get you." I walked around the corner. Maybe "big girls did not cry," but I had to or I would burst. It felt unbelievably good. I could now wipe my eyes and believe that Mother, realizing how late we were, might ask Uncle Carl to get his car and find us. And I would learn to read the print in the papers that told how much movies cost.

We were almost home when Uncle Carl honked the horn of his car. My feet hurt a lot and Bobby was crying hard by then. Mother was sure I had spent the bus fare on candy.

After my marathon walk, no one questioned my ability to walk the eight blocks to the Llewellyn branch library. From then on, I climbed its wide marble stairs with delicious anticipation. The librarian pretended to wonder where my voice came from when I stood at the counter that was over my head. Leaving with my arms full of as many books as I could carry, I always glanced over at Barker High School across the street. Someday I would be old enough to go there and really learn.

By third grade I had finished the last of the fairy-tale books that the library owned. By fifth grade I had read through the huge section of biographies for children.

Reading about Thomas Edison, Queen Victoria, Florence Nightingale, and John Paul Jones, I identified with each in turn. Being a queen was beyond me, but running a ship might be fun. On second thought, Queen Isabella had sense. She sent Columbus out into the ocean and got what he brought back.

Madame Curie's accomplishments came as no surprise. Girls, I had noticed in school, "buckled down" and did their work while boys threw spitballs and fought. Fighting, in fact, might be a male occupation. Grant, Lee, and Napoleon mostly made war. Well, at least Audubon, Fulton, and Alexander Graham Bell avoided bullets and did important things.

My best friends, Jean, Jenny, and Martha, did not care to talk about how it might be to invent radium, or light bulbs, or to do any of the things Rosalind Russell did in the movies. We were inseparable, but their lives and attitudes were different from mine. Their mothers made them help around the house. Grandmother pronounced me incompetent even for dusting. We had long ago agreed that the best place for me was out of the way. Their fathers, for reasons mysterious to all of us, forbade them to walk home from school with boys. I had no such silly rules. The Maleski boys were still my neighborhood friends. So were Warren, Lenny, and Jack. Since my girl friends lived in opposite directions, it was natural for me to walk home with the boys. Warren and Lenny lived nowhere near me, but *they* liked to talk about inventing radium.

It was fun, I thought, to think about the future and watch other people at work. Jean, Jenny, and Martha did not seem to give it much thought. We all laughed over some of my dreams, but they never mentioned theirs.

My most outrageous dreams took place in the Bay View Theatre when Ruby Keeler, then Ginger Rogers and Eleanor Powell, danced. Mother had once decided that my legs were too thin, and I had taken dancing lessons for years. I loved the way the taps sounded and the way my body felt as I moved to the music. Now that I was twelve years old, I was allowed to invent my own routines adapted from Keeler and Powell, but mostly from Fred Astaire. My dancing while jumping rope, on roller skates, or up and down a set of wooden stairs Grandfather had been persuaded to make was often the highlight of Mrs. Artinian's recital. For the last recital I had combined all three. Mrs. Artinian's husband, who sold insurance finally said, "No more of that." But sitting in the dark movie house, watching Ruby Keeler plucked from the chorus to be made a star, I dreamed.

Mother's ambition for me was to be a secretary and join her and Grandfather at his office. Since the dancing school was in her building, I had had plenty of time to watch Mother work. Grandfather was the director of a small German-American insurance company. Mother typed letters full of numbers and, in her tiny handwriting, put more numbers in enormous ledgers. It was odd, but at school I did well in all my studies except arithmetic. Since I could not put accurate numbers in ledgers, Mother would have to see that I could never follow her. In fact, if I became a movie star, I would quickly whisk her and Grandfather out of the dark, dingy office where even the window plants failed to survive.

At home, Grandmother never pushed marriage as a potential career. By now I had noticed that there were no hugs or kisses between her and Grandfather. They had both come separately from

17

Germany—Grandfather to escape the draft, Grandmother brought over by an older sister. While Grandmother worked in a hat factory, her sister served meals to the young Rheinhardt Wolf—along with propaganda about his need for a strong, healthy wife who could cook for him at home.

I firmly believed that, for all our sakes, Grandmother should have stayed at the hat factory. The only time she smiled was over those memories. After her morning appeal for more food money, she created gray stews, black-bordered eggs, and cardboard pork chops. She had scars from burning herself on the iron and from innumerable cuts. Grandfather treated her as if she were a purchase he could not return.

I seldom saw the mothers of my friends. They were shadowy figures who went in and out of rooms where Jean, Jenny, Martha, and I giggled. Their fathers were equally shadowy, forms to be glimpsed behind newspapers if I visited on Sunday. They had jobs I could not possibly study. They worked "for the city," doing things even their daughters did not understand.

No one spoke of college. Martha, Jean, and Jenny were all planning to take the secretarial course in high school. Aunt May, I knew, had gone to normal school for two years to learn to teach. So had Uncle Carl. Uncle Bernard did something in a factory. Mother had never gone to high school at all.

I had thought of—and reluctantly dismissed—a career as a teacher. I admired my teachers at Fernwood. They were all friendly, helpful, and happy. But how could I teach children arithmetic when I could not learn it myself? Adding rows of figures, I never got the same total twice, and I suspected that seven times *anything* would always remain a mathematical mystery to me. I hoped I had some other talent.

Just before my thirteenth birthday, my life took on a whole new dimension. Mother had been taking a great deal of interest in my underwear. One Saturday she left a booklet on my side of the bureau we shared. Since Mother never gave me anything to read, I assumed this must be an Occasion. When I scanned the booklet, published by a company named Kotex, I found that it was. This was absolutely fascinating! I knew that I was due to develop breasts. Jean, Martha, and Jenny had them, but they were all a year older than I. But I had faith and two definite bumps. Until I read the incredible Kotex booklet, however, I had no idea what else my body had in store. I had something called a uterus (or womb), and each month it prepared itself to nourish a baby. "The weeping of the disappointed womb" was the blood that would come out. The poor thing would be disappointed for a long time, I realized, but it felt special to own one, along with ovaries and Fallopian tubes, and to know that one of my openings was called a vagina.

I was also glad Mother had given me the booklet. From somewhere way back in a time I could no longer recall, I had formed the impression that it was best to check up on what Mother said. But here was the information—in black and white with a light-blue cover.

Mother was washing her underwear in the bathroom when I burst in to thank her. It was, I said, a wonderful booklet.

Her face, mysteriously, was crimson. "Well, you had to know," she said. "You might become a woman any day."

I sat on the edge of the tub. "Really? I'm a *woman* when I menstruate?" I had thought I had to wait until I was twenty-one, an official adult. This was great.

Mother closed the bathroom door and lowered her voice. Between her back's being toward me and the swishing of the soapy water, I could hardly hear her. She whispered, "And now you'll have to be careful."

"Of what?"

"Of boys."

"Why?"

Mother wrung out her heavy cotton brassiere so hard that her knuckles turned white. "You'll find out. Just don't let them touch you." She picked up her small basket of laundry and left the bathroom.

I stayed where I was, trying to connect all this information. I seldom understood exactly what Mother said or what she felt. She seldom laughed, never hugged me, and answered most questions with "I don't know." Her definite statement about boys was, therefore, quite unusual. But so was the booklet and her statement that I was going to become a woman—any day.

Perhaps she meant that I should not play rough games with the boys. My uterus and ovaries might need to be protected. But I had long since stopped playing baseball with the Maleski boys, and I had absolutely no desire to play football. If I sat on the steps with Warren or Lenny, there was no need to touch. We talked.

19

In the movies sometimes people kissed. That required touching. I had heard of parties where kissing games were played, but had long ago decided that I could not possibly kiss any boy assigned me in a game. If Dick Powell or Nelson Eddy came along, that would be different. Warren and Lenny were not like either one.

Bobby pounded on the bathroom door. I decided to phone Jenny, Martha, and Jean to share my new information and maybe get some answers.

Martha said, "I thought you already got the Curse."

The Curse?

Jenny said, "Wait until you get cramps!"

Jean sounded uncomfortable. Apparently menstruation was something "nice girls" never discussed. But this was 1937, not the Victorian days. Surely the Llewellyn library had something about this new, intriguing phenomenon.

The librarian blushed, glanced toward a locked bookcase, and said, "When you're older, dear."

My periods began that summer at Aunt May's new home in northern Wisconsin, where she now lived with my new Uncle Gus. Averting her eyes, Aunt May handed me a belt, a pad, and a bag for used pads to be put into the trash. No one shared my delight at being officially a woman. Even the slight cramps were exciting. They were, I felt, the complaints of my "disappointed womb."

By then I had gathered a bit more information from Uncle Carl's anatomy book stored in the attic. Men did not have wombs, according to the drawings, but they did have—although the drawings were not very clear—those dangling parts I had seen on Bobby. Males and females, obviously, had several differences. Sitting among the cobwebs and discarded clothing boxes, I had totaled them up.

Now that I was functioning as a female, I could admit that the cramps and messy pads were inconvenient. But grown-up *men* had to shave. I had watched Grandfather and heard his German curses when the razor slipped. Men also had to lift the toilet seat when they urinated. Grandma even yelled at her beloved Bobby when he forgot. Very well, men had to shave every day and could not produce people. I menstruated only three days a month. In the physical arrangements of men and women, women came out ahead.

When my last semester of elementary school started in the fall, I wondered whether Warren and Lenny were aware of our differences. The implications of those differences now seemed to extend beyond whether we stood up or sat down to use the toilet seat. My friends who were boys would have to think of their future just as I was doing—and it looked as if females held all the best jobs. Except for Grandpa and the grocer, I had no specific idea what the men in our neighborhood did. Most of them came home in rumpled blue clothes, carrying empty lunch boxes as if they were still heavy. The people who came to collect garbage were all men. Men stooped under the heavy blocks of ice they delivered, or climbed up the electric pole in front of our house, or worked in the sewer. The cleaner, easier jobs were obviously reserved for women—my cheery, brightly dressed teachers, the nurse in spotless white who had come to see Bobby when he was sick, the librarian, the women who sold tickets at the movies.

To my great relief, Warren, who slipped me answers during arithmetic tests, planned to be a painter like his father. I considered this a vast improvement over collecting trash. Lenny's parents expected him to take over their grocery store someday. But both boys said they might have to go to war. Some man named Hitler might have to be stopped, their fathers had said.

I listened to them both, glad no one expected me to go to war, but uncommitted to my own career. My dream of dancing with Fred Astaire was fading fast. In all those movies, only one girl was picked from the chorus to star. The odds looked long. Sports were out. "Babe" Didrickson had broken four Olympic records, but gym class bored me. Amelia Earhart flew planes and wrote books, but she had crashed.

Our principal, Miss Leiser, had talked to me of college. All during my school years she had given me special chores. She had assigned me to take care of a second-grade class while their teacher coached my class in singing. It might have been because of my terrible voice, but I had enjoyed it. My latest job was writing a mimeographed newspaper for the school. I loved that too, but school newspapers were not a career. Miss Leiser said that whatever I decided to do, college would help.

She had also supported me in my fight against eighth-grade sewing class. I did not need or want an apron, I explained, certainly not one I had to sew myself. Woodworking would be much more useful. The boys were making bookcases. That was a skill I could use.

Miss Leiser nodded her regal head. "That makes sense. But I'll have to get Mr. Schulz's permission. It is, after all, his class."

In a few days I had my reply. "Lois, I'm truly sorry. Mr. Schulz said no. He feels that a girl in the class would distract the boys."

"But a boy in the sewing class wouldn't distract *me*."

Miss Leiser nodded. "I'm sure you're right, but can you understand that I don't want to force a teacher to accept my views? Unfortunately, it is Mr. Schulz's class. And he has a right to say no."

Doomed to sewing class, I was as inept as I had expected. So much for the dress-designing career I had casually considered. But the easy "distractibility" of boys stayed in my mind. There must be something about them that I did not understand.

At the Llewellyn library I had been following a system of taking three biographies and three just-for-fun books each week. The fun books were mostly mystery stories. The biographies were selected at whim—Marie Antoinette, Pasteur, Mark Twain, and Catherine the Great. Then—on the just-returned cart—I picked up what seemed to be a mystery: *Man Against Himself* by Karl Menninger.

At home I knew immediately it was not a novel. Instead, if I could decode the words with a dictionary, it might yield a lot of answers to questions I had been wanting to ask. Men, Menninger wrote, had powerful sexual drives. In woodworking classes?

I had a vague idea of what *sexual* meant, but the dictionary was little help. "Divisions of two organisms" was less to the point than "the attraction between the sexes." *Intercourse* was listed as "Communications or dealings between people or countries." That did not fit Menninger's text. "The sexual joining of two individuals" could mean Siamese twins, but probably not.

If there was already a heated national controversy over whether Clark Gable could say "damn" in *Gone with the Wind,* there were obviously other words people did not say aloud—or in dictionaries—but I plodded on.

Intercourse, in any event, was, according to Menninger, an expression of love—pleasurable, necessary, and healthful. Marriages often failed because people believed unconsciously that it was "dirty" or "bad."

The one word I could not decode was *masturbate*. It was a verb, I knew, and not "harmful" as some people believed. The dictionary ignored it completely. For weeks I tried to figure it out.

As long as it was not harmful, I decided to show off my new vocabulary and possibly get a clue. At the dinner table one evening I said cheerily, "Do any of you masturbate?"

Grandfather's forkful of cucumbers stopped midway to his mouth. Mother turned the color of tomatoes. Grandmother closed her eyes. Only Bobby spoke. "What's masturbate?"

Everyone began to speak at once—about the weather, President Roosevelt, the price of meat. Such lively conversation was decidedly atypical. All right. They knew something I did not and I was not going to find it out from them.

A few days later, Mother made the unusual request that we go for a walk after dinner. I was so pleased. Even though we had shared the same bed for most of my life, we had seldom talked. On walks you had to.

I chattered on about school as we traversed the three blocks to the lake. Mother did not respond. She walked with her head down.

Finally she glanced at me and said, "Lois, I thought you knew not to touch yourself 'down there.' That's what *masturbate* means."

I worked to keep quiet. So that's what it meant! And I thought I had invented this delightful activity myself. Thank heavens Menninger approved. Mother, I was now sure would not approve of Menninger.

Mother continued, her head down and her hands in the pockets of her last year's black coat. "Somebody has to tell you this. You're old enough to get pregnant now."

I felt very close to Mother. At last we were having an intimate talk. I had so many questions. In addition to Menninger, I was also reading the *True Confessions* magazines I had found in her drawer. People in the magazine were always allowing "wild ecstasy" to carry them away, and I was curious how. I put my arm through Mother's, but she had to adjust her coat and moved away.

"Lois, someone has to warn you about men. Don't let them touch you. They only want one thing and it's bad. What men make women do is filthy."

I could not take my eyes off the gray cement sidewalks that stretched straight and interminably in front of us. With the bright autumn leaves above us, I concentrated on only the hard drab surface beneath my feet. Mother was trying to tell me what she thought I should know, what she believed, and what she had felt. For a moment I considered explaining to her what I had read. I said I was getting chilled and asked if we could walk back.

Now, walking home, I was as silent as Mother. Her words explained why she never talked to men as friends, never smiled or laughed with them in her office. She had probably, with great strength of will, defied her father to marry a Catholic, "put up with" my father to have Bobby and me, and now lived with "I told you so" from everyone she knew. How could I tell her what I had read?

Aside from anything else, it would be like being a mother to my mother. I wanted too much to keep the only parent I had left.

Still, it seemed wrong to pretend I accepted what she said. At the door to the house I touched her arm. "Mother, thank you for being honest, but that isn't the right thing to say to a young girl." She could read into that sentence whatever made her feel best.

My questions—not urgent anyway—would have to wait. Between Menninger, the movies, and Mother's *True Confessions* magazines, I could piece together enough to get me through. Menninger's "pleasurable, healthy" sex was obviously to be reserved for after marriage. Every woman in *True Confessions* who gave in to premarital "wild ecstasy" ended up in disgrace, homes for unwed mothers, poverty, or all three. In the movies, anyone who—*off-screen* of course—had unmarried sex was predictably dead by The End. Since none of the boys in my eighth-grade class were likely to inspire wild ecstasy, I put it down as hardly a pressing problem.

As elementary school graduation came closer, preparing for the future seemed much more urgent. Jean, Martha, and Jenny were still planning to take the secretarial course in high school. It was now as embarrassing to talk careers with them as to talk about sex. My dreams were too hazy to risk their giggles.

Instead I sat at the movies, knees up on the seat, and watched Roz Russell succeed in a dozen careers. The newsreels showed me "Ma" Barker and Bonnie Parker, but a life of crime seemed insecure. Frances Perkins had been made secretary of labor by FDR, whom I dearly loved, but I had no idea what she did or if I could be good at it. Occasionally, a tall, round-faced woman, Dorothy Thompson, appeared on the screen. She was a newspaper woman. Hitler had kicked her out of Germany and the whole world seemed to listen to what she said.

Those women on the screen were as far from my life as women on Mars. I had never met a successful career woman—or a successful career *man*. Grandfather and my uncles never talked of their jobs with enthusiasm or mentioned promotions. Mother and Aunt Jane went to theirs as if serving a sentence. Yet some people, I believed, felt joy in their work. If college made this possible, then college was for me.

Perhaps, as Grandmother said when she was angry at me, I was not as smart as I thought. I might fall flat on my face halfway to Mars. Still, halfway was better than what I saw around me. Secretly, so that no one would laugh, I was going to try.

The day we filled out forms for high school, I wrote in "English course." Miss Wulff, my teacher, had told me that this would prepare me for college. Domestic science or the secretarial course would not. I took the forms home for Mother to sign.

"No, Lois, you did this wrong. Erase it and write 'secretarial course' here." She smiled one of her rare smiles. "Just think, in four more years you'll be able to work with Grandpa and me."

As during our talk about sex, I found I could not speak. Different as we were, I loved her and knew she loved me. She never hugged or kissed me, but she never yelled at me either. She had never gone out at night, as some mothers did, and left me alone. She spent her money on things for me and Bobby, not on herself. She had gone to that office every day so that I could eat. How could I tell her now that I could not fulfill her dream?

Miss Leiser, the principal, was the only person to whom I could turn. I wept in her office. "I don't want to hurt Mother, but I can't take the secretarial course."

Miss Leiser asked Mother to come to school. Having her take a day off work increased my guilt. In Miss Leiser's bright, sunny office, I could hardly breathe as she spoke gently, tactfully, to Mother.

"Lois has the ability for college. Why not let her take electives in shorthand and typing, but take the English course? Then she can be ready for college *or* a secretarial career."

Mother and I walked home past the brown, gray, and tan houses of our neighborhood. It was frightening to want more than I saw around me and painful to feel I'd hurt Mother. She walked slowly. Her dark-brown dress blended with the drab houses around us— and with my feeling that I had betrayed her.

"Lois, I can't give you one cent to go to college."

"Mother, I know. I probably won't go. I just want the choice."

"Wouldn't you like working with Grandpa and me? We could all take the trolley together every morning. You'd like that."

This was no time for honesty, no time to tell her that the 7:20 trolley would take me only where I did not want to go. I said, "I could never be as good a secretary as you, Mom. So I'd like to try

25

something else." I cringed. Fate might punish me for lying and perhaps for the arrogance of reaching too high.

I took Mother's arm affectionately. She looked uncomfortable at this unaccustomed touching, but she said, "Well, maybe it will turn out all right," in a voice that said it would not.

Chapter 3

IN 1939 I entered Barker High School with the same high expectations that had been fulfilled at Fernwood. It took only one semester to find out that the situation at Barker was entirely different. By force of habit, I worked hard the first semester and made the honor roll. By the second semester I knew that something was distinctly awry.

My classmates were a much more interesting mixture than those at Fernwood. There, nearly everyone had been German-American. At Barker, I now had classmates named Klukowski, Pegis, Morales, and Ginsberg. The corridors of this enormous more-or-less-middle-class school were teeming with fascinating new friends. It was the classrooms that presented the problem.

Dr. Helmut Schnell, Barker's principal, I finally reasoned, was the source from whom all tensions flowed. He looked and behaved much like Joseph Goebbels. He was short, with a gray-green pointy little face and an air of constantly confirmed suspicions. No teacher, I reasoned, would *willingly* work under him. Therefore, the teachers he commanded were very old, very young, or very peculiar.

Some were merely timid, twitchy, or irritable, but we also had Mrs. Arbuthnot, who would touch no object without first wrapping her hand in a paper towel. Mr. Fletcher grabbed girls' bottoms, and fat Mr. Buber grabbed at the boys. We always knew

27

when Miss Whitley was drunk; she dropped books and mumbled. Two teachers committed suicide during my four years at Barker. There were, however, a few determined teachers who apparently wanted to prove that they could teach under *any* circumstances. Through them I hoped to survive.

Clues accumulated almost immediately to indicate that Barker High and I were not entirely suited to each other. In English class I dutifully plowed through *Silas Marner* but was much more interested in why Mary Ann Evans wrote under the name of George Eliot.

I asked the teacher, Mr. Trent, a man with a gray face, gray hair, and angry gray eyes.

"Writing, Miss Mark, was not considered a ladylike occupation in those days."

His answer confused me. Had not Jane Austen and the Brontë sisters written under their own names? I was still timid in this new school, but I wanted my confusion cleared up.

Mr. Trent listened to my question, glared, and changed the subject. School, apparently, was not the place to ask questions.

For algebra I had drawn the coach of our school's championship swimming team. We were both better suited for swimming. I was already blocked on numbers. Adding *letters* made my confusion overwhelming. No one explained the use for this mysterious system, but I plodded on, resigned to flunking. The boy who sat next to me wrote me love notes but no test answers. He couldn't catch on either. If math was required, we could both forget college.

At the end of my first semester, my passing grade in algebra baffled me. Maybe the teacher realized it would take a lifetime to teach me math, or did not want to flunk an otherwise honor student.

I gave the second semester a test run. My biology teacher was also the football coach. In class we read from the text. My geometry teacher gave up a few days before I did and answered my anguished questions with "Don't worry." American history was another read-the-chapter, discuss-in-class course. Art class presented no problem but staying out of Mr. Fletcher's reach.

In English composition I worked hard on my first assignments and got 90s. I worked less hard—and got 90s. I experimented with scribbling my homework while others recited. I still got 90s—once a 98. Nice, but I was not learning a thing.

Gym class presented a problem. I did not mind so much romping around in a gym suit designed for a pumpkin who was afraid of rape. But Barker High had a swimming pool. After swim class I had to walk past all those good-looking senior boys in the corridors, my hair a mess. Then I learned that to be excused from the pool, girls could simply but *M* on the roll-call sheet. Two months later, Miss Luell called me into the gym office. I had better, she said, see my doctor. It was unnatural to menstruate for sixty days straight.

Around the middle of the second semester, I knew that somewhere young minds were being challenged, new vistas of knowledge were being revealed—somewhere, but certainly not at Barker High. And I had a future to prepare for.

Jean, Martha, and Jenny still seemed unconcerned. They were learning shorthand and typing. They would work for one of the enormous insurance companies until.

Until what?

Martha, always the most outspoken, looked at me as if I had questioned the rising of the sun. "Until I get married, of course. What did you think?"

Getting married as a means of survival had simply never occurred to me. Mother had tried it unsuccessfully. Aunt May's husband had died. At best, it was risky. At worst, it could be like Grandmother's life, arguing for grocery checks and hanging out wash. I might marry someday, but only for love—someone like Cary Grant, perhaps.

Meanwhile, boys were fun. I liked their attention and liked them as friends. Our differences were fascinating to try to figure out. At dances I enjoyed the challenge of anticipating a boy's sometimes stumbling, sometimes smooth steps. A girl, I decided, must have some special sensitivity to know what her partner would do next. I was also fascinated by how seriously boys took sports. Bob voluntarily got muddy and bruised on the football field. Leon got floor burns from basketball. When they lost a game, they were bereft. Their worlds seem to hang on the throwing or carrying of *balls*.

In spite of what I felt was a too-round face, a too-small bust, and the glasses I had worn since second grade, I was having more success with high-school boys than I had expected. Most of them said they liked to talk to me. That was fine. It avoided the "getting fresh" problem girl friends reported. I had let Carl kiss me to see how it felt. He acted as relieved as I to go back to talking.

Bob and Leon never tried, but they asked me to wear their rings. Someday, Bob said, he would marry a girl just like me. That was nice to hear, but I hoped his someday was a long way off.

Mother inspected me closely after my dates. She also patrolled the porch. "And what does 'going steady' *really* mean?" she asked with suspicion. I was not sure. Some girls, I had heard from gossip, "went all the way," but they seldom went steady. They seemed, instead, to be passed around. Some suddenly disappeared from school—to those homes for unwed mothers, I suspected. I wished Mother knew that "going all the way" seemed a profitless activity to me. But inspections continued.

"Going steady," moreover, was not working out. It was nice to be asked, but after wearing Randy's swimming medal or Joe's ring for a week, some other boy would catch my eye. Since my interests were apparently brief, early marriage was certainly risky. And an old feeling persisted. I was, after all, responsible for my own survival. I had better make plans. Almost fourteen, I had not yet decided what I wanted to do.

One evening, family talk turned to Grandpa's "election" as it did every two years. The members of the fraternal insurance company where Grandfather—and Mother—worked elected their officers. Each year, for as long as I could remember, Mother had predicted disaster. Grandfather's job as secretary-treasurer was the only paid position among the officers, and Grandpa had hired Mother. If he was not reelected, he would have no job and neither would she. Early in the spring, before the summer elections, familial predictions of doom began. "With the Depression so bad," Mother said this time, "someone else will want the job and Pa will be out." Grandmother and Mother compared convictions that soon we would all be "on relief." Grandfather never spoke. Nor did I, but my stomach clenched as I listened, as it had all my life. As a child there was nothing I could do but wonder how it would feel to be hungry. Still, Grandfather always won the election, and for two more years I could push the terror from my mind. Now the election was coming again.

The next morning at school, I walked from art class to study hall, avoiding my friends. I had to decide how to earn a living myself. But how? My saddle shoes squeaked on the dusty terrazzo floors. The long, narrow, green-painted lockers formed a dark line along the walls.

A dancing career, I admitted sadly, was out. No moving to

rhythms on spotlighted stages for me. Milwaukee did not even have a chorus line where I might get a start. Anyway, I consoled myself, dancers eventually get too old to dance. Then what did they do?

I thought of my mother's doctor, a pleasant, gentle woman. But medical school cost lots of money and required math. Scratch that. My approach should be through a *proven* ability. I assessed my rank in art class. At least ten students were better than I.

By now, head down and still thinking, I passed Miss Wilder's room. I had her for English. And then I stopped, literally in my tracks. Someone bumped me from behind, but my mind was too busy to care.

Miss Wilder openly disliked me. She had once accused me of plagiarism, but by now she knew I did my assignments in class. She had caught me unprepared when I was asked to recite first. But she had recently said to me, "Lois, I have to admit you write well."

Praise from friends on my letters or rhymes was to be discounted, but praise from someone who disliked me carried weight. I had taken my 90s in English for granted, but Miss Wilder's remark had made me wonder whether I might not have special ability after all.

But how did people earn a living from writing? I clutched my books tighter and, as fast as the school rules allowed, rushed past those green-painted lockers to my personal source of all wisdom— the library.

The book was on a middle shelf. It was blue and of average thickness. It was remarkably realistic. Poetry, it pointed out, was hard to sell and paid little; novels were gambles and took years to write; articles and fiction for magazines needed years of acquired skills and the income was spotty.

Then I reached the chapters on advertising copywriting and news reporting.

Reporters, I read, earned relatively low salaries but could start on small papers and work up. Advertising was highly paid but highly competitive. It was "selling through words."

If the author of the book used *his* and *him* or warned that few women were in either field, I missed the point. My mind was too busy sorting the other pieces to fit them in place. The previous summer at Uncle Gus's "trading post," I had cajoled him into buying beaded rabbits' feet from a Menominee tribesman who lived nearby. I had promised to sell every one, and I had. I had even persuaded another Menominee tribesman that he should have a token of his culture. Uncle Gus, a gregarious, fun-loving man, enjoyed telling the story. "Forget about iceboxes to Eskimos! That little girl sold an Indian souvenir to an Indian!"

All right, if I could sell and write, advertising might be within my reach. As for newspaper reporting, I could start right now. I closed the blue book and, feeling as if I had just found a road map, headed for the school's newspaper office.

For the next three years, I did manage to get an education out of Barker High, but exclusively through its newspaper. After an unexpectedly easy sprint from cub to star reporter, I stopped doing homework entirely. I did not have time. And I learned that Miss Salem, the faculty adviser, could get me excused from classes. I stopped buying texts.

Conveniently, I had already been labeled a problem student after a violent confrontation with the principal, Dr. Schnell. Bobby, now also in high school, got caught playing hooky. Mother, I decided, could not properly defend him. I had gone with her to the scheduled conference.

Dr. Schnell glared down his narrow nose at Bobby. "Boys like you go from skipping school to stealing cars! Without a father, I knew you'd turn out bad."

Both Mother and Bobby looked about to cry. This was obviously up to me. I stood up.

"That," I said, my indignation covering me like armor, "is a terrible thing to say to a young boy—and to my mother."

Dr. Schnell did not take kindly to the opinions of others. His sallow face turned puce. He sputtered. Then he waved a bony finger at the door, commanding me to leave with my "worthless brother." As I herded my family in front of me, he screamed at Mother, "If I ever had a student headed for the penitentiary, that girl is it!"

Outside, I comforted Mother. Dr. Schnell had forgotten to give Bobby detentions, I reminded them both.

From then on, teachers treated me in one of two ways. Some who may have loathed Dr. Schnell as much as I did were exceedingly patient with my spotty attendance and missed homework. Others treated me gingerly, as a problem with which they did not wish to get involved. Mother wondered why my grades were barely passing. I wondered why I was passing at all.

I was, however, learning. Long, convoluted answers by a teacher meant he really did not know the answer. In English literature I got mental exercise discussing books I had not read. (*Lady of the Lake* and *The Mill on the Floss* were the teacher's choices; *Sister Carrie* and *Vanity Fair* were mine.) In class, by listening to others, I could pick up the plots and discuss side issues endlessly. I was learning that teachers bluffed and I could too. And soon I would be learning the most valuable lesson of my life.

On the school newspaper I was resigned to never being editor. The editor, I knew, had to have an 85 average. Mine was barely 70. I was content as features editor, writing, helping paste up the layouts, and learning about type at the printer. School rules, unfortunately, were rules.

When Miss Salem, the newspaper adviser, sent for me at the end of the semester, I expected another lecture on "tact." Earlier in the year, a coat rack had fallen on the physics teacher. I had accurately reported his response. "Oh, shit," Miss Salem had explained, was not an acceptable quote.

Miss Salem smiled broadly when I entered her room. She was a tall, thin woman, reserved and quiet, but helpful and fair. She leaned against the window wall with her arms crossed.

"Lois, the faculty has discussed this at great length—great length."

My stomach knotted despite her smile. Maybe they had decided my grades were too awful even for my features editor job. I winced, expecting the worse.

"We have decided to appoint you editor in chief for the coming semester."

At first I felt only overwhelming enthusiasm. I had a dozen ideas for changes. But I merely beamed, thanked her, and left. In the corridor my other reaction surfaced.

Something was terribly odd. Much as I wanted the job, rules, I assumed, were rules. There were plenty of other staffers with qualifying grades. Why choose me? Some articles of mine had won prizes in a city-wide high-school competition, but my grades were at their all-time low. Surely Miss Salem knew the rules.

I walked toward my locker past Dr. Schnell's office. He was standing at his door as he often did, watching for victims. Usually he glared at me. Now he looked away. According to Miss Salem, he had been in on this incredible appointment.

At my locker I was still in a daze. Our swimming coach passed by and the pieces clicked. Barker High stood out for only two activities: the paper and the swimming team. Our football team never won a game, never even made touchdowns. Our band played out of tune and marched out of step. We firmly held the bottom rung in basketball. But the *Barker Oracle* and the swimming team were city-wide champs.

Apparently I was needed, low grades and all. I did not feel triumphant. Instead, the blow to my idealism hurt. So this was how the adult world worked! If you were good enough at something, rules were no longer rules.

I now attended even fewer classes. Why listen to Mr. Mann drone dully on about economics, sounding more bored than the class? Sociology had intrigued me at first, until Miss Fastnect dodged all my questions on slavery and southern segregation. Why waste time there? I had work to do.

Outside school, my "work" now involved Bobby. For years I had settled our arguments simply by twisting his arm. Then Bobby spent a summer at Aunt May's while I got a summer job. When Bobby came home in September, he still looked like Bobby to me. One night, there was a question about who would choose the radio show. Unexpectedly, I found myself sprawled on the floor. In three months Bobby had grown. Contemplating the weave in the rug, I switched to persuasion. Brawn had been handy, but those days were gone.

With persuasion I could handle—but not understand—my brother. He was a sophomore now and had not even thought about goals. I still felt responsible for Bobby, and a little guilty. In school he was, and had always been, "Lois's brother." In high school, at least, not much was expected of him academically because of my record, but my newspaper work was his cross. Unlike most other boys I knew, he did not care for sports. Maybe, I suggested, he could join the club that broadcast through the school's public-address system. Would he want a radio announcing career? He was not sure, but he joined the club. Well, at least I had persuaded Mother to let him take a college-prep course.

He was, I found out fast one day, well informed on sex. I had been worried. When Bobby reached fifteen, I knew someone had to tell him the facts of life. Grandfather seldom spoke to Bobby at all, nor did Uncles Bernard and Carl. Mother's speech to me about "filthy men" was hardly appropriate. The job, I decided, was mine. At least I had Menninger to back me.

As Mother had done, I asked him to take a walk. It was time, I said, to talk about the facts of life.

Bobby, now eight inches taller than I, grinned down with sophistication. "Yes," he said, "and what would you like to know?"

I had the startling realization that he knew much, much more than I. And I planned to keep it that way. Bobby, in that area at least, was on his own.

In June of 1943, Barker High gave me my diploma. It was certainly not for my work in class. On graduation night, Mother sat in the auditorium while I walked across the stage. Both of us were amazed I had graduated.

Many of my male classmates had not. World War II was in progress and they had been drafted or had enlisted. So had Tony, the college man with whom I was very much in love.

That night I grabbed my diploma as if it were a parole. I believed I would now go on to college. I had earned the money, and in 1943 deserted colleges accepted anyone. I also believed that, after college, I would marry Tony.

Chapter 4

TONY BRONSKI had entered my life soon after my career decision in the halls of Barker High. Tony—unknowingly—had guided me through my adolescence. I would—also unknowingly—take more from Tony than I gave.

Tony and I met on March 28, 1940, at a party given by my new friend, Grace. Grace's aggression with boys amazed me. She could ask them to dance, phone them, and, in this case, invite a group of *college* men to her party. While her parents were busy in the tavern they ran downstairs, Grace walked provocatively through the apartment upstairs and turned out all the lights.

Perhaps Grace could sit kissing some boy she hardly knew, but I could not. I groped to the bright square of a porch door. On the porch I planned to wait, watch the traffic, and decide if I was irredeemably square.

The door opened behind me. A deep masculine voice said, "Hi!" Lights from passing cars lit up his face as he asked if he could sit with me. I saw brown eyes, fair hair, and features like those of a friendly bulldog. His shoulders were unusually broad. Even when I moved to the corner of the porch steps, they hardly allowed room for an appropriately impersonal arrangement.

He quickly established, however, that he had come to talk, not to neck. His name, he said, was Tony Bronski. He was a college sophomore, had just turned twenty-one years old. He played football and hoped to be a high-school English teacher. He asked about me.

Well, if God could not forgive me for the lie I was about to tell, He would at least have to understand. I wanted to see this gentle, intelligent young man again, but a twenty-one-year-old college student was unlikely to date a fourteen-year-old high-school sophomore.

"I'm eighteen and a senior at Barker High." That, I figured, was as far as I dared stretch things.

It was far enough for Tony. He asked if he could drive me home.

As we talked in his car in front of Grandfather's house, I wondered how long my luck would last. Tony was attractive, polite, easy to talk to, and a genuine college man, the only one I had ever met. I knew I was socially in over my head, but this young man with the bulldog face was worth my best try.

My luck, I thought, had run out fast when Tony took me to the door. It was locked. Mother had often threatened to lock the door if I came in too late. "Too late" had never been defined. To my humiliation, it was now.

Tony suggested the back door. It opened. We stepped into the dark kitchen. By now, I wanted Tony to kiss me.

Suddenly the lights flashed on. When my eyes adjusted, there was Mother, and in her homemade pajamas with their built-in bowlegged effect. "Lois, it's after midnight. You tell that boy to go home."

I stared at her, shocked, shamed, and stricken. Tony would surely lose interest in a girl whose mother had bowlegged pajamas.

Tony politely apologized to Mother as she stood silently, her face greasy with Pond's cream and her hair in a net. He had not realized, he said, it was quite that late.

He kissed my forehead and left—forever, I was sure. In bed I pulled as far away from Mother as I could and cried while she snored.

Tony phoned at 5:23 the next day. Had Mother forgiven him and would she let him come to see me that night?

For the first time in twelve hours, I spoke to her and got a reluctant yes. Back to the black candlestick phone, bearer of news of miracles. He would be there at seven.

That gave me seventy-seven minutes to beg, bribe, cajole, and rehearse the family to support my "eighteen-year-old senior" lie.

37

Mother said, "What will you do in June when you'd be expected to graduate?"

What I was going to do was think about it later.

Bobby said, "I get to choose the radio shows for a whole month, right?"

Right. For a year, if need be. With luck, I would not even be home. I would be at football games and college proms with Tony.

By June it had all come true, but not without crises. Too soon, Tony's college had its spring prom. He invited me. I was terrified. I would have to fit in with *real* eighteen-, nineteen-, and even twenty-year-old girls. What if I wore the wrong clothes or said the wrong thing?

Even Grace was no help. She had not acquired a college beau in that darkened room. She was thrilled with my "success," but her only response was "Wow." Mother could not help. Nor could Jean, Jenny, or Martha. They were not yet even allowed to date. For a moment I envied them.

I could not confess my fears to Tony. To him I was eighteen. I could, however, ask what he'd like me to wear.

"I love you in blue. And something simple. Just something pretty, long, and blue."

Ah! It had to be long.

Mother sewed the dress. The zipper bulged. I bought a white ribbon to tie at the waist and lash down the zipper.

The orchestra was playing "In the Mood" when we entered the gym. Tony had said I looked great. But almost at once his friends gathered around us. Mike and Millie, both short, dark, and vivacious; tall, blond Dick and his girl friend, Betty, who looked like a model in *Mademoiselle;* Sylvia and Joe were actually Mr. and Mrs. They were all sure to guess I was only fourteen.

Talk of college life swirled unintelligibly around me. I smiled a lot hoping no one would talk to me. What if one of these sleek, confident people had a relative at Barker High?

Suddenly I felt as if I had been dropped into the center of a whirling stream, miles from shore. I could never keep up this charade. Tony would tire of a tongue-tied date, and if I spoke, I would say something wrong.

Unexpectedly, thoughts of heroic escapes from fires, floods, and earthquakes came into my mind. They had always failed to impress me. Now I knew why. In a terrifying situation, you obviously had two choices: fight your way out or sit still and perish. The choice did not take courage; it just took sense. All right. I would not stand there, stupid with fear, and perish. Fighting my way out meant studying the sophisticated girls around me and picking up clues. It meant listening until I could find something *not* dumb to say. If I could not swim yet, at least I could float.

Listening to Tony's friends and picking up clues was a lot like faking in English class when I had not read the assigned book. "Herman," I figured out, was the football coach. The Drama Club was "doing" Odets—a playwright, I guessed. And Tony, I learned, had just been elected both president of his fraternity and captain of the football team. As Tony's girl, I was unquestioningly accepted. His tender looks helped me relax.

Each college event became easier. At football games I had only to yell and wince—and after the games, listen as Tony, Dick, and Mike relived each play. The dances were great; I could not discuss football with Tony's friends, but I could follow their leads. After Drama Club plays, I listened and learned. I had thought Odets's *Awake and Sing* was to be a musical.

It felt odd to go back each week to the immature world of high school. But on weekends and evenings, I was where I now felt I belonged—with Tony.

To Tony I could confess my dreams of a career in journalism or advertising. Tony too wanted more than he had been born to. His parents were Polish immigrants who ran a small grocery store. His mother could not speak English, but the family obeyed her rapid-fire Polish commands with love and alacrity. Tony was the only one of six children going to college, and he encouraged me to go too.

"Lois, honey, you *do* write well. College will help you write better."

"Mother said there's no money. When I graduate high school, I'll have to pay rent."

"You can work in the summer."

I had thought of that. If Tony believed I was eighteen, employers might too.

Tony was my guide to the world I hoped was out there. He was also my guide to the outskirts of sex.

Menninger and *True Confessions* took me only so far. *Ladies' Home Journal*'s Teen Pamphlets filled in a gap. But swimming cannot be learned by reading books on dry land. Shy, awkward high-school boys had presented no problems. Tony was a man.

The first time Tony touched my breast, I pushed him away,

wept, and sent him home. In 1940 the *Ladies' Home Journal* pamphlets said "nice" girls did not pet; "nice" boys did not try.

I sat on the porch swing alone, bereft, confused, and upset. To whom could I talk? I knew what Grace would say. She laughed at my pamphlets. Jean, Jenny, and Martha would not know. I wished for an older sister, but Mother was all I had.

Right after dinner, Mother listened to my garbled story. It was hard to get to the point. I tried to read her face. She looked resigned and distressed. Finally I managed to say, "And then he touched my breast."

Incredibly, Mother laughed. "Oh, for God's sake, is *that* all? What a relief! I thought you were pregnant!"

I sat on the edge of the bed, trying hard to juggle my thoughts. I was obviously more innocent than Mother knew and, as always, there was no way to talk.

Tony called that evening. He wanted to come over to explain. I said he could. He was my only source of information now, and I trusted him more than I had known.

We parked in our favorite spot near the lake. Tony held my hand. His bulldog face was serious and stiff. He loved me very much, he said, enough to marry me someday. Meanwhile, he had a problem to solve.

"Maybe girls don't understand, my darling, how strong male passions get. Especially if you love someone. But I promise I'll control them. Will you give me another chance?"

Of course I would. I loved his arms around me, and now I could relax. As the months went by, I could enjoy what I guessed was called "heavy petting." It was not, I knew, entirely fair to Tony to push his control, but it felt so nice. I threw the *Ladies' Home Journal* pamphlets away.

In my high-school world, things bobbled along. When I finally turned fifteen, I "confessed" to Tony I was only *now* eighteen and only a junior, that I had thought he would feel a seventeen-year-old was too young to date. I decided I would have to repeat the "confession" for three more years.

When I was given the newspaper editorship in spite of my grades, I did not share my cynical new insight with Tony. His ideals were so high, I thought it might hurt.

I did, however, share a wild, crazy idea that had been nagging at my mind for a while. Would one of the big department stores be interested in a fashion column for teens written by a teen-ager? *I* knew how quickly teen clothing fads flashed and then faded. Could I write a shopping column for, say, the Boston Store? It would surely, I figured, advance my career.

Tony put his arm around me as we walked to the lake. "Well, honey," he said, "you have nothing to lose if you try."

I made up a sample. To Mother's relief and my teacher's regret, I took typing now. Fast I was not, but with time I managed to copy my copy. I telephoned the advertising manager to ask for an appointment. I had, I said, an idea.

My enthusiasm carried me as far as the door of the store. My feet alone got me to the door of the bustling, messy, noisy advertising department. I was told to wait. I wanted to run.

Tony, I thought, had been wrong. What I had to lose was a nice cozy dream. What if the manager laughed at me? It would have been better to have kept my dream and stayed at home. I stood up to leave.

Then I sat down. If I left, I might wonder forever if I might have succeeded. Which was worse: humiliation or eternal regrets? Humiliation, at least, was over fast. I decided to stay.

Mr. Sawyer, the advertising manager, was tall and skinny and looked amused. He arranged his limbs between desk and chair and listened to me talk. I sold with the passionate sincerity I had used to sell the souvenir to the Indian.

He reached out a long, bony arm to his phone and dialed a three-digit number. "J.D.? Something here you oughta see. Her name is Mark."

He pointed to a brown door at the end of the hall, yawned, and shuffled some papers.

As I walked toward the brown door, I wondered whether I was a joke Mr. Sawyer wanted to share or if it was his way of getting rid of me. The door had a gold-lettered sign: "J. D. Daniels, Publicity Director." Publicity director sounded more important than advertising manager. I opened the door. Yes, it must be. The secretary's office was bigger than Sawyer's.

The gray-haired secretary looked at me questioningly, but a voice boomed from beyond an open door. "Miss Mark? Come in."

A tall, bald man with a broad smile met me at his door and settled me into a chair next to his desk. He acted as if I were an adult instead of a ready-to-run fifteen-year-old. He asked Miss Kuswa to hold his calls, sat back in his chair, crossed hands over a

41

slightly bulging waistline, and asked, "Now, what can I do for you?"

J.D. nodded occasionally as I spoke. What, he asked, had I written before? Quite a lot; I was editor of my high-school paper.

J.D. nodded again and picked up his phone. He made two calls, each time repeating my idea.

Then he reached across to shake my hand. "O.K., let's try it. A ten-inch column on Saturday. How's four dollars a column?"

Somewhere in my mind, bands played and fireworks went off. Oh, Lord, what if I had lost my nerve outside the advertising manager's door! Dreams—my goodness!—did come true. I grinned, shook J.D.'s hand, and nodded.

"Miss Mark, I think you should also work as a salesclerk. There's nothing like direct contact with customers to help an advertising writer."

If J.D. had suggested it, I would have worked as a lion tamer. He had called me an advertising writer!

For the next year I considered my life idyllic. My column was published weekly; I had my school newspaper work and sold sportswear on Saturdays; and my college fund was building. And I had Tony.

On December 7, 1941, I was sprawled on the floor in Grandfather's house reading the comics. The news of Pearl Harbor struck from the big Majestic radio behind me. I slipped on the papers in my rush to phone Tony. Did this mean he would have to go to war?

That day Tony comforted me. He could be deferred until his college graduation. But as the weeks passed, Tony spoke of his obligation to enlist.

I countered with every objection I could muster—his education, my education, the education of his future students. I wept and begged. I needed him more than the army. And men got killed in wars.

Months later, Tony and I were holding hands at a movie when James Stewart's face filled the screen. Another recruiting film. I felt Tony's grip tighten as Jimmy Stewart exuded sincerity. While Stewart talked of the Army Air Corps, I looked at Tony's face. And hated Jimmy Stewart.

On the day Tony left for basic training as an air cadet, I hardly saw the train station. Somewhere around me, his family moved and talked. The dingy train station felt smaller, dark, and threatening.

Tony said, "I'll be back."

I had heard those words before. My father had said them and they had been a lie. When the train pulled out, I was sure I would never see Tony again.

But daily letters crisscrossed from Florida to Milwaukee. Gradually I stopped weeping each time "our" song—"I'll Never Smile Again"—was played on the air. When my junior year ended in June, I wrote to Tony, I would try to find a really good summer job. There was not much time left to accumulate money for college.

The classified ad in the *Milwaukee Journal* read: "Writer wanted, American Legion magazine. Experience preferred." If experience was just preferred, my limited credits might do. I answered the ad. "Age: nineteen." If I could lie to Tony, an editor might believe me too.

On the day of my appointment, I entered the editor's small office. He was a short man himself and introduced me to another, taller, blue-jowled man.

"This, Miss Mark, is Judge Joseph R. McCarthy. Remember the name. He'll be famous someday."

The blue-jowled man looked me over. I looked away. I had never met a judge. I did not like his eyes.

The editor said, "Now, you understand the job is in Appleton, Wisconsin."

Short interview. I stood up to leave. "I'm sorry, but I can't move out of town."

Joe McCarthy waved a large hand. "Oh, you'd like Appleton, Lois. There're no niggers or Jews there."

I stared at this blue-jowled man with his strange, lopsided grin. I had just read a book on the "mental illness of bigotry," and here was a victim of the disease.

As gently as I could, I said, "Judge McCarthy, psychiatrists feel that bigoted people are mentally ill. I'd see a doctor if I were you." Joseph McCarthy leaned back and roared with laughter. I fled the room. His eyes had crawled over my body and I was repulsed. I felt safe only when I reached the street.

Later, in my summer job with a neighborhood newspaper, I read that McCarthy had joined the Marines. My boss on the newspaper was Irish too, but red-headed, cheerful, and liked by us all. I hated to leave to finish high school.

When Tony called long distance on my graduation night, I had wonderful news to tell him. I had been accepted at the University of Wisconsin and had a marvelous summer job. We could not talk long. Air cadets were paid very little. But just hearing his voice was enough.

Yet when I hung up the phone, I felt sad for Tony. Here I was, excited about jobs and college, free to plan my future. Somehow it seemed unfair. *All* the men I knew were away at war, losing time at best and at worst losing their lives. That possibility, applied to Tony, did not bear thinking about. I pushed it aside.

I had not approached J.D. to ask for a summer job. I had had to stop writing the column for him when I worked full-time the summer before. He had said, "Remember, you have a job here the day you get out of college." His jobs, I decided, were for those with degrees.

But the classified ad run by Gimbel's did not mention degrees. "Sign writer wanted" was all it had said. The advertising manager, a dark-haired, red-faced man, glanced at my application. On it, with another beg-your-pardon to God, I had written: "Age, eighteen." Well, I would be—in less than three months.

Mr. Anderson looked at me over the rim of his glasses. "Well, at least you're draft-proof. Sign writers have been going in and out of here like cats through a swinging door. Stay here, do a good job, and you'll get a promotion."

This was not the time to mention that I would be leaving for college in September. But I would work extra hard. I would also look hard and learn and be prepared for when I finished school.

The job, Mr. Anderson admitted, was "crummy." I was to fill requests from buyers for counter signs, write them, and have them printed and installed. But the salary, to me, was great. Jean, Jenny, and Martha were at Northwestern Insurance for $60 a month. I would be making $17.50 a week.

As I zipped from the sign shop to the selling floor to my desk in the corner of the artists' room, there was a lot to see. One male and three female copywriters sat in small offices. Jim was elderly and wrote men's department ads. Flo was chubby, fortyish, and wrote ads for the children's department. Shy, quiet Betty, I learned, was a graduate of the prestigious Milwaukee Downer

College. She handled drugs, notions, and shoes. Maureen Maynard was high on the rungs. She wrote copy for middle-priced dresses and coats.

At the top of the ladder, Kay Daly glowed. She did the high-fashion ads and looked it. For me she was a daily fashion show as she swooped from her elegant office downstairs to our messy quarters above. Here, I decided, was someone worth studying.

Often she returned from her business trips to California and New York to storm at Mr. Anderson and our top boss, Jack Niefer. I walked *very* slowly past his door while Kay berated them for some mistake. Even important Mr. Niefer apologized.

Then came the news that Kay Daly was leaving for a fabulous job in New York. I would miss this colorful model of mine, but as I carried a "Vassar Bras—Reduced for Clearance" sign back from the print shop, I gave it some thought.

With Kay gone, would everyone else move up? Would Maureen get Kay's job, Flo get Maureen's? If Betty moved up, the bottom rung would be empty. But I had been at Gimbel's only three weeks!

In the elevator I weighed, once again, the humiliaton of being turned down against the chance I might not be. I could at least write some samples and see how they looked. If I did write the samples and thought they were good, I would talk to Mr. Niefer, not Anderson. Anderson stared at my blouse and my legs. Mr. Niefer was businesslike. And he was the top boss.

Two days later, I prayed to the top of Mr. Niefer's bald head as he read the samples I had written. He finally looked up. "I wish you'd been with us a little bit longer, but your copy is good. I think, Miss Mark, you deserve the chance. The salary we'll pay is twenty-two fifty a week. All right with you?"

I managed to nod. This could hardly be true! I would bless Kay Daly for the rest of my life. Twenty-two fifty a week! For doing work I loved to do! A big store was paying me all that money—and I was still only seventeen. I walked down the hall to my desk in the back, to sit, to hug this incredible fortune inside. And to sneak peeks at Betty's office, which would soon be mine. And to write, on my lunch break, to Tony.

That evening, Mother's disbelief—and then suspicion—did not put out my glow. "Twenty-two fifty is a lot of money to pay a young girl. What's Mr. Niefer like?" Mother herself made only $25 a week.

I described Mr. Niefer—medium height, bald, and very nice. Did Mother think he would pay me that much just because he liked me? He hardly knew me, only my work.

Mother and Grandmother both shook their heads. Only Grandfather smiled. Grandmother said, "Something will happen. Just wait and see."

For two wonderful months I reveled in my job as a full-time real-life copywriter. Two days before my eighteenth birthday, Grandma's prediction came true.

Mr. Anderson sent for me. When I entered his office, he closed the door. He was not flirtatious or joking. He was red-faced angry.

"You, young lady, have committed a serious offense. You are *not* eighteen and you've been working here without a Child Labor Law permit."

I was afraid to ask him how he had found out. All I could do was let him shout and say meekly that I would be eighteen on Monday.

"*That* is immaterial! You've worked over two months against the law. Do you realize you've put Gimbel's in serious trouble? We could be ground to powder legally for hiring a minor."

A vision of crumbled stores—in Milwaukee, New York, Philadelphia—came to my mind. Crumbled stores with me standing near them in rags. Grandmother had been right. It had been too good to be true.

While Mr. Anderson continued raging, I wondered where I could get another job . . . if ever. My criminal record might follow me to college! Would I end up in jail as Dr. Schnell had predicted?

Finally Mr. Anderson's tirade stopped. He shuffled some papers. I was now, he said, to take my "seventeen-year-old fanny home." On Monday I was to put my correct birth date on the store records before starting work.

I took approximately six steps down the hall before I realized I had not been fired. During the next slow five steps I wondered why. Then I remembered Barker High and the editorship that broke the rules. My, my, Gimbel's must need me badly not to bounce me out on my underage rear. I took three more steps grinning, then turned around.

At Mr. Anderson's office door I grinned some more and said, "As long as I'm not fired, I've been meaning to ask you for a raise."

Mr. Anderson stared, gasped, and then guffawed. "Kid," he

said, when he stopped laughing, "if only for having that much goddamned nerve, you deserve one. It's worth five more dollars a week."

I was suddenly "rich" and I loved it, but soon I would have to quit to start college. I had already paid my tuition and my first deposit at the dorm. Tony, however, was much more excited than I. His letters were filled with praise and advice: "Don't study *too* hard, just hard enough. Leave time for social life, too." I hoped I could study at *all*. I hadn't had much practice at Barker High.

But it had to be done. Tony—and that blue book I had read long ago—said a degree was important. I would have to go to college and I would have to quit my job.

At the end of August 1943, I went into Mr. Niefer's office to give my two weeks' notice.

"I'm sorry to lose you, Lois."

"I'm sorry to go."

"What are your plans after college?"

"To write advertising, Mr. Niefer."

He glanced up at his own diploma, framed on the wall, and then back at me. "Perhaps I shouldn't say this, but you *are* writing advertising now."

"But to get a top job, don't I need a degree?"

He paused, moved his ashtray, looked out his window, lined up his pens. "This is, my dear, only one man's opinion, and you must decide. I don't know who has a degree in my department and who does not. I only know who writes well. In four years you can have a degree—or four years' experience. You must decide which gamble to take."

As I sat in Mr. Niefer's sunny office, observations I had largely ignored filed through my head. There was no diploma in Anderson's office. The head of our store was *proudly* unschooled. Four years from now—with my degree—I might be looking for the job I was holding down *now*.

I was making a decision that would affect my life forever. But classrooms, I knew well enough, were not for me. I loved the world I was in right now and it felt right to stay.

"May I take my resignation back, Mr. Niefer?"

Tony understood my decision. So did the University of Wisconsin, which refunded my money. I would use it to visit Tony in the fall. By then he would be in Union City, Tennessee, not too far away. Meanwhile, I settled in happily to what I thought would be a long and successful career at Gimbel's.

My career seemed easy to map. People, I noticed, moved around often in advertising. Kay had left for New York; our top artist had moved on to Chicago. Betty was pregnant and might leave. Even Mr. Niefer or Mr. Anderson might get better offers elsewhere. I had the luxury of time to watch, to learn, and to move up ladders.

At the office, chubby, fortyish Flo and I had become friends. She was divorced, maternal, and amused by my dreams. "So you want to aim for Niefer's job, eh? Well, good luck to you, honey. I don't have your ambition. You're sure they'd let a woman run this department?"

Flo smiled at my indignation. "Sure they would," I said. "Look at Bernice Fitzgibbons. She created 'Does Macy's Tell Gimbel's?' She practically runs all the advertising in New York!"

As far as I was concerned, if one woman did things, so could the rest.

Flo continued to smile. I knew her life was focused on Bill, the sweet-looking guy she intended to marry if he ever stopped drinking. Then, she said, she would sit home and write her book. It was hard to understand her choices, but she was nice about listening to mine.

Women, I reminded Flo, ran all kinds of corporations. Helena Rubinstein had built her own company. So had Coco Chanel. Through the store I had learned about Elizabeth Arden, Hattie Carnegie, and Adele Simpson. It was not all Roz Russell fiction. This was real life.

Flo continued to smile.

Back in my office I gave it some thought. People did choose different goals and that was all right. Not everyone could run General Motors. Someone—man or woman—had to run the grocery store and deliver the mail. But it was hard to understand the goals of my classmates. For Mother and Grandmother it was probably too late, but why had Jenny, Jean, and Martha—and even Grace— settled for jobs they admitted were dull?

Martha was engaged now. So was Jenny. Grace talked of being a nurse, but *only* talked. All of them, Jean included, had almost disappeared into the big gray stone insurance building up near the lake. Along with hundreds of other young women, they worked with cards, numbers, and files. Jean hoped to get promoted. Martha and Jenny planned to go from files to keeping house. Did they not *want* to test the world? This was 1943, not some dark-age time when women had no choice.

Martha said, "Well, you're different." I did not feel different. Only more curious, perhaps, as to what the world was like and how I might fit in. I had had some "crazy" dreams, but so far they had all come true.

When the men came home from war, my dreams might not come true so fast. There would be more competition for jobs. But as a draft-proof female, I had gotten a wonderful start. No matter what happened now, I had tested the world a bit and found I could fit in just fine.

It was like learning about Grandma's cooking. I was eating in restaurants now, amazed to find that steak could be juicy and tender, that eggs were not black-edged and hard. There was a lot more out there that I wanted to taste.

And then it was November. I arranged for some extra days off to visit Tony in Tennessee. It would be so good to see him. I could talk with him, hold him, and feel warmed by our love—and come back to continue my life.

Chapter 5

THE TRAIN I TOOK to visit Tony was crammed with wartime travelers—servicemen going home or back from leave, their wives and children who were following them. Men in khaki stood in the aisles. Babies and children fussed and cried. The women's room was the diaper-changing center. Sleepy, red-eyed women—some of them young girls—changed red-bottomed babies.

I felt sorry but proud for those women. That was what wives should do, follow their husbands no matter how hard it was. Sometimes I helped them. I held diaper pins or the patched rubber pants. I gave up my seat for a while.

When I changed trains in Chicago, the cars were less crowded. I sat near the window and watched the scenery. The train reached Indiana, my father's home state. I could hear Mother's voice: "He doesn't love you. If he did, he'd at least send you a [birthday, Christmas, graduation] card." Still, I watched for any tall, slim, fair-haired man who just might come into view. I saw nothing but flat plains.

Finally I was in Union City, Tennessee, and in Tony's khaki arms—arms I had once believed I would never feel again.

As we walked to the Davy Crockett Hotel where he had reserved a room for me, we both talked at once—Tony about his cadet training, I about my career. That night we slept side by side. Someday we would make love, but not until we were married.

The next day I met Tony's friends—all married men whose wives were with them. There were jokes about living on an air cadet's pay, much lower than a private's or corporal's.

Millie, a freckled blond from Ohio, said, "They want to discourage cadets from getting married. But Pete and I fooled them. I learned to eat less."

Pete, "Rube," Jack, and Tony talked of finally being allowed to fly small planes alone—of Immelmanns and outside loops. Amy, Millie, and Carrie talked of the fatal crashes that were frequent among cadets. My stomach contracted. I had thought Tony was safe for now.

That night, in my hotel room, Tony asked me to stay and marry him. His bulldog face was soft and his brown eyes misty. He said, "I know it's selfish, but I want you here so much. Just think about it, honey."

I tried to hide my dismay. "I *will* think it over." I kissed him good night. He went back to his barracks. I smoked cigarettes.

Tony had never asked me for anything before. He had always been the one to give—to give comfort after hurts from my mother, to give advice, encouragement, and unending love. How could I tell him I did not want to get married? I owed him so much. He might never come back from the war. A few months together might be all we would have. It was selfish to think of my job when Tony might have no future at all.

The ashtray was full. There was only one chance to escape with my conscience intact. I could telephone Mother. She might forbid me to marry so young.

I prayed while the operator handled the call. Please, please make her say no. I had seldom asked—or followed—her advice before, but just this once I fervently wished her to be stubborn and firm.

"Mother, Tony wants me to stay here and marry him."

"That's nice, dear."

"Mother, don't you think I'm too young to get married? I'm barely eighteen."

"But he's such a nice boy. He'll make a good husband."

When I stood next to Tony at the altar of the Methodist church, I waited for God to strike me down for my unbridelike thoughts or to send me some sign. Tony, a casual Catholic, believed he knew why I did not want a priest. He thought it was because of the bitter feelings my family had for my Catholic father. But as I stood there, pushing thoughts of divorce away, I knew I had chosen that Protestant ceremony for Tony. A Catholic marriage could make difficulties for him someday.

The ceremony began. No thunderbolt, no sign. As the little fat minister spoke words I did not hear, I noticed a vent in the floor. I bargained with God. If Tony dropped the ring and it rolled into the vent, that would be the sign. I could plead superstition and stop all this.

Tony placed the wide gold ring securely on my finger. I would now have to send my telegram of resignation to Gimbel's.

Reluctant as I was to be a wife, I would be just as happy not to be a virgin. Finally I would find out what all the mystery was about. Tony, typically, was tender, gentle, and enormously patient.

"Are you *sure*," I asked, "that this is how it's done?" How could *that* enter my very small hole?

Tony, who had waited four years for this moment, could stop, grin, and say, "Honey, there really aren't many alternatives."

Finally it worked. It felt good to have Tony that close. The wild ecstasy I had read about would come, Tony said. There was no hurry. I enjoyed being cuddled and petted, enjoyed Tony's shuddering gasps.

For me, eating had a higher priority than sex. Millie had been accurate. The Air Corps discouraged marriage—and eating too. Tony's pay was $70 per month. Rooms rented for $10 a week. Even my bad arithmetic showed that this left $30 for luxuries like food.

I was determined to be as cheerful as possible on an empty stomach. It was *my* problem. Tony lived and ate in the barracks all but two nights a week. No need to worry him, but I could ask him to bring things from the mess when I went to the field. The bus fare, I figured out, was the cost of my meal. For lunch I went to the USO, where leftover food was half-price.

How Millie, Amy, and Carrie managed I did not know. Perhaps they got money from home. I could not ask Mother or Grandfather. They probably missed the rent I had been paying. Tony's folks sent "special treats." I examined the candy, cookies, and homemade fruitcake, mulling over the relative merits of hunger pangs versus stomach cramps. I took on the cramps.

Getting a job, I was told by my friends, was impossible. No one hired cadet wives who were transferred every two months.

In December we were transferred to Newport, Arkansas, Tony by transport plane and I by train. As I got off the train, I made a vow: I was going to get a job. Tony had noticed how thin I was, and even I was beginning to worry. Since I had lied about my age so often, I could lie about Tony's being an air cadet.

A short, stubby woman owned the *Newport Gazette*. "Miz" Ella listened to my credentials and asked my husband's rank. I gulped and said, "Private." If she saw us in town, maybe she would not notice the small cadet wings. If necessary, I could hug him and block them out.

Miz Ella said, "If you work out all right helping Joe, I can take some time off. You write the features and soldier-boy news. And light that damn gas burner soon's you come in. Everyone's late around here."

Lighting the gas oven proved to be the hardest part. Joe, the editor, was a nice little man who shook when Miz Ella spoke. When Miz Ella left to "visit down Georgia," Joe let me write whatever I chose. I lit the gas burner, made friends in the print shop, and interviewed everyone in town. Tony was transferred before Miz Ella came back. I was sorry I never got to know her, but glad she never knew of my lie. Miz Ella's wrath, I suspected, had driven poor Joseph to his tremors.

Our next stop, Moultrie, Georgia, had no newspaper—and the room rents were higher: $12.50 a week for Mrs. Spencer's back room. That left about 66 cents a day for bus fare and food. The weight I had gained in Arkansas disappeared. Several times, in desperation, I raided Mrs. Spencer's kitchen. One cracker, three grapes, a piece of ham, would not, I hoped, be missed. I now understood how people could steal, but I never dared steal enough to fill myself up.

I still did not want Tony to know how hungry I was. He had worries enough in those planes.

When I heard that the USO needed a secretary, I felt I had no choice. "Must take shorthand and type fast." I could do neither, but before they found out I might earn a week's pay.

Mr. Cullom, the USO director, was a tall, sandy-haired Georgian with an infectious grin. "Wal, li'l lady, you're the only one to apply. Sure looks like the job is yours."

Thank heavens he talked very slowly. I had already decided that people probably did not remember *exactly* what they dictated. If I got the names right and the gist of the letters, I might squeak by. I made squiggles on my pad and listened *hard*. When Mr. Cullom left the office, I was alone. I could laboriously type and retype until it looked right. The first day he signed my letters without complaint.

It was on the second day that I asked him about the "colored" signs. There were none at the USO, but I had seen them now in three different states—in waiting rooms, rest rooms, and even drinking fountains. I had tested the fountain marked "colored" and been surprised when the water was *white*. From then on I ignored the signs at my convenience. If the line at the "white" rest room was long, I moved to the "colored." No black or white person had ever said a word. But I was curious now, and this friendly, easygoing boss of mine was someone to ask.

For the rest of the day, Mr. Cullom "explained" segregation.

"*They're* not as clean as you and me," he said.

"But they cook in white houses and take care of white children. They have to be clean for that." I knew southern ways were different, but I wished they made some sense.

For the next four weeks, Mr. Cullom worked hard at answering unanswerable questions. And dictated few letters.

I never started the discussions. Mr. Cullom did. He seemed determined to persuade me—and perhaps himself as well—that southern-style segregation was right. I merely asked questions. "If *they* don't pay taxes to build good schools, why don't *you* build good schools so that *someday* they can pay taxes?"

Mr. Cullom often disappeared for hours, only to return with new arguments that made no sense. I was gradually losing interest in the subject, but on he went—and so did my paychecks.

After my hard days of office discussion, I would meet Tony at the base, always relieved to see him alive. He was in advanced fighter-plane training now, and planes crashed often. Usually we would join Amy and Rube at the Cadet Club for dancing or Ping-Pong or talk. We talked about rumors—that the Japanese had some new secret weapon or that there were too many pilots waiting on bases for planes. Their whole class, Rube had heard, might be "washed out."

One Monday night when I stepped off the bus at the base, I knew something had happened. Tony's face was pale, tight, and working for control. He led me away from the lights to a place behind the club.

"I washed out today." And his voice broke.

Inside, I was glad. Anything was safer than flying fighter planes, but Tony looked destroyed. I held him, urging him to cry. For once he needed me.

Rube, he finally told me, had washed out too, both of them on minor technicalities. So the rumor had been true. This class of pilots had not meshed with plane production. I tried to make Tony see it that way.

The Air Corps moved fast. Tony and Rube would leave for radar observer training in a week. Amy and I would follow them to the new field at Boca Raton, Florida. I would have to resign as Mr. Cullom's secretary. At least he could now get one who knew how to take shorthand.

When I explained I had to quit, Mr. Cullom, to my mystification, looked sad. "I'm really sorry to see you go. You're the best secretary I ever had."

I hardly had time to ponder his remark. Tony's transfer coincided with another significant event. I had missed two periods and was fairly sure I was pregnant. With savings from my salary, I could take a trip home to break the news to my family and Tony's before joining him in Florida.

My emotions about being pregnant were mixed. Tony was simply dismayed. "Baby," he said. "I don't need a baby. I have you. And we don't know what the future is. I might not come back."

But if Tony's child was the only future I had, I wanted the baby. I was, I felt, awfully young to be a mother, but I really had no choice. The thought of a small person growing inside me was endearing. On the other hand, if I had a child I could never leave Tony. I would never take a child from its father as I had been taken.

With my sketchy knowledge of birth control, it was surprising I had not gotten pregnant before. Condoms, I found out, could burst, and I was too embarrassed to ask advice from other wives. I bought some vaguely worded product from the drugstore. Amy saw it in my drawer. "Worried about venereal disease?" she asked.

Amy, a former nurse, explained about diaphragms, but it was too late now. Perhaps that was how Fate arranged things. I would have Tony's baby and stay married forever.

Tony left for Florida and I for Milwaukee. Wartime traveling was bad enough, but it seemed as if no one but me h.d ever wanted to go from Moultrie to Milwaukee. I crisscrossed the South, changing trains, it seemed, hourly. When I found a seat where I could drop off to sleep, it was time to change in Atlanta, Memphis, Nashville, Chicago. I reached home feeling beached and bedraggled, but full of my news.

Mother said, "That's nice, dear." Grandma said, "Now you'll find out." But Grandfather twinkled.

Tony's parents were delighted with the thought of a grandchild, even a Protestant one. They offered to pay for a *plane* ride back south. With thoughts of those trains still clear in my mind, I accepted with thanks. I had never flown, but it had to be better.

As I waited to board the twin-engine plane, I looked at it closely. What if those rivets and bolts worked loose during flight? Too late to turn back. What I could do was sit in the rear. Planes crashed nose down, did they not?

In the swaying tail I was airsick before our first stop in Chicago. By Indianapolis, my fear that the plane would crash had given way to fear that it *wouldn't*. My only hope was being "bumped." At any stop, military personnel could claim my seat and leave me behind as I wanted to be.

At every stop I staggered off the plane, hoping some soldier was assigned to Miami. Smiling airline clerks instead praised my "luck," stamped my ticket, and sent me back to filling airsickness bags.

As the plane took off from Jacksonville, an army colonel came to my messy, smelly seat. "Young lady," he said, "I've watched you since Chicago. If you'd move up front where there's less motion, you'd feel a lot better."

I did. But why had he waited so long to tell me? Men like *this* were running the war?

He had indeed waited too long. That night in the motel room Tony had reserved for me, the terrible cramps began. I felt too sick, exhausted, and pain-racked to think. Raw-liver-like chunks came out of me. I decided I was not really pregnant after all. Tony, I knew, would be glad. I was not sure how I felt.

Time passed quickly and pleasantly in Florida, though the newspaper had no job for me. Instead, I wrote ads for a restaurant in return for whatever I ate. My biggest problem was shoes. My only pair had a hole in the sole and Florida sidewalks were hot. I planned my day carefully: to the USO early for Ping-Pong and bridge, then home after dusk.

Sometimes, as I waited for the Florida sun to abate, I felt sure that being "poor" had its advantages. I had learned a great deal and had managed, so far, to survive. Living on little would never be frightening again. By now I knew that some couples lived on their savings and some received money from home. Tony and I had married too quickly to save, and money from home never came. That, I decided, was just as well. Soon Tony would get his lieutenant's commission and wings. The lean days would end, but I didn't really regret them.

In the last weeks before our husbands got their wings, Amy, of all the wives, became my best friend. I liked Carrie all right, but she treated Jack like a child. "Men just don't know how to take care of themselves" was her favorite theme. She had Jack's postwar career planned: law school on the GI Bill, then corporate—not criminal—law. Millie was the opposite with Pete. She asked him, Amy said laughingly, when to wash her hair! Amy and Rube seemed ideal: caring, cooperative, and equally matched. That was the way a marriage should be.

Still, the other marriages looked happy. Maybe, I thought, Carrie *liked* mothering Jack, and Pete *liked* playing father to Millie. I liked leaning on Tony at times, but it had felt good when he leaned on me, brief as that episode had been. Wartime marriages, Amy said, were all "happy" for wives who followed their husbands. With death looming on the training fields and ahead in the war, who, she said, bothered to quarrel?

"After the war," Amy said, "we'll all find out who's matched up right."

"After the war" was a vague, misty era to me.

Just before our men got their wings, Amy told me her news. She was pregnant with a child she wanted badly to bear. She was appalled at my plane ride experience, sure it had made me miscarry. No planes for her.

The solution was simple. Tony wanted to buy a car, and his new lieutenant's pay made it possible. We would drive, all four of us, to the next base, at Fresno.

On the used-car lot in Florida, I saw only one car—a black, four-door Ford convertible. Tony pointed out its impracticalities. I saw my hair streaming in the breeze. It was, Tony admitted, mechanically sound. Thank heavens. I would have pushed it across the country if necessary.

With the top down as often as possible, we drove to California. Neither Amy nor I could drive, but the men took turns. I reveled in the scenery of exotic Louisiana, flat Texas, the mountains of New Mexico, Arizona's deserts, and, finally, Fresno.

I had only time enough to find and rent another room when rumors began of a transfer back east. The colonel on the plane with his too-late advice was now a symbol to me of army intelligence.

Amy said, "Where will they send us?"

"Back to Florida, of course. Remember, Tony and Rube scored highest on *navigator* aptitude tests. So they trained them instead to observe radar. To predict the army, just take logic and reverse it."

I won $5 when the orders came through.

There was only one enormous problem. The men were being flown back to Boca Raton on Monday. How could we get my precious convertible there? Three days was rather a short time to learn to drive.

Tony and I had our very first quarrel. We compromised. *If* I could pass the driving test on Monday, I could drive to Florida. If not, I would sell the car and fly.

On Saturday, Tony explained the clutch, the gears, and the accelerator. On Sunday, I managed to lurch around the deserted parking lot nearby. Monday morning, Tony left, confident that no sane policeman would pass me.

The Fresno motor vehicle office was crowded when I arrived. One state trooper behind the desk looked resigned. The other looked harassed. I passed my written test without a mistake. The short, harassed trooper waved me outside.

"Just drive around the block," he said while he sat in my car and sorted papers on his lap.

Luck— I guessed—was with me. The stoplights were all green, and the parking space I pulled out of and into was clear and wide. The trooper scribbled on a piece of paper, handed it to me, and hurried inside.

I had passed.

As we packed the car on Tuesday, Amy, I felt, was weighing me against flight. If I had been unselfish, I would have suggested she fly. Road maps, however, had calmed me. They were easy to read. I found I could get around cities and take mountain roads instead. Cities were humiliating for me. I could not yet coordinate the gears and the clutch, and I lurched from stop signs like a drunken turtle. Mountain roads would have very few signs.

I had no idea, until we reached them, that mountain roads were quite so narrow or that my car would seem so wide. Amy, a devout Catholic, held her beads. I tried to smile reassuringly as I looked at rock walls to my left and sheer drops to my right. In an emergency there was only one way to go—nowhere at all.

I remembered how I'd felt at my first college prom. I could stop and perish, or push on ahead. I might *perish* ahead, but there was not much choice. I had written to let Tony know we had left. I watched other cars. They were managing. So—please—could I.

Somewhere near Las Cruces, New Mexico, I found I had relaxed my white-knuckled grip on the wheel. By Van Horn, Texas, I was ready to try city stop signs. By Houston I felt I could actually drive. By New Orleans it seemed safe to phone ahead—to reserve a hotel room in Boca Raton and leave a message for Tony that we would arrive.

When he saw us, he hugged me as if he had never expected to see me again. I never told him I had had my own doubts.

In Florida the weeks passed too fast. Training there would be short and then Tony would go. At least, I decided, we could rent a small house. For the last few weeks I could be a *real* wife. Now that he was allowed off the base each night, I could—well, at least sew on his buttons and cook.

The first day I stood in the kitchen of our tiny furnished house, I realized I was starting below scratch. Grandmother had always chased me from her kitchen. However, the local library had cookbooks, the best way to start.

The cookbook I chose was not as specific as I had hoped, but I made out a list. Veal scallops sounded easy, though the recipe did not specify what kind of veal to use. Cooking peas could not be hard, and when I got to the grocery, I found round tubes of biscuits with exact instructions printed on the package. I handed over the ration stamps I had never used before and asked the grocer for one pound of "veal."

"Veal breast or veal steak?"

Breast sounded more tender to me.

The meat with its creamy white membrane was hard to cut up. While I struggled, the biscuit tube stood on the range. I "sautéed" the veal and put on the peas.

But "sauté until tender" took awfully long. The squares I had measured and struggled to cut seemed to get tougher the longer they fried.

Well, at least the biscuits would be good. I heated the oven while they stood on the range.

"Tap tube sharply on the table edge," it said on the tube. Easy enough.

And then the room was filled with flying biscuits, their huddled masses yearning to breathe free. It was easy to throw away the ones on the floor, but tears filled my ears as I scraped others off the ceiling. I baked the three that had stuck to the sink.

Tony chewed manfully on the shriveled squares of veal, ate the peas that tasted scorched. "Honey," he said, "you're too precious to risk in a kitchen. You weren't meant to cook." He held me, dried my tears, and took me to the Officer's Club for dinner from then on.

My feeling of failure did not fade. I wanted Tony to *want* me to cook. To him, nothing I did was wrong. That was how it had always been. Unquestioning love was a father's love, and at times it felt good. But children had to grow, and if Tony made no demands, I could not grow. Lovely as being loved was, there had to be more.

Tony got his overseas orders. We would have one week together back home, then he would leave for San Francisco and for some unknown destination in the Pacific. On our last night, he brushed my hair back from my face, traced my eyebrows with his blunt fingers, and said, slowly, "I never expected you to stay married to me for long. I just wanted to have you as long as I could."

"Tony, why would you say such a silly thing?"

"Because I was thinking it, honey."

At the airport, I realized I had never gotten used to good-byes. The pain was as bludgeoning as ever. When Tony's plane took off, I walked around the airport until the dizziness of terrible loss subsided.

Work, I knew, was the anodyne to pain. "Tomorrow"—or the next day at the latest—I planned to visit Gimbel's and see if they wanted me back.

But instead I wrote letters to Tony while Grandfather's house ran as before. Nothing had changed, including me. I did not feel married at all. Marriage was a house, a husband coming home each night, and children to love. My months with Tony had been wonderful. I loved him a lot. Real marriage would come after the war.

But meanwhile I could do *something* wifely. Grandma could teach me to knit. I would start out with socks for Tony—and went to get the materials at once.

My dark mood brightened a bit as I wandered through the Boston Store. Here I had had my first real-world success, as a frightened high-school girl presenting her idea for a column.

I wondered how J.D. was faring and if he knew I would always feel a special gratitude to him for giving me my first important boost.

Then I heard his voice behind me. "Lois! Where have you been?"

I told him about Gimbel's and about my marriage.

"But why did you go to Gimbel's for a job? Why didn't you come to me?"

"You said, J.D., to see you after *college*. I never went."

"Hell, neither did I. Listen, are you looking for a job now?"

I nodded.

"O.K. I've got something in mind. Hang on and I'll call you in a day or two." His tall, bearlike figure disappeared into the crowd. I went to the notions department to pick up the yarn, needles, and instructions for Tony's socks. I could knit, perhaps, on the trolley back and forth to a job.

J.D. phoned the next day and announced as calmly as if he were giving the time that I would be writing a radio show.

"But I don't know how!"

"You'll learn."

In his office J.D. explained it was "all very simple." The store had bought a broadcast package of classical jazz. I would write the record introductions from the information on the jackets and write the commercials for the store. I was to go over to WTMJ, the station broadcasting the show. Frank Hunt, the station's copy director, was expecting me at two.

As I drove to the station, I reflected that, this time, things had moved too fast. I had taken wild gambles before, but only when desperate. Now I was not. Driving through the mountains was all very well, but if I had failed there, I would have crashed on some deserted curve. A failure now would be public and awful.

Dark, bushy-haired Frank Hunt seemed the only person who

shared my lack of confidence in me. Had I written for radio before? No, I had not. He scratched his ear.

Frank explained the tight timing of radio. He pointed out that
the exact length of each musical selection was printed on the records. "Your commercials should run sixty seconds, so with your
record intros, it must all add up to thirty minutes. Do you have a
stopwatch?"

Not yet. But with my incredible $50-a-week salary I could cer-
tainly buy one.

"The continuity," Frank said, "should be here on Tuesday for
your Saturday show."

Asking him what *continuity* meant could have depressed us
both. It was probably the script.

Back in my office in the advertising department, I wrote as best
I could. The jazz information was fascinating and the commercials, I thought, were a breeze. Adding up numbers of seconds was
hard, but by concentrating, using my fingers, and checking three
times, it seemed to come out right.

Then came the broadcast. I sat in the client's room with the
time salesman, the program director, and Frank. The broadcast
was piped into the room.

The men around me were silent. I wished the announcer were
too. The script I had written was terrible. Writing *spoken* words
was far different from writing words meant for print. Each awkward phrase I had written hit me like a bullet. The ego drained
out of me like blood until it could have covered the floor.

When the interminable broadcast finally ended, the men were
polite. After all, I did represent the client. The salesman and program director escaped when they could. Only Frank hung behind.

In the cream-tiled corridor of the radio station, I glanced up at
his strained face. "Frank," I said thoughtfully, "I think that must
be the worst script in the history of radio."

Frank's face relaxed. "Thank God! I didn't know how to tell
you."

We went into his office, where he dug through piles of paper for
the sample scripts I should have asked for before. No one could
tell me how to write for radio, but by studying good scripts I
might figure out why mine was so bad.

At the store, J.D. insisted he had missed the broadcast, but he
added, "Don't worry. You'll learn."

I would not—I shuddered—be fired. The radio contract had

twelve more weeks to go. But listeners could simply change stations. Even I could not stand twelve more weeks of my terrible scripts.

That night, and for the next few days and nights, I studied the scripts Frank had given me. I read my own copy *aloud,* as an announcer must do. I wrote with my *ear* instead of my eye. The next script was better. Not great, but not bad.

Frank relaxed. So did I. This time I had suffered the humiliation I had dreaded before, and I was still alive. Humiliation was bad, I had learned, but not fatal.

For the next few weeks I wrote my scripts and explored the store. Often, when I took work in for J.D.'s O.K., he would wave me to a chair while he made or took a phone call. After the call he would explain the problem he had dealt with and how it had been solved. I was getting, I knew, a superior education just listening to his phone calls. I noticed he focused on the *tangle* in a problem, then, without assigning the blame, found the solution. The advertising manager, Bill Sawyer, reversed this procedure, putting the blame first without solving the mess. This, I decided, was why J.D. was Bill Sawyer's boss.

As I drove to the store from the radio station one day, I realized that, educational as it was, my days at the store might end with the show. And the show had only nine weeks to run.

By now I had realized that no one ran the world for my convenience—or anyone else's convenience, for that matter. Tony was overseas being shot at. If I wanted to continue to work, I had better think of a way to expand my job.

Back in my cubicle, I stared at a blank piece of paper, waiting for ideas to come. The chore was to think of some way I could make or save money for the store.

I scribbled threads of ideas. Some sounded good in my mind and faded to nothing on paper. At least, I consoled myself, I was finding out what would *not* work—holding live jazz concerts at the store was really a dumb idea.

Crumpled paper piled up around me. My idea for a teen fashion column had come so fast. Why would nothing come now?

Then it did. Teens were still a big—and growing—market. I was nineteen myself, so it was a market I knew. Teens liked music, dancing, a place to gather. What if the store opened a "Teen Canteen" with a jukebox and a place for dancing? When teen-agers came to it, they would have to pass through the store and be tempted to buy. The radio show could publicize it—and I could supervise it—for a long, long time. Teen fashion shows, war-bond drives, and even art competitions could easily be tied in. As I scribbled my notes, the idea held up. I typed a proposal and took it in to J.D.

He read it, nodding, and made four phone calls. In the morning we would meet with the teen department buyers, Bill Sawyer, and Vince Sommer, who was in charge of window displays.

At the meeting J.D. said, "Miss Mark has an idea. Explain it, Lois." Then he crossed his arms over his waistline and looked at me.

"Well—" To my surprise, I spoke coherently. I answered questions and countered objections. I was actually leading a conference of experienced, successful adults! J.D. had pushed me into the water and I had not drowned.

When there were no more questions, J.D. said, "So let's try it." When the others left, he said to me, "Get a week ahead on your radio scripts. I want to send you to New York. There's a fashion promotion being put on by some new teen magazine. You ought to be there."

That night I began my daily letter to Tony, sharing my exciting news. I was being sent to New York! And my job would continue, even expand! But as I scribbled my usual "Can't wait 'til you're home," my stomach contracted. Yes, I wanted him home, prayed for it nightly, yet tonight I realized with shame I did not want him home *right now*. I wanted much more of the life I was leading. I did not want it to end. With a feeling of selfish betrayal, I sealed the letter.

My roomette on the Twentieth Century Limited was wasted on me. I never closed my eyes. Outside the window, towns rushed past. Each town got me closer to New York, the city I had never really expected to see. This was where the giants lived—writers, actors—the top of the world. I would move among them, at least for a little while.

At the New York station I was surprised I could keep up the pace. People moved with practiced haste and I felt gloriously pulled into the rhythm. It felt like dancing, moving my body around, between and past a chorus of crowds.

In the taxi, the cars around us had the same rhythm and there were so *many* of them. Each one knew the split-second timing to avoid a crash. My cab moved upstream like one salmon determined to spawn.

J.D. had said, "There are better hotels than the Astor, but on your first trip, that's where you should stay." I knew now what he meant. The Astor was right on Times Square—noisy, perhaps, for someone who slept, but wonderfully magical for me.

The next day, at the magazine's fashion show, I was sleepy but surprised that I could see several ways to improve it. A male commentator would have been better. The audience was entirely female and would have enjoyed the sight of a man for a change. Boys' clothes, I thought, should have been included too. Girls care how their boyfriends dress. I made notes for a show I would put on back at the store.

When I boarded the train to go home, I felt different from when I had arrived. Something had happened; I was not sure what. Could a person be changed by a city?

The young woman I sat with in the dining car was friendly, witty, and warm. She talked largely of her husband, a medical officer with General Patton's troops, and of her two children. Her life in suburban Lake Forest, she said, would be heaven on earth when her husband came home. In the club car we talked until late, of houses, committees, and kids. She excused herself to go to bed.

I went to my roomette and wept.

There was, I felt, something terribly wrong with me. I had a wonderful husband who loved me. I loved him. But I did not want her kind of life. Maybe this was what Grandmother meant when she said, "You're too smart for your own good." I *knew* there were challenges out there, and I wanted to meet them all.

Some women combined marriage and a career. That was impossible for me. Marriage meant children, and my children must have the full-time mother I had not had, not someone on the end of a phone line or drained from a hard day of work.

Once again, the roomette was wasted. I sat in the bed, smoking, weeping, and watching the landscape rush by. I *did* love Tony, so much that I did not want to ruin his life or the lives of the children we might have. Tony deserved someone who put him first as he put me—not someone who would always wonder what she might have done. If I chose love over ambition, I might demand more compensation from Tony than even he could give, might demand from my children the success I had not reached for.

And if I chose ambition over love? Well, I might never meet another man as wonderful as Tony, might never be loved in the same way again.

The train was now stopped just over the Indiana border, Father's home state. I had survived without his love and had found Tony. But I had also found something within myself. I needed to know how much I could grow as a person. That curiosity would not go away—and in the end I would hurt Tony more than I could hurt him now.

It was time to change trains in Chicago. I saw the woman from the dining car as we disembarked. We wished each other good luck as she rushed for her suburban train.

She was so sorry, she said, that we were going in different directions.

Chapter 6

ON MY FIRST DAY BACK from New York, even familiar sights looked subtly different. I willed the screeching trolley to hurry past houses and factories and into downtown Milwaukee.

Milwaukee was not fast-paced, tumble-jumble New York, but it was my arena for the future I planned. If I could first make it there, I could go on—I could go on anywhere. Suddenly I felt as I had when I was three years old and the world outside my door had been welcoming. Now, at nineteen, I had had some successes to bolster that belief.

As the trolley stopped and started on its slow trip downtown, even grimy brick buildings had a new sunlit sheen. There were shadows too. Telling Tony of my decision would not be easy. Then I remembered a statement he had made: "I never expected you'd stay married to me for long." Tony may have known, better than I, what I needed to do.

Finally the trolley reached my stop. I jumped from its side to walk the three blocks to the store. On the street I tried to match my pace to those around me. I gave up. Glum-faced businessmen might lag if they wished, but my feet had acquired that fast New York pace.

A truck driver whistled. I waved and danced on, through the door of the store. Inside, I collided with Ella Leet, our advertising department messenger. "Lois, how was the trip? Shit, I've got these proofs to deliver, but I'll be back in an hour."

We arranged to have coffee. I grinned as Ella glided away, hips swaying, bust thrust out. I moved through the crowd of employees and boarded an elevator.

And at last I was in my small, messy office. Even that looked different, lighter, larger, and ready for work. I began to type my report. My typing had miraculously improved! The words came out fast—not my excitement, but the facts J.D. would want to know.

The report was finished when Ella burst into my room and moved some papers from my one extra chair. Ella's deceptively innocent sea-green eyes sparkled with thirst for my news. "Did you meet any men?"

I laughed. Such a typical question for Ella. She was, she had told me, a "displaced party girl." "Why did I have to hit my prime during a war?" She had taken the messenger job at the store, she had said, as a not-too-bad way to meet men—"a better class than you meet in bars." Ella had set her "career" goals long ago. She wanted to be kept. "Mistresses get treated better than wives." But what about children? "I'm not cut out for kids. I'd be a worse mother than Mom."

Different as we were, I enjoyed Ella's friendship immensely. She was shocking, outspoken, profane, but after I learned to stop blushing, I found her delightful, direct, and sincere. She was also a source of knowledge that might come in handy someday.

"Never sleep with a man who tells you he's great. They're always flops. The ones who are good never brag."

And, with a nod toward a salesclerk in notions, "She tried the bedroom route up. In Chicago. Shit, it never works. Screw the buyer, you gotta screw the merchandise manager. And if they don't come across, what do you do? Take the screwing back?"

Ella's knowledge might never have a practical application for me, but it was a side of life I had never known of before. At twenty-two, Ella knew more about sex and store politics than, I suspected, the store president.

According to Ella, sex in business worked only if you were terribly smart. "And if you're smart enough to make it on your back, you're smart enough to make it—and keep it—on your feet."

Meanwhile, Ella was simply having fun. "I wiggle my ass while I'm carrying proofs and practice for bigger game. But the only *job*

I'll settle for is holding some rich guy's hand twice a week when his wife doesn't 'understand.' Hook the guy right and—shit, Anne Boleyn changed the religion of England."

Store politics there, Ella admitted, was not much fun. "Except for Sawyer wanting J.D.'s job, there's not a lot going on. With Kimmelman as president, nothing will. He doesn't play games."

I had already realized that politics would not work for me. If I did not like someone, I could not pretend, could not laugh at Bill Sawyer's cruel little jokes. It would be like sleeping with someone I did not love. Lucky for me, I respected Mr. Kimmelman, head of the store, and admired J.D. with what amounted to awe.

Ella brushed back her long brown hair, widened her eyes, and repeated her initial question: "Did you meet any men?"

Not that I had noticed.

She teased me for "wasting my time." Then she was off, tight skirt wagging.

Time now for me to write the formal proposal for the Teen Canteen I had suggested before the trip. Yes, we could advertise the new promotion on the radio show.

But we could do more than that. Why not invite kids to come to the studio and dance during the broadcast? I had noticed several studios at the station that would work out fine. It would cost the store nothing and would bring kids in to pick up their tickets. I typed up the idea.

J.D. looked over my New York report and my expanded version of the new teen promotion. "Guess the trip was worth it," he said. Yes, he liked the dancing.

"The background noise will add to the show," I said.

J.D. grinned. "Right!"

To be sure I had checked all obstacles, I phoned Jack Beahn. Short, bald, chubby Jack was the station's chief engineer and also my friend. "Jack, are there any union or technical problems that could mess us up?" Jack thought it out and said no. We could, he said, use Studio Two. Plenty of room.

I put in a call to copy-director Frank Hunt to let him know.

In thirty minutes Frank called me back. "Ben Hill says no to the dancing." But why? He lowered his voice. "Maybe he'll tell you."

Indignation made me grab my handbag and head for my car. I had expected to butt heads eventually with the station manager, but not this soon. He looked a lot like my Uncle Bernard: red-faced, arrogant, with the scrunched features of a colicky baby. Often I had heard him yelling at underlings. I had heard the station president yelling at him. Some companies, I suspected, worked this way—ill temper at the top dripped inexorably down. At the time it had not been my problem. Now it was.

As I drove to the station on the outskirts of Milwaukee, I kept my belligerence fueled. Friendly people could be dealt with in friendly ways, but not this fool. Bullies, I suspected, had to be bullied back.

Parking my car in the station lot, I wondered if Ben Hill knew my age. No time to think about it now, but I fervently wished for some way to reach forty fast. Meanwhile, I strode into the station. Nineteen I might be, but I was angry enough for fifty.

Ben Hill's door was open, and I had no intention of losing my pace by stopping at his secretary's desk. I could see he was alone and reading the paper. Hands on hips, I glared down at him. "Why did you say no to the dancing?"

Ben Hill glanced up at me as if I were a bothersome fly. "Because it's against the rules."

I was glad I had double-checked. "It's not against union rules, and whatever insurance you have for your tours will cover my audience too." I was not sure about the insurance, but it sounded convincing to me.

The fly was becoming more irritating. "Well, it's against *my* rules."

"In that case, I'll take the program to a station with different rules." I almost looked around. Had *I* said *that?*

Ben Hill's florid face got redder. "Oh yeah," he sneered. "We'll see what J.D. says." He dialed his phone.

Too late to back down now, but J.D. and Hill had lunch frequently. I might have grossly exceeded my authority and put J.D. in a bad spot personally too.

I sat in a chair, trying to look calmer than I felt. There had not really been a choice. If I caved in now, some even more important benefit to the store might be denied in the future. I raised my chin to look angrily sure that J.D. would back my ultimatum. I arranged my posture as I had seen models do. If the limb I had gone out on was to be sawed off, at least I would fall gracefully.

J.D.'s family was apparently fine. So, Ben Hill reported, was his. Ben Hill glanced up at me contemptuously and said into the phone, "Listen, Joe, *your girl* here has some silly idea about kids dancing in the studio and—" he chuckled—"she says she'll take the program elsewhere if we don't agree."

This his face changed. "Oh. Sure. Listen, I'm sure Miss Mark and I can work it out."

He put down the phone. His look wished me damnation no more than I wished it to him. "J.D. says you're in charge."

I tried to act as if I had known it all the time. Bless J.D. with a hundred years of good fortune. He had backed up my impulsive threat.

I rose to my full five foot five. "Studio Two will do fine. I'll tell Frank and Jack. We'll give tickets away at the store."

He bent to his paper, but as I walked out my back felt warm. In the hallway I tried not to dance.

Department stores move fast. In a week, Vince Sommers, our display manager, had constructed the Teen Canteen. Bill Sawyer ran my ads, and the young people came—to the store and to the studio. The Saturday dancing was more popular than even I had suspected.

Ben Hill's only revenge was to preempt my show for every conceivable "special event." No problem for me; it lengthened the contract.

Some special events were justified. When President Roosevelt died, no one thought of dancing. He had been elected when I was seven years old. I had grown up with his strong, simple, reassuring words. It was almost like losing a parent.

Victory in Europe preempted a broadcast in May. But Tony was in the Pacific. No one could guess how long it would take to end the "other" war.

On a day in early August, I was in J.D.'s office when Bill Sawyer strode in, grinning. "We just dropped something called an atomic bomb. Wiped out a whole Jap city."

J.D. straightened in his chair. I stood up. If, as Bill said, it would shorten the war, that was good. But somehow, inside me, horror and patriotism collided.

Bill announced the second bomb three days later. He put his head into my office and laughed when I winced.

"Listen, kid, if they hadn't dropped those bombs, they'd have started drafting women. Count your blessings."

I had. Long ago.

On August 14, 1945, Japan surrendered. The store, the streets, the city filled with jubilant people. Our men would now come back—and I would have to tell Tony what he was not coming back to.

According to the point system the papers announced (points for combat, length of overseas service, number of children), Tony would not be home for a long time. It was hard to read his letters filled with plans; kinder, I decided, to tell him now.

My tears made the ink run, but I finally wrote: "I love you and I always will, but I don't want to be married."

In a while his reply came. "Honey, I got drunk as a skunk when your letter came. I hurt, but I understand. No matter what you think, we're still going to be friends for the rest of our lives."

As always, Tony made it easy.

The world settled down to normal again. No more plugging war bonds in store ads or on my show. No coupons for gas or sugar or shoes. Even my job was becoming routine. It was time, I decided, to look around. The store was filled with people from whom I could learn.

I had learned from my friend Marie. All through high school she too wanted to write. Her family, unlike mine, had tried to help. So had I. When Bill Sawyer needed a new receptionist, I had rushed to Marie.

"It's a start! You'll know when copywriters leave and you'll have the jump on other applicants."

Marie was hired. Her ebony hair and translucent white skin had visitors taking extra looks. I knew she could write, better in some ways than I. It could not be long before she moved to a copywriter's spot.

Suddenly Marie was gone from her desk. I phoned her at home.

"Lois, I quit. Sawyer hired someone else for Bill Curry's job. He doesn't want women writing housewares, I know. My father is sending me to school. I might as well go."

The next morning I went to see Sawyer. Why had he skipped over Marie?

Sardonic and callous as Bill Sawyer was, his reaction this time seemed sincere. He clapped one bony hand to his head. "Why didn't she say something? I'd have been glad to give her a try!"

Marie, I learned when I called her back, had said nothing since the day she was hired. That day, months before, she had told Sawyer she wanted to write.

"He should have remembered," she said.

"You can't *count* on that!" But Marie had thought she could.

I had always envied her her warm, caring family. I wondered now. She had learned to expect that people would care, remember, and act. Perhaps it was better to expect that they would not.

I was learning from others too—the fiercely competitive whom nobody liked, the cooperative who seemed to elicit from others that little bit of extra effort, the confident, the self-effacing. I studied them all, carefully noting what seemed to work and what did not.

Activities in the dozens of departments sparked ideas. The rough sketches for a chinaware ad excited me. Why not have an expert—a home-economics professor from nearby Marquette University—come in to demonstrate the proper way to set tables? J.D. liked the idea. Do it, he said.

Why not a men's wear fashion show now that men were coming home? (Marie's sister let me borrow her baby for the male model to carry as he walked down the runway in pajamas and robe.) A high-school art show built traffic in our teen department. And when a new cookware line was being promoted, we had a mini quiz—lotteries in Wisconsin were illegal—and gave some away to the winners.

Even my errors were helpful to me. I was learning to think on my feet. Moments before a disk jockey was to broadcast from the store window, promoting a new line of records, a police sergeant walked over to announce that loudspeakers were not allowed on city streets. I held my breath, hoping some thought would come. By luck, I did not close my eyes. Three of the teen-agers I knew from the Canteen were standing near me, waiting for the show to start. One carried a portable radio.

Radios were not illegal on Milwaukee's streets. We had time to send the young people into the store for two more portables, and to hire them to stand there for the rest of the week—the sound turned up loud.

Then one Monday, J.D. called me into his office. "This," he said, "can't go on." He looked seriously at me.

Quickly I searched my mind file for what I had done. Nothing at all I could think of.

"You've been doing your job—and more. I think the store can afford a raise and promotion. That is if you *want* to keep up this pace."

Want to? I was having the time of my life! I said so.

"All right, then which title do you like, Lois?" He was smiling now. "Assistant to me, or something I made up—promotion co-ordinator? Whatever that means."

I had to grin too. Promotion coordinator did sound important. If I ever left the store, it would look good on a *résumé*. "Assistant" to anyone was not as good. I stated my preference.

He nodded. "And I got you a raise. How does a hundred a week sound for now?"

It sounded as if I had not heard him right. Good Lord, I was making $75 already—more money than anyone in my family had ever made. I sat there, unable to close my mouth.

J.D. said, laughing, "One piece of advice. If you ever leave here —and I hope you don't—*try* to keep a poker face when people offer money. You're good. You deserve it. Now get back to work."

I could not quite follow J.D.'s advice. In time I might develop the poker face, but I could not go back to my office. Instead, I had to go to the corner table in the cafeteria to be alone for a while.

The coffee I was learning to drink tasted sharp and hot. Four hundred dollars a month? If I took another sip, perhaps I would come awake. I drank some more. It really was true and it had happened so fast. Wonderful, wonderful!

Wonderful, but scary too, and I didn't know why. I warmed my hands on the cup.

I should be delighted, and part of me was. I had been successful—on my own, hurting no one. Things that I had heard and read were untrue. You did not have to step on others to get ahead. Yet I felt fearful. Why?

Then, at the thought of telling my family, I knew. Grandpa would be pleased. He'd had a stroke that kept him home now. Mother had taken over his salary and his job. She would say my promotion was "nice," but she would look hurt. She must be so tired of being proved wrong. Since the day I fought to escape the secretarial courses, her dire predictions had proved false. And, step by step, we had moved farther apart.

Well, the only alternative was to fail on purpose. And that I could not do. Somehow, it would have to work out.

I left the cafeteria. Four hundred a month was twice what Grandfather—now Mother—made. But I would spend it well. Mother thought the expensive watch I bought her was "nice."

During the next months, life—and I—moved fast. Now I planned two, three, sometimes four promotions at a time for different departments. J.D. sent me off on more trips to visit our "sister" stores—not to New York, but to Cleveland and Detroit.

Ella giggled. *"I* knew you'd do it, but people do talk."

What did she mean?

"Hey, don't get upset! Folks say that you're J.D.'s girl friend. Shit, nothing you can do. If you stick your head out of the crowd, people throw tomatoes."

Yes, but it hurt. What if J.D.'s pretty blond wife heard this trash? And it hurt me too to think that people felt I had not earned my promotion myself. Yet Ella was right. There was nothing on earth I could do—except remember never to believe such gossip.

I was reading an article on something new called television when Ella burst into my office. "Have you met him yet?"

Met who? Whom.

"Our new co-worker. David Cohen. Absolutely gorgeous and *not married.* He worked here before the war. Now he's out and he starts work today."

I said, "Hmm," and went back to my reading. The store would soon be sponsoring a demonstration of this new television, one of the postwar "miracles" people had predicted. Jack and Frank were talking of the station's broadcasting television soon. The store demonstration would send pictures from one end of the main floor to the other—hardly a practical invention, but one never knew.

Then a masculine voice interrupted my reading. "Hello, I'm David Cohen." I looked up. Ella had been right. He was *gorgeous;* thick, brown, curly hair, brown eyes with a sparkle, and startlingly white, straight teeth. The brown eyes were looking for a place where the rest of him could sit. I swept unfiled folders from the chair.

David said he would be writing furniture copy and asked what I did. Explaining "promotion coordinator" was never easy, but I tried. He looked at my hands. I had removed my wedding ring after writing the letter to Tony, but a new romance was not, just then, for me. I talked about Ella.

Later, over coffee, I told her, "He might not be rich right now, but I'll bet anything he's got a terrific future." There was something in the slow, careful way he talked and the specific plans he had talked about—a few years at the store, then to Chicago, and someday an advertising agency of his own. He had said he felt he could trust me. I knew he could. If he hoped for the job as Sawyer's assistant, I certainly was not competing.

Ella said, "I'm not the type to struggle, pal, while some guy works out his future. Anyway, he's wild about *you*. Shit, he's asked me everything about you but your shoe size."

I was, I pointed out, still legally married. "And business and romance don't mix." I had seen some examples around the store, ex-lovers working together in terrible tension, or one of them having to leave. "Not for me, thanks," I told Ella.

There was no reason, however, why this tall, rather shy man and I could not be good friends. Over coffee in the cafeteria, I learned that he too was an eldest child; that his father was dead and his mother ran the family dry-cleaning shop ("in some ways better than Dad did"). His sister was going to law school and his brother, Sammy, was still in his teens.

David adored his mother. "She's been through a lot and handled every bit of it well." He puffed on his pipe. "After Dad died, she never looked at another man. Probably never will. That's really love."

Like me, David had set his career goals early. The war had set him back. "I had just gotten a start and then—three years out of my life." He would, I assured him, make it up. He had his degree in merchandising and a minor in journalism. His agency dream would come true.

I was not really sure what an agency was, but David explained. Agencies counseled companies on how to advertise. They made their money from commissions paid on newspaper space and radio time. It was, David said, a "cutthroat" business—clients wooed by other agencies, new ideas needed for each campaign—but he thought he could survive.

"The only problem is I'm not much of a salesman, not a razzle-dazzle guy." He puffed on his pipe again. "Better at details, I guess."

But the world needed people like that! My razzle-dazzle father, I told David, would have let us starve. It was my quietly reliable grandfather who had kept us alive.

Coffee—then lunches—with David were becoming regular. It felt good to talk to someone as ambitious as I, someone I learned from whenever we talked. I had not even known advertising agencies existed—or public-relations firms or business consultants. At the moment my own ambitions were vague. I had moved so far so fast that it was almost frightening to plan any more at present. I had to catch up with my dreams.

I loved the store. It was like a family with J.D. in my eyes, at the head. It was good to know everyone's name and to know they knew mine—from the stock boys who helped me move heavy things to the merchandise manager and the head of the store. I walked the aisles feeling as if I belonged.

When I allowed a dream to sneak in, it was of J.D. running the store while I had his job. But there was no rush. I had just become twenty years old.

When lunches with David turned into evening dates, we still talked of his dreams. One evening, as we walked near the lake, David puffed on his pipe and said there was someone he would like me to meet.

"I'd like your opinion on Murray." Murray, it appeared, was an old college friend who had managed to stay out of the war. "Heart ailment," David said, "so his father bought him a partnership in an agency. Now he wants to leave and start one with me. He *is* a razzle-dazzle guy, but maybe too much so."

Yes, I would like to meet Murray. He could be just the partner David needed.

David continued, talking slowly as always and puffing on his pipe, "There's something else. I've fallen in love with you and I don't know what to do about it."

Neither did I. I was divorcing a wonderful man because I could not be a proper wife, because I did not want children right now, and because our careers were so different.

David said, "We'd make quite a team. I don't expect children for a long, long time, and we *can* hire people to cook while you work. Would you consider marrying me?"

Consider was just what I did when David went home. On the same porch where I had sat so often with Tony, I tried to think.

David had made it sound so easy: two people with their separate careers, but each understanding what the other did.

"Great as your Tony sounds," David had said, "you'd never have made a good schoolteacher's wife. You like the business world. You're terrific in it."

As a few late-night cars hurried past, I wondered if it really would work. I did love David, I could admit that. His warm brown eyes and slow, careful ways made me feel safe. At the same time, his ambition and knowledge excited me.

I had loved Tony too. He had given me so much for so long. I

77

respected his choice of careers. Teaching young people, as Tony would do it, was important and wonderful. But it was not exciting to me, and it would have shown. With David, perhaps I could have the best of both worlds—marriage to someone I loved and the freedom to have my career.

I felt it was wrong to decide before Tony came home, wrong to let him find me engaged to another man. David would understand. And now *I* would go to sleep.

David did understand about waiting, but Murray Cantor did not. Murray, it appeared, waited for nothing. Small, red-haired, and always in motion, Murray had hugged me. "Ah, David's betrothed."

"Not yet," I said firmly, but it was hard not to smile. Murray looked like one of Santa's elves and acted as if Christmas were *now*.

We sped through the store. Keeping up with Murray was a complex task. Even David looked strained. Fragments of sentences whipped back to me as I tried to keep up his pace.

Finally, at a table in the restaurant, I could hear what he said. "Advertising is where the future is for young people. The wartime paper shortage will be over soon. Magazine space will be available again. And it's young ideas companies want. We're young. What are we waiting for?"

His present partner, Joe Eagles, was forty-five. Murray, I learned, was twenty-four. If he was David's classmate, he must have sped through college quickly too. David was twenty-five.

Murray was finished eating almost before I'd begun. "There're millions to be made out there," he said to David, "and we're the ones to make them." Murray's freckled face flashed his enthusiasm like neon. David puffed on his pipe.

Murray looked at his watch. "Jesus, I'm a half-hour late! David, I'll call you tonight." He grabbed the check and disappeared in a wave of *Hi*'s and *Hello*'s.

David refilled his pipe, then asked, "What do you think?"

I thought Murray and David might make a good combination. "Murray," I pointed out, "does have experience." He and his partner had operated profitably for three years, he had said.

David puffed on his pipe. "I wish I were your age," he said slowly. "Taking risks at twenty is not like taking them at twenty five."

Suddenly, I felt sorry for David. He was a man, and success was

78

serious to him. The world expected it from him—or he felt that it did. For me, it had all been fun. If I reached my goals, great. I had set them for myself. David seemed to feel that society set them for him. What a terrible burden to bear!

David decided to "think it over." We both went back to work.

For me, life at the store resumed its carousel pace. The television promotion had gone well, although why anyone would want to talk from one booth to another stumped me. That over, I went on to other things—a visiting author, a new type of glove. On an impulse, I had written up our Teen Canteen promotion for a department-store magazine. We had won an award!

J.D. made fewer and fewer corrections on my proposals. In April he announced he would be in New York for a week. I was to sit in his office, handle his calls, and "keep things running" until he got back.

I was not enthusiastic. Would anyone take me seriously? After all, I couldn't even vote yet.

J.D. crossed his hands over his waistline and pushed his glasses back up on his nose. "Don't worry. By now you know how I'd decide on the ordinary problems. If there's an emergency, phone me in New York."

Back in my office, I saw Murray's bright-red head bobbing in David's office. When he left, David asked me to go for a cup of coffee with him. All the way up to the employees' cafeteria, David shook his head but smiled.

When we settled down with our coffee, David said, "Murray was selling me hard. I wish I didn't know how often he goes off on tangents."

"Well, maybe it's right for both of you. He obviously respects you and would listen. He wants you to handle everything but sales."

The smoke from David's pipe reached for the ceiling. "It would take eight to ten thousand to start up. And there are a lot of big agencies in town. How could *we* compete?"

I should, I told myself, stop encouraging David. It was his decision to make. But Murray was right about youth. I had read the same thing in business magazines.

"Look," I said, "you compete on the basis of young, fresh ideas. And even if it fails, starting over at, say, twenty-six is hardly a tragedy. If you don't try it, David, wouldn't you always wonder if you might have succeeded?"

David nodded and puffed. He would think some more, he said.

His mother would lend him money, he thought, to supplement his own. She too was pushing him to take the chance.

I had to leave. J.D. was leaving on Monday and I had to get my own work done by then.

The first few days in J.D.'s office were easy, but David was acting oddly. I put it down to the strain of decision-making. He did not come into J.D.'s office to invite me to coffee or lunch.

Then came a minor meeting, a furniture promotion planned long before. It was a matter, merely, of checking J.D.'s memo to remind everyone—Bill Sawyer, Vince of display, and David, of course—of deadlines set by J.D.

Bill Sawyer slumped in his chair as usual, ad layouts dangling from his hand. Vince Sommers, always enthusiastic, described how the windows would look. Only David seemed ill at ease.

When the meeting was over, he left abruptly with no word of good-by. Something was bothering him. I went to see what.

"Well, if you must know," he said, "it was not becoming of you to act so important behind J.D.'s desk." He "had an appointment." He left.

I stood in the hallway trying to understand, until Ella came by. I had not even *felt* important during the meeting.

Ella pulled me down the hall, back into J.D.'s office, and closed the door.

"Maybe you'll have to choose," she said, after she heard the story. "Some men don't like women who are smarter than they are. Shit, it bruises their little egos."

I had heard that theory before and ignored it. I wasn't smarter than David, I said, only luckier. I was a woman—David had lost three career years to war.

"Have it your way, pet. But I can see lots of rocks up ahead."

That night I drove home automatically. Ella, in this case, was wrong. I was not smarter than David. In important ways he was smarter than I. He could handle figures, for one. I was simply luckier. In the three years he had been at war, I had been building a job that could have been his.

Ella was also wrong about some types of men. I had heard the "play dumb" theory before and, in high school, had tested it out. Playing dumb had led to incredibly boring dates. Being myself had been better. The right ones didn't seem to mind if I made suggestions about their problems. They even came back to discuss them some more.

There were, of course, some men (and women) who liked their mates to be not too bright. It apparently made them feel superior to play Mama to "Jack" or Papa to "Jill." Those men would automatically avoid me and that, to my good fortune, was that. I would not want to feel superior because my partner was dumb. It seemed a pretty cheap way to try to inflate your self-esteem.

I guided the car between parked cars and the trolley. David was certainly smart. But David was also human. It must have hurt him to see *anyone* five years younger than he in a job he might have had. If I had spent four years in college and then three years at war, I too might feel envious for a moment, just as David had.

I parked and locked the car. Inside, Grandmother told me that David had phoned. I was to phone him back.

"I'm sorry," he said. "Just a brief attack of insecurity. You handled that meeting just fine."

In May, Murray Cantor became an almost daily visitor. David and I began talking of the future as if we had one together. I waited for Tony to return. He wrote of "monumental snafus" in his records: "My God, I could be the last man home from this goddamned war." David soon got a bad blow too. Bill Sawyer hired an assistant advertising manager—from outside the store. Murray increased his efforts. I found myself more and more on Murray's side.

At the end of the month, over coffee at the store, David tapped out his pipe and announced, "I've decided to go into the agency business with Murray, Lois."

Wonderful!

"But only if you'll join us."

Chapter 7

DAVID SEARCHED MY FACE for an answer. The noise of the cafeteria faded as I searched within myself.

I wanted David to fulfill his dream but felt empty at the thought of leaving the store. "I don't know *anything* about agencies," I said. "You can do fine by yourself."

"No, I need you," David replied in the slow, deliberate way I had come to admire. "You give me confidence, Lois. And I need you to keep Murray in line. He and his father want to put up seventy-five percent of the money. If I let them do that, it means I'd be outvoted on everything. If you and I put up twenty-five percent each, we'd control fifty percent."

But that was $2,500. My conflict was over. There was no way on earth I could produce $2,500. I had banked Tony's allotment checks, but he would be home soon. To me, that money was his, badly needed to start civilian life.

David offered to lend me the money. No. Bad for our relationship, and if the agency failed, there would be no way to pay him back.

"Then," David said, "I'm not going to do it." His brown eyes looked sad but his chin was firm.

Although I was relieved I could stay at the store, I regretted not being able to help David. It made sense that he wanted the protection of equal stock. Murray *did* go off on tangents.

"David, why don't you just buy fifty percent of the stock?"

"Honey, I need you for a lot more than the money."

For the rest of the day I tried to push the money issue out of my mind. I had happily squandered my salary on gifts for my family, clothes for myself. It was silly even to ask Grandmother or Mother for a loan. No one I knew had ever had $2,500.

The challenge, like an unsolved riddle, nagged at me. That evening, as David and I walked to the lake, I said jokingly, "The only person I'm not absolutely *sure* does *not* have twenty-five hundred dollars is my father.

Even David knew enough about the circumstances to laugh.

Father, I was sure, was alive. His sister, Aunt Josey, sent cards every Christmas. She would tell me if anything had happened to him. I had no idea where he was, but all my life I had believed I could reach him through her. I had never tried. He knew where I was and, as Mother said often, "If he cared, he'd at least send a card." He did not care for me; I would not care for him.

But when David left, sleep chose not to come. Perhaps I had an obligation to David to explore my only, wildly unlikely source. For all I knew, Father's outsized dreams may have come true.

The next day Mother laughed. "Hah! If he *had* it, he wouldn't give it to you. He's ignored you all these years."

Grandmother said, "He wouldn't lend you gravel."

Grandfather, crippled and helpless, simply shook his head.

Bobby, almost eighteen now and headed for college, said in his newly superior way, "You're out of your mind. We're nothing to him."

I said, "Well, I probably won't do it." But I realized I probably would.

It took two days to gather the courage. I walked the four blocks to a drugstore with a phone booth, knowing why I had not phoned from Grandfather's house. I might need the four blocks back to digest my disappointment.

At the drugstore counter I sipped a lemonade. Perhaps Aunt Josey would not know where he was. She might also tell me he did not wish to talk to me. He might even have forgotten me in the new life he had built, might be married again with other children.

I stirred my lemonade. I remembered so little about him—nothing, really, except what Mother had said: "Lazy, irresponsible, a dreamer." I knew his face only from pictures—a slim, light-haired man, smiling in his wedding picture next to serious-faced

Mother; a snapshot of a man on crutches holding the hand of a five-year-old, me.

That visit had been his last. My memories were both sharp and vague—some scary adult conspiracy, a movie, the zoo, Father struggling on crutches, and—oh, yes, the silver dollar.

He had given me one. I had lost it. He gave me another before he left. When he was gone, I had found the first dollar in the lining of my coat. Mother had praised me for being "clever." She never believed I really thought I had lost the coin.

Did his quick replacement of my misplaced coin make me believe my father cared? A small wisp to cling to for all those years? I looked at the phone booth in the corner of the store. If I used it, I might lose that fragile hope. Did I really want to call him and find out for certain he hardly remembered? Or would it be better just to walk past the phone booth on my way out the door?

That, I realized, I could not do. Once again, it was better to risk the pain than to wonder what might have been. I asked for some change for the phone.

In the tiny Indiana town, Aunt Josey's voice answered.

"Do you know where I can reach my father?"

"Lois? He's right here."

With not a moment to think, I was talking to the strangely familiar voice of my father.

"Lois, are you all right?"

"Oh, yes, I'm fine. I just want to come down to talk about some business."

"Sure, sure. When can you come?"

"Next weekend?"

"Sure. I'll meet the train. There's one that comes in at nine in the morning. Can you make that one?"

He wanted to see me! He had not even asked what kind of business I wanted to talk about. He wanted to see me!

The train ride took two hours. This time I did not search the Indiana landscape for someone who could be my father. This time he would be there, waiting.

Grandmother had laughed openly at my journey. Mother had said, "Don't believe anything he tells you." Grandfather again silently shook his head. I felt unexpectedly disloyal to him. He had been there when Father had not. But I was not going to my father to *give* him something, only in the hope of getting something. I kissed Grandfather on his bald head as I had done as a child. I was making this trip only out of obligation to David.

84

When the conductor called out my stop, I waited with a dozen other people for the train to slow down. Finally, the door opened. Nearly everyone was embraced by someone on the platform. I looked for the tall, slim, fair-haired man I remembered from the photographs.

Inside the train station I continued looking. Obviously I would have to pick him out. He could not possibly recognize the five-year-old he had last seen.

As I stood against the wall, searching faces, the small station began to empty. People were leaving, either alone or in happy, laughing groups. I began to feel cold inside. Was Father as unreliable as Mother had always said he was?

Finally, there was only one person left, a white-haired man with a red face and a pot belly. He too had been searching faces, futilely, it appeared. I wondered who had disappointed him. He looked at his watch and then limped toward the train schedule on the wall.

Limped! The tap of my heels across the marble floor made him look up. I said, "Excuse me, but are you my father?"

His embrace knocked off my hat and sent my handbag sliding across the floor. "Goddamn, son of a bitch. Goddamn, you sure grew up. Goddamn." My cheek felt wet, but it was not I who was crying.

He wiped his eyes, picked up my suitcase, and retrieved my handbag with one skillful motion, hugged me again, and limped on ahead. "Jesus Christ. You're grown up, for God's sake. Son of a bitch." Walking in the backlash of my Catholic father's blasphemy, I tried to put the pieces together and to keep pace with this man who was swinging his stiff leg so expertly. No one had told me he was permanently crippled.

He led me to his car. "Have to have cars fixed special so I can drive." This one had seen better days.

But drive Father did. Off with a squeal of tires, past policemen who smiled as they waved. At each stop sign someone said hello. Father yelled back, "Hey, goddamn, this here's my daughter." I was meeting the town on wheels.

Off the main street onto dirt roads and into a farmyard where Father honked his horn. Two dogs, four young men, and a tall, gray-haired woman responded.

"Son of a bitch," my father said. "Would you believe it's Lois?" Five people and two dogs looked at me as if it were a miracle that I had grown up. "This here is Aunt Sophie."

I had gotten as far as "It's nice to . . . ," when off we sped, churning up dust, to another farm. Three farms later, I wondered when the inner music would stop. I was laughing with Father, not sure at what.

Another farmyard with a trailer out behind. "This is my place," Father said. "Used to be your grandma's. Remember it at all? No, Jesus Christ, you weren't but a baby when you were here."

Father limped ahead of me into the house. "I'm fixing it up." It had a long way to go.

"You can come down," Father said, "and live with me here. I'll fix it up any way you want."

My inner music stopped abruptly. *Now* he wanted me. Not until now.

Father changed the subject when I did not reply. "Aunt Josey's waitin' a meal. Goddamn, she'll be mad if we don't get there fast."

He limped along a well-worn path to Aunt Josey's house.

Aunt Josey had never married, I knew. Instead she had raised Ruth, daughter of my Uncle Pat, when Aunt Kathy died. Aunt Josey, Mother had said, "ran her farm like a man," driving tractors, chopping trees.

But she was so small. She was also a woman of few, but direct, words. "How come it took you so long to visit?" Cousin Ruth introduced her husband and son before I had to reply.

Her little son, Chris, had made a rush for Dad's arms the moment we entered the house. He now sat contentedly on Father's lap as if it were his own special place. Father obviously loved— and was loved by—children. Then why?

Homemade butter, homemade bread, beans from the garden, and family talk flowed around me. Father made everyone laugh and made little Chris eat his vegetables.

Then we were all in the living room. A big family photograph hung on the wall. These were my ancestors too. Funny, I had grown up feeling that I had only one set of relatives.

Father interrupted my thoughts. "Now, what's this business you came down here to talk about?"

Good heavens, I had almost forgotten.

In leading up to the idea of an advertising agency, I had to explain my career so far. Father knew as little about advertising as did Mother, but he "goddamned" and "well, son of a bitched" through it all.

"Josey, hear that? She wrote a radio show. Christ Almighty, you must be smart."

When I finally reached the point of my story, Father wanted to know only how much it would cost if I did not have partners but owned it myself.

"Father, I don't know how to run an agency myself."

Father was another of those people who believed I could learn. Ten thousand dollars for *all* the stock stopped his belief fast.

"Holy Christ, I'm gonna have enough problems getting the twenty-five hundred."

Holy Christ, he was going to lend it to me! He was taking, he said, a second mortgage on his farm, but $2,500 was all he could get. He grinned. "And that's gonna take a lot of persuasion down at the bank. But next year, maybe, if things go right, you can buy your partners out. Wish I could do better now, but at least you'll have a start."

My father was easy to hug. It felt so right to walk into his open arms. But still so much did not make sense. Why now when all those dreary years had passed without a card?

At the train station Father said, "The check should be in next week's mail. Christ, shouldn't take more than a week."

The train pulled in. I hugged him hard. His cheeks were wet. "Now, Lois, don't take so long to visit next time. Jesus Christ, it's been such a long time."

I wondered if he felt me stiffen. *Me* wait? Where was he when I was too young to write or phone or get on a train? I could not make myself ask. For now I would just enjoy his good-by hug and the fact that he cared enough to lend me this enormous amount of money.

Mother said, "He was always quick with promises."
Grandmother said, "You'll never get a check."
Bobby said, "What is he like?"
Four days later the check arrived.

That evening David lifted me, check and all, into the air. We could be, he said, incorporated and operating within two weeks. Murray knew of office space.

"I'll give my notice to Sawyer," David said, "and you give yours to J.D. No reason we can't both do it tomorrow."

In the excitement of being with Father, I had almost forgotten

I was now committed to leaving the store. The loan from Father had wiped out my only excuse. But perhaps it was for the best. I could give David the support he thought he needed and, at the same time, develop new skills myself.

Walking into the store the next morning was poignant. I would be leaving these people who smiled and greeted me. Giving my notice to J.D. would be like ending a part of my life. But he needed to know, and I needed to get it done fast.

J.D. greeted me with a what's-up-now grin. When I blurted, "I'm leaving the store," he rose from his desk, told Miss Kuswa to hold his calls, and closed his office door.

"What's wrong?" he asked. "What can I do?"

"I'm going into the agency business with David Cohen."

For the next hour J.D. presented all the advantages of the department-store world versus agencies: more flexibility, more stability, better suited to my particular talents. Finally, I simply told the truth. David and I were thinking of getting married and he felt he needed me in the agency.

J.D. leaned back in his chair. "All right, it's not my place to talk you out of *that.*" He paused as he always did before an unusual announcement. "But I'm not going to let you leave the store completely. You'll have to take the store as an account for the agency."

I was too shy to hug the man who had begun, guided, and constantly advanced my career, but I wanted to. J.D. continued. My present salary would be the retainer fee for the agency. We had our first account and a $400 monthly income!

At his office door I shook his hand hard. In a way it was an ending, but J.D. had made it painless.

Murray was already in David's office when I rushed in to share the news. His bright-red hair stood out as I glided down the hallway, still absorbing the realization that I would have the best of both worlds.

Murray was ecstatic. "The store is one of the most prestigious accounts in town! How'd you pull it off?"

While I explained I hadn't pulled anything off, I thought I saw a brief unhappy look on David's face. He had planned to solicit the account when we got organized. But in a moment he smiled.

Our lunch hour the next day was spent in the office of Myron Welby, the attorney for Murray's father's real estate company, who was incorporating us at no charge.

David and Murray had signed the papers. I was about to.

Mr. Welby gave me a jolly little smile. "Hate to ask a lady her age, but you are over twenty-one, aren't you?"

It was deflating to have to take the papers home for my mother's signature.

On my last day at the store, J.D. said, "Come back if it doesn't work out, but you know I hope it will." It had to—for David's sake much more than for mine. I was taking little risk. My job was waiting, and if I could not repay Father, it was only a small portion of what he should have sent to his children over all those years. For David, I suspected, the gamble was more serious. As a man, he might feel pressures I could only imagine. If he believed I could help, I hoped he was right.

The day I first saw the offices that would be ours I felt like part of a Mickey Rooney—Judy Garland movie: young people taking on the big time. Murray had made a convincing case for using much of our investment for impressive offices. Murray also insisted that, as a woman, I was the agency's biggest sales point and should have the most elaborate office.

"Listen," he proclaimed, "eighty-seven percent of the products manufactured are sold to or through women. Think about it. Food, most clothing, appliances, furniture. We're the only agency in town with a woman executive. Manufacturers need Lois's viewpoint whether they know it or not."

An interesting thought, but I reminded Murray that, woman or not, I knew nothing about the agency business. His "Don't worry" sounded too much like my geometry teacher's.

Learning the agency business did prove easier than learning math. What I had learned from promoting departments in the store was, more or less, applicable to the small companies Murray and I would be soliciting. I was beginning to learn the language. "A twenty-four sheet" was a billboard; "spots" were radio—and someday television—commercials; agencies got 15 percent commission on the advertising they bought for clients. The goal, as I saw it, was to sell the clients' products at the lowest possible cost. I had come reluctantly into the agency business, but it was beginning to be intriguing. Whether being a female in this field was an advantage had yet to be proved.

Meanwhile, David and Murray had already quarreled about what kind of female to hire as secretary-receptionist. Murray believed that, like our impressive offices, a stunning secretary was important window dressing. David believed secretaries should type. Della, Joyce, Victoria, and Francine made entrances, and departures when David found their spelling less acceptable than Murray found their bustlines.

Murray protested we were not "using" attractive women as client bait any more than the women were using us. A recent magazine article had stated that the best place to find a husband was as a receptionist in an agency. David said that nonetheless, *"Deer* Mr." was no way to start a letter.

Sally was the compromise. Pretty, intelligent, and married, she was putting her husband through medical school. Murray liked her figure; David liked her typing; and I liked her good sense.

My advantage as a female had not yet been tested when Murray and I made our sales calls on potential clients. Our first calls had been to Murray's relatives, all of whom dealt with things like auto parts, wholesale tobacco, and boat trailers. Then Murray made a date with the Neuman Chemical Company, a relative many times removed, who made a special cleaner used largely by auto mechanics. Murray insisted that my presence at least made us more memorable.

By now I was used to buildings in the grimy industrial sections of Milwaukee, to iron stairways, unwashed windows, and elevators that heaved, grumbled, and only reluctantly agreed to move. Mr. Neuman's office was small, dark, and unadorned, much like Mr. Neuman himself.

He moved boxes of hand cleaner from two chairs, asked us to sit down, and introduced us to his friend and attorney, Irving Rock, a short, husky man with amused gray eyes.

Murray made his usual sales pitch about a "young agency with young ideas" and the conversation then lay down, about to die. I asked if I could see the hand cleaner. Mr. Neuman reacted as if I had asked to see pictures of his grandchildren.

He proudly opened a jar of white goo. Would I be willing to participate in a demonstration? Of course.

Mr. Neuman produced a can of black grease. I was to rub some on my hands. Now try to wash it off with soap and water, he instructed. The mess only distributed itself equally between my hands and the towel.

"Now try getting it off with my hand cleaner."

It really worked. The pleasant-smelling white goo removed the grease. Warm water flushed it away. The towel stayed clean. There was a woman's angle to this after all.

"Mr. Neuman, this should be advertised to *wives*. They're the ones who have to wash the dirty towels."

Mr. Neuman beamed and nodded. Even Irving Rock stopped looking amused.

The problem was how to reach the wives. Mr. Neuman's office did not look as if he could afford space in *Good Housekeeping*. "You could get a department store to stock the cleanser, and then you could pay for their ads. Local rates are half the cost of the national rates you've been paying on the sports page." This co-operative advertising was common at the store. How nice that it had popped into my mind when I needed it.

Mr. Neuman beamed; Irving Rock asked if I could have lunch with him the next day; and Murray waited until we were on the reluctant elevator to explode.

"Lois, you messed it up. There's no agency commission on local advertising. We won't make a nickel."

I thought Murray would be pleased that his "women's angle" theory had proved true. No one had told me that there was no commission on local rates. But it still seemed to me that if we helped Mr. Neuman's business, we would somehow profit.

Murray looked as if I had told him about the tooth fairy. "Well, have lunch with Rock and see if you can't talk him into convincing Neuman to give us a retainer."

David was unhappy about my impending lunch with Irv Rock. "Don't be silly, David. It's business."

"But what kind of business?"

At lunch, Irving was friendly but not a bit flirtatious. He had been curious about my background and my age, he said. I told him the truth but asked him please not to tell anyone. His amused gray eyes looked more so. Of course he would keep my secret. He had had the same problem when he graduated from law school, the youngest in his class. "So I just grew a mustache." He laughed. "Frankly, I wouldn't recommend that for you." He assured me that it was only because he had fought the same problem that he guessed it of me. "Don't worry. You'll get older fast enough."

By coffee, I had learned that Irving practiced law but also played the stock market, that he had never married ("a born loner—and I like it that way"), that he supported and was active in scouting, Junior Optimists, and a group that helped delinquent boys: "Real fathers don't seem to have the time."

I told him about my father, surprised to find that my voice

broke as I described our reunion. This short, husky man, I decided, was going to be a good friend.

I also decided he would be a good lawyer for the divorce I was soon going to need. I had discussed the divorce briefly with a lawyer in our building who had tried to make me greedy and bitter. Irving understood why I wanted Tony to have the car and the allotment money I had banked.

As I walked back to the office, I felt confident that he would handle my divorce with sensitivity and pleased that he had agreed to a retainer for Neuman Chemical. David, I was sure, would be pleased about both.

Instead, he quizzed me suspiciously about everything Irving had said. "Don't tell me he only talked business!" But he had, and there were many other men I would have to have lunch with. It was frightening to see David's gentle face harden into angry rigidity. I retreated to my office.

Sally, our receptionist who had become my friend, saw my face as I passed her and followed me into my office. She sat on the zebra-striped chair that looked so good with the dark-brown walls. I was beginning to love my office, my clients, and this new challenging work, but I was also beginning to see pitfalls.

So did Sally. Murray made some impossible promises to clients, and Sally's job was to tell them he was out until the printing, photographs, or artwork finally arrived. She had also overheard my conversation with David.

"Why don't you just marry David, stay home, and have babies?" she asked, almost maternally. "If you stay down here I can see a lot of problems."

So could I, but marrying David did not seem the way to solve them. I had never faced that kind of jealousy before, and baseless jealousy could only grow, no matter what I did. If I stayed at home, David would be jealous of the milkman, the mailman, the man who read the gas meter.

Sally, I knew, lived for the day when Phil graduated and they could have children. For me that would solve nothing. In fact, it worried me that I had no desire for children of my own. All my friends from high school had at least one child. When I visited them, I saw their pride and tenderness toward those small bundles, but I also saw fatigue that their protestations of happiness barely hid.

Marriage to David had meant to me five years or so of working together until, I hoped, the idea of children finally appealed to me. Working together, it now appeared, was not working out. I had always had men friends, hoped always to have them, and in business there would always be contacts with clients, most of them men. David's jealousy would only create constant crises.

Sally handed me a tissue. "Mother says women can fulfill themselves through their husband's success," she assured me.

I had never heard that before, certainly not from my mother. Even Grandma focused on the grocery money rather than Grandpa's achievements. How would it feel to stay home and help David become a success?

Photographs of prominent men flashed through my mind—smiling men with smiling women next to them, the women just slightly out of focus. General Eisenhower's wife, apparently, raised the children and saw that uniforms, utility bills, and underwear were all taken care of. Eleanor Roosevelt had had a mind of her own—sometimes to her husband's annoyance. On the other hand, Ernest Hemingway was going through wives rather quickly. How would it feel to help a husband become a success and then be traded in for a different helpmate?

David was not the type to trade me in, but I would feel as if I were patronizing him, coaching from the sidelines. It also sounded boring. David would come home evenings to discuss moves in a game I knew. I wanted to be *in* that game, not on the bench.

There was, I realized, much more of Eleanor Roosevelt than Mamie Eisenhower in me. I had better wait until that changed rather than marry David hoping it would.

I told Sally, "It will just have to work out."

Sally said, "Lots of luck."

Father now telephoned occasionally to find out how things were going. "Fine," I lied. David continued to glower, though business was building quite well.

I had found a book on how to sell and, against Murray's predictions, it worked well for me. Murray believed that "socializing" was the way to get business. He wined and dined people, hoping it would help. I simply made calls. The book said that ten sales calls would produce one sale—if you could take the nine turn-downs. With companies selected from the Yellow Pages, I found I did better than one out of ten.

Murray, however, was right about the advantage of being a

woman. Several clients admitted they had made an appointment largely out of curiosity. One client added, "But you're very smart, Lois. You think like a man." I stifled a giggle. He was trying to be nice. And he had just signed a contract for an enormous amount.

There were disadvantages too, I reflected one day, as a creaky elevator took me down to the street. But I had learned another lesson that would probably serve me well.

An hour before, with great naïveté, I had gone up in the creaky elevator to Mr. Shalitto's office. It was a Saturday and his dress factory was silent. He had asked me to come then so that "we can work undisturbed."

When he offered me a drink, I politely refused—and tried also to persuade myself that I was imagining the look in his eyes.

He asked me to put the ad layouts on the coffee table near the sofa instead of on his cluttered desk. I sat on the edge, but Mr. Shalitto moved closer. The silence around us got thick. Why had I agreed to come on a Saturday? He probably thought it meant I was ready for his advance.

His hand moved closer to my thigh. In a few minutes, I reflected in panic, I was going to have to hit him with my briefcase and lose a good account. I played for time, rose, and went to my briefcase "to get a better pen." And stopped to look at the family photographs on his desk.

"Oh, what beautiful children!"

After five minutes' talk of the talents, ages, and future goals of his children, I could see his passion had cooled. Like baking soda on flaming grease, his pride in his children snuffed it out. Just to be safe, I admired his wife. "Someone I'd like to meet."

A half-hour later I was safely outside, layouts O.K.'d and my virtue intact. God bless his family, I thought as I fled—and no more appointments on Saturday afternoons.

So when, during Father's calls, he asked if my clients "got fresh," I could now tell him no. No more had even tried. It appeared to me that people sent messages. My message was no. No drinks, no private meetings, and no hint of flirtation. If David only knew.

J.D. phoned to say he had just heard television was coming to Milwaukee. The store wanted to be among the first to try this new form of advertising. Could I—expenses paid, of course—go to New York to see how television functioned there? I said yes. It was an obligation—and an exciting opportunity to learn.

It would also mean leaving David and Murray alone. Their quarrels were increasing each day. Murray, David fumed, spent too much on client lunches. David, Murray said, "thought small." Both had shocked me by suggesting we leave with our accounts and start business together.

Irving Rock suggested I leave, but by myself. "Get out. You don't need to play peacemaker to two neurotics. You're smarter than both of them and more professional. Open your own agency."

Despite David's jealousy, Irving and I had become friends, strictly platonic friends. But David's attitude forced me to sneak off to see Irving. I had to consult him about the upcoming divorce —and I badly needed someone to talk with about the increasing tensions at the office.

Irving said, "Leave those two. I'd be delighted to be a silent partner with as much money as you need. You're a damned good investment."

I thanked Irving for his confidence but shook my head. "I didn't want to be in this agency. Certainly not in one of my own. If I left, I'd go back to the store."

Irving signaled for the check in the obscure restaurant where we had sneaked lunch. "A damned waste, Lois. Do you realize what those two jerks would do to your clients if you left? They'd mess them up in a month."

I hadn't thought of that. Mr. Neuman was finally making money with his hand cleaner; my candy account was expanding its markets. If I left, Murray might sell them things they did not need. David might *not* sell them things they did need.

Walking back to the office, I thought of the David I had first known—tender, slow-talking, reliable. But reliable had turned to stubborn and tender to suspicious. The possibility of my marrying David now seemed more and more remote. All I wanted to do was find some way to keep the agency together.

I had hardly entered my office when David strode in and slammed the door. "You had lunch with Irving Rock. I followed you. If you don't promise never to see him again, you're not going to New York. Murray will back me up."

The David whose quiet I had once seen as wisdom was now red-faced and shouting, unable to see that his silly revenge would only hurt a client.

I felt unexpectedly calm. "Do you want to lose the store's account, David?"

"I don't care." The man I had once admired and loved looked like a small boy about to stamp his foot.

Words I had not planned spilled out. "All right, then I'll go back to the store and leave the agency."

David sputtered, "But . . . why . . . you can't."

I picked up my handbag. "Watch me." As I left, it seemed that to stop loving someone must be just as sad as finding someone had stopped loving you.

Irving's office was the only place I could go. While I fumed my rage, he grinned. "Now you've come to your senses. But don't go back to the store."

I stood, looking out Irving's window at the crowds of people below. Some walked toward the center of town, some away. If I walked away from the agency, what would it mean? I could go back to the store, to the comfortable, predictable life I had enjoyed. And never know what I might have done for clients who trusted me.

Still, it seemed wrong to ruin David and Murray's business. I wasn't angry at them. They couldn't *want* to be the way they were.

"Hasn't each one of them tried to get you to take accounts and go off into business with him? Believe me, they'd do it to you if they could."

True, but that didn't mean I should do it to them. On the other hand, it was the clients' choice. And I shuddered to think of what Murray could do to the trusting clients I had nurtured.

Then I realized the decision might be out of my hands. "Irving, Murray and David control most of the stock. They might vote not to buy me out. I might have no money at all."

"That's true. They could also put in a clause preventing you from going into the advertising business for a specific number of years. But, Lois, it's worth a try."

I smiled at Irving suddenly, aware that I had learned at least one thing. "If it does work out, and if you are a partner, I'd like to sell you only forty-nine percent of the stock. I want fifty-one. I never want to feel outvoted again."

Irving laughed. "Now you're learning, kid."

Any lingering doubts were quickly slain when I returned to my office and Murray sneered, "We don't have to buy you out, you know."

My casual shrug took Murray aback. "You mean you'd let the money go? Well, just like a woman. No business sense."

Murray had just given me a clue as to how to conduct myself during this cliff-hanging period. I shrugged again and looked as vague and vacant as I could. I gathered my papers clumsily and stumbled off to a recording session. I wanted to stay in this interesting world. If my acting ability held up, perhaps I could.

By the time I got back, Murray had changed his attitude. "Sure, we'll buy you out. Let's stay friends. We'll even give you a kickback on advertising for the store."

I only shrugged again and sighed. "I think I'll take a trip before going back to the store . . . or maybe I'll buy a fur coat."

Sally had said that men believed women were emotional and flighty. None of my clients seemed to think so, but with Murray and David I intended to act as unstrung as I possibly could until I was safely out.

David barely spoke to me during the next few days. I was openly going to Irving's office. Murray delighted in my scatterbrained plans—a trip, a coat, my own apartment.

From Irving's office I could make real plans. I called Mr. Bazarian, the owner of our office building, and told him the truth. "*If* I get my money, I'd like to rent some space. Could you hold it without a deposit?"

I breathed through his silence until he said, "O.K. You a smart girl. Got a high forehead. That means brains. I go along."

Well, the forehead I had always hidden with bangs was proving advantageous after all. Mr. Bazarian was holding space just across from his office—and two floors below the agency I was leaving.

Sally was waiting to join me—again, on that "if." She had to give two weeks' notice, I said. All right, then she'd help me at night. Her husband wasn't home much anyway.

Finally, papers were ready to sign. David, Murray, and I gathered once more in attorney Wembley's office. I tried not to stare at the papers in front of him that would release me and my money. There was no way to guess if he had inserted the clause about my not going into the agency business again.

David puffed on his pipe and looked at the floor. Murray was eager to leave. He was taking a new girl friend to lunch. He looked at his watch while I tried my best to keep my hands from clenching.

Attorney Wembley cleared his throat. "I'm so sorry it didn't work out. But the papers are ready to sign." He scanned them, and then he looked at Murray and David. "Oh, did you want me to add a restriction on Lois's operating an agency in the future?"

The traffic sounds outside Mr. Wembley's office froze into silence along with his ticking clock. Murray eyed me speculatively. Could he tell my heart had stopped?

I managed a casual gesture. "Put it in. I never want to hear the word *agency* again." I looked at my nails, praying that Murray remembered my silly babbling and that his ardor for the new girl friend was strong.

Murray looked at his watch. "Oh, let's not waste time. I'll sign it this way." He picked up a pen.

David signed next, then me. Mr. Wembley gave me a check. I held it in hands that no one had guessed were sweaty.

Murray rushed for his lunch date. I rushed for the bank—and then to Mr. Bazarian to give him the rent and pick up my keys.

Mr. Bazarian, from under his bushy eyebrows, muttered to me, "I bet on you, girl. Fixed up that office some for your first day. Phone company come this afternoon. Want the sign painter now?"

Oh, yes.

I opened the door to my brand-new office. Mr. Bazarian had lent me a desk, a chair, and a table. A fairy godfather with bushy eyebrows had given me someplace to sit.

While I watched the sign painter completing his work, a familiar figure passed the door—then reappeared.

Murray's bright-red head poked inside, looked at the name, then at me. He opened his mouth, then closed it, then laughed. "Well, I'll be. We fell for that dizzy-dame act. O.K., gotta give you credit. You did pull it off."

"Just," I told him, "barely."

We shook hands. Yes, we could be friendly competitors. He left. Ten to one, he would rush upstairs to call our clients and break the news. Then we would see if Irving's optimism had been justified.

Until the phone company came, I could only gaze at the unlikely lettering: Lois Mark & Associates.

Chapter 8

THE NEXT MORNING there was only one thing to do: telephone my clients, announce the change, and find out if I had a business to run. If not, I could still return Irving's and Father's money and go back to the store.

I took a breath and began to phone. To my slight surprise and vast relief, every client I phoned chose to come with me. J.D. said, "Good. I'll send your new address to Accounts Payable right now. You're still going to New York for us, aren't you?" I told him I would, of course.

Late in the day, Murray's cousin, one of our clients phoned. "Blood is not thicker than that jerk's craziness. If you'll have me . . ." Sure I would.

Sally came down to visit. "Lord, I need a break. They're up there blaming each other as the phone calls come in. When can I give them my notice?"

I had just added up our potential monthly income. It was hard to believe. We were a thriving business after all.

Sally sped up to give notice and returned with a grin. "*You* wanted to be nice and give them two weeks' notice? Well, they fired me so I couldn't carry 'secrets' to you! When do I start?"

Right away. She went out to buy the file cabinet we would need.

In the temporary quiet, I moved paper clips around my desk. How had it happened so fast? And, really, was I glad? I was happy to be rid of the constant crises with Murray and David, no doubt about that, but I had taken on an enormous chore. From now on I would be responsible for people's salaries—Sally's to start and others I would have to hire soon.

As I formed the paper clips into a circle, I wondered for a moment what it would be like to go back to the safety of Tony. I was no longer eighteen, almost twenty-two in fact. My early curiosity was gone. I had moved much, much faster than I had ever dreamed possible. Was this what I wanted to do? With Tony I had to do nothing but simply, as he teased me, "breathe and be you."

In this new job I had taken on, there would be much more than that. I had been incredibly lucky so far. Bad breaks were sure to come along. I had worked hard before. I would have to work harder. Employees and clients depended on me.

The paper clips, I noticed, were formed into a spiral. That was how I felt. It had started so small and grown, outward and larger so fast. I could still gather up the paper clips and throw them into a box—or I could see where the spiral led, how far luck and hard work would take me, what the real world of running a business was like.

Sally came back. The file cabinets would be delivered in an hour or so. Then she sat on my desk.

"You know, I really feel good. I never knew women could do things like this. Not that *I* could, but it's nice to know some women can." She looked down at my spiral and added a clip.

The earliest problems were easy. Newspapers, radio stations, and magazines all gave me credit. Only Irving was surprised.

"You don't even have a Dun and Bradstreet rating yet."

Oh, yes, I did. I had forgotten to tell him. Joe, an old friend from high school, now wrote reports for D. and B. He saw my name and came to see me. We joked about all the English essays I had ghostwritten for him. He would, he said, make me sound as much like General Motors as the facts would permit.

Other friends, I found, came through. An assistant buyer at the store now wrote for the newspaper's financial page. "Send me a picture," he had said. The "New Agency in Town" story was big, prominent, and enthusiastic.

The story brought me, just as I was thinking about it, some associates to hire. Even working nights, I could not keep up. I needed a production director to get bids on artwork and printing, an assistant to share the work with me. I knew I should call an employment agency, but I had never hired anyone before. How could I choose among, perhaps, several applicants?

The newspaper article brought two immediate if vastly different applicants. Joe Santos, swarthy, shy, and grossly obese, but awfully sincere about a job, would start, he said, for whatever salary I offered. He had studied production in college but had had trouble finding a job. His nearly black eyes in their blanket of fat looked eager and hopeful and honest.

When could he start? He took off his coat.

Then Sally came into my office to say that Jane Kane was outside. She lowered her voice. "She wanted to know if you were really a woman or if the paper had run the wrong picture and spelled 'Louis' wrong. She sure is suspicious."

Jane Kane entered my office with an air of belligerence. "Good heavens, you're *young!*"

I sighed. "Does it show *that* much?"

"I'm sorry. No. I just thought you might be some babe who uses a photo fifteen years old."

This small woman with the unadorned face was surely direct. If she wore brighter colors and form-fitting clothes, she would be quite attractive. I asked her to sit.

Jane brushed preliminaries aside. She had read the article and thought perhaps she would have more chance for advancement here. She was now an assistant ("secretary, it says on the record") to an executive at Milwaukee's biggest agency. "But after five years of doing his work when he comes in hung-over, I've given up. They won't promote a woman. Maybe you will. If you're interested, I'll take a salary cut. Fifty dollars a week is fine."

Later, I realized that I had just hired two people on instinct, but my theory was if they came to me, they were eager and alert. Irving met them both. "I think you did well. How did you get them to work so cheap?" It was, I pointed out, their idea, and I hoped it would not be for long.

I knew Tony would be phoning any day, but time had passed so quickly that I was stunned when he did. No, he would not come to my office. "I want to see you, Lois, where I've known you so well—the front porch of your house. Tonight? O.K.?"

I sat on the porch, waiting for Tony's car to stop at the sign and make the left turn to the front of our house. I thought of how much had happened—to both of us—since the too-young high-school girl had waited here for her college beau, always afraid he might guess her age. Tony knew my real age now, but he did not know how much I had changed. Somehow I didn't want him to. He had raised me—and I had gone ahead and grown up away from him.

But when the car did turn the corner and Tony's husky figure and bulldog face emerged, it was possible to turn time back. I could feel fourteen again, enveloped in his embrace, as safe as a child with a parent who loves her.

We talked of Tony's experiences—his flights, his narrow escapes, his trip home, the fate of mutual friends. I minimized my own experiences; I was trying to run an agency and would "probably get tripped up by my own terrible arithmetic." Tony patted my hand. No, I was a smart "little bug" and could do it.

Then he toyed with my fingers. "How about if you go ahead with the divorce as you planned, and we'll kind of take it from the beginning again? Maybe in a year or two you'll be ready to settle down."

Again, Tony was giving me all the best choices. I could go out into the world, knowing that a home was always waiting. I felt a flash of unfairness, but Tony insisted he *wanted* to wait.

"Now," he said, "tell me about your father."

Tony never visited my office. I saw him often but talked little about what went on in my business world. I was no longer the girl he had helped to grow up, but I found I could feel like her when Tony wanted me to. Irving went ahead with the divorce. I asked him to use the mildest possible grounds. One day I sat before a judge, lied, and was no longer married.

With Jane, Joe, and Sally to run the office, I made my trip to New York to study the new electronic miracle and returned with the reassuring opinion that no one knew exactly what he was doing. Television was happily experimental. *Whatever* program I put together for the store could not be a total failure in these hit-or-miss times.

At the station the two iconoscope cameras and engineering equipment were installed, but even surly Ben Hill knew so little about how it all worked, that he kept out of our way. Big, pudgy Al, the station's first TV producer; short, mouselike Jesse, who was in charge of scenery; and I simply learned what these cameras could and could not do.

Colors reproduced unexpectedly in front of those black-and-white cameras. Shades of red either disappeared or turned black. White flared badly. Men, we learned, must wear light-blue shirts. Anything that sparkled or glared could wipe out the picture entirely.

Faces were also unpredictable. The most skilled radio announcers sometimes looked like "Wanted" posters and were quietly relegated to being heard, not seen. Men adept at sportscasting were replaced by men who looked good. A famous woman broadcaster was tested and declared unfit. The camera made her look like a bowl of dough left to rise too long. Careers were advanced or ended by the mysterious workings of cameras whose decisions were not open to appeal.

Jack, my engineer friend, predicted that someday there would be national networks. Hollywood and New York programs would be seen world-wide . . . and in color. Ridiculous. It had even chilled me when Al, who I knew was two rooms away, said, "Lois, would you move that red vase two inches to the right? No, two more." Jack laughed at my alarm. Someday, he said, I would watch a camel race in Egypt.

Meanwhile, just filling air time was a tremendous chore. The few people with television sets watched films on herons, swans, and sparrows. Jack took his "remote" truck to every high-school football game around.

The store had bought thirty minutes of television time, and I was responsible for its content. "Do whatever you want," J.D. had said. "Just being first is worth the money."

I had already decided that television was an *intimate* medium. It was not like a theater where hundreds of people gathered to watch. These pictures were going into homes where one—or maybe five—people sat looking into the box. The program had to be intimate, one person talking to another.

How about, I wondered, a series of demonstrations? Like "How to Pack a Suitcase," which would be helpful and would also show the store's newest luggage lines. A cooking show might display the latest gadgets from housewares; "How to Arrange Flowers" would show vases from the china department. Unless Ben Hill realized I was doing thirty-minute commercials, these shows could be helpful to viewers and profitable for the store.

Ben Hill never bothered me. On the few occasions when he came into the TV studio, I tossed technical terms around with

Jack and Al. I used "pan," "Go to black," and "superimpose" lavishly in my scripts. Frank O.K.'d them, and Ben Hill went along.

At the store I had a wealth of experts available to demonstrate their expertise. Mrs. Bisby, a glowing, white-haired woman, was perfect for showing how to care for house plants—and to show the house-plant equipment for sale in the store. She was willing to do our first shows.

Steve Rodway was the best-looking announcer at the station, and I chose him as the program's emcee. I could only hope his good sense matched his looks. He was charming, enthusiastic, and adept during rehearsals. Mrs. Bisby was superb.

On the night of our first telecast, Steve, Mrs. Bisby, Jane, and I sat in the client's room waiting for our cue. Mrs. Bisby was digging in her vast black handbag. She finally held up a small vial of pills.

"Got to keep these handy," she said. "Nitroglycerine. I do have a very bad heart."

Steve's handsome face turned gray. Mine felt hot. Jane's lips moved as if in prayer. We healthy people were tense enough. Any unexpected crisis in this untested medium could throw Mrs. Bisby into the first on-camera coronary. I joined Jane in prayer.

Ten minutes later, Jane and I sat in the engineer's booth while Steve and Mrs. Bisby faced the cameras, her pills tucked behind a pot of violets. Al pressed the button for the title card, then for a medium shot of Mrs. Bisby and Steve. The script called for Steve to get up from his folding chair. He started, then stopped. The camera held the close-up of his stricken face.

Mrs. Bisby said cheerily, "What's wrong?"

Before the hundred or so viewers in town, Steve answered, "My pants are caught in the chair."

"Oh," Mrs. Bisby said maternally, "let me fix that." She freed Steve's trousers and went gracefully on with her demonstration. The only heart that stopped was mine.

The program ran ten minutes over schedule. I had not yet learned how to time people's movements as well as their speech. Al shrugged. Until networks came in, it did not matter. What did matter, he said, was that it was an entertaining show. Hair-raising, I thought. I planned to run health checks on experts from now on.

Al said, "Well, pal, you're now part of history. First commercial television show in town."

During the next weeks the shows were equally entertaining, if not as cliff-hanging. Viewers learned how to dress for figure problems and how to choose a pipe. On Thanksgiving, of course, we showed "How to Carve a Turkey." We needed, I said, one turkey for rehearsal, one for the show. The prop men, cameramen, and assorted studio personnel ate very well that night. Even Ben Hill came in to gnaw on a drumstick.

Meanwhile, I was training Jane to take over. Everyone liked her. She thought through her requests of the crew and seldom changed her mind. As we nibbled on turkey, I introduced her to Ben. Gracious as ever, he gave her a glance and a brief "How d'you do?"

Driving home, Jane said, "Ben Hill doesn't like women in charge."

"Ben Hill," I informed her, "doesn't like anyone in charge but himself."

Jane and Sally, I reflected, certainly believed in some rather strange myths. Sally "never knew women could run agencies." I had never heard they couldn't. Jane believed she had been passed over for promotion because of her sex. Chances were, it seemed to me, that her hung-over boss had wanted to keep her just where she was—and would have done the same if she had been a man.

So far, for me, being a woman had been nothing but good. If I had missed out on anything because of my sex it was never apparent to me. The contrary seemed to be true. My clients listened when I gave my "women's view" on products that females would buy. I even got a bonus when "space reps" who traveled around selling the benefits of their magazines and taking ad people to dinner came to town. Cal Hummel, a rep for a teen magazine, said, "Heck, I'd rather smell perfume than some guy's cigar." I got good dinners—and valuable tips on clients who were dissatisfied with their present agencies.

I was gradually becoming aware of still another advantage: all the helpful men I knew did not see me as a threat. My success as a woman had nothing to do with them. Some lovely form of gallantry made them feel good when they helped. They might have helped some other young *man*, but I doubted it would feel the same.

So why had Sally and Jane clung to those depressing myths? Myths, perhaps, were persistent until people tested them. I had just heard some myths about Jews. A loud-speaking woman outside Grandfather's church had said, "Jews are slick businessmen and they sure stick together." I was tempted to tell her about Murray and David. Slick they were not. And Irving, Jewish, had "stuck" with *me*. So what were those myths all about? The "good" myth of close, loving fathers and happy mothers had proved untrue. The "bad" myths were equally false. Eventually Jane would see what advantages we females had.

She sometimes shook her head at my theories. "You remind me of the child who found a room filled with manure and said, 'Somewhere in here, there's got to be a pony.' " I could admit there was a lot of naïve Pollyanna in me, but so far things *had* worked out well.

Running my own agency was, I was learning, a lot of very hard work. Three clients often wanted attention at once, and some were late with their checks. My days now stretched from eight to eight and sometimes well past that. My arithmetic had not improved, but with a special kind of finger counting, backward figuring, I could work out the numbers all right. I had also reversed Murray's procedure and set deadlines artificially ahead. When printing or proofs were delivered before the deadline, clients were pleased and surprised. I did the same with cost estimates, figuring high. When things cost less, clients felt they had saved money. It all seemed so simple; I couldn't figure out why everyone didn't use the same system.

By now my family had no idea what I did, and it was hard to explain. Mother cared only that I never came home to dinner on time and sometimes forgot to call. Time did slip away when I was trying to figure out how to solve a problem, and it was wrong, I knew, not to phone. I tried to get home to see Grandfather whenever I could. He was bedridden now, but I could still make him smile.

Then, on an April morning in 1947, Mother called my office to say that Grandfather had had another stroke and was in the hospital, not expected to live. He was asking for me.

In a cab I prayed silently: Grandpa, please wait. I found that he had. He was tossing in bed when I entered the room. Grandmother sat in a corner. When I took his hand, he smiled and said, "Lois, you stay here, *ja?*"

Of course I would. I held his hand as tightly as he had held mine when we crossed streets long ago. I stroked the veined, spotted hand that had made dollhouses and child-sized chairs for Christmas after Christmas. Like Tony, he had been there when I needed him most, and I was there for him now.

His breathing became irregular. The nurse caught my eye and

shook her head. Mother and Grandmother left. I would not go. Grandfather's grip was still strong. I would wait, as I had waited for that 5:32 trolley, for the one reliable anchor I had had in my childhood.

The minutes passed and his hand slipped away. His breathing stopped, then started again. "He's all but gone," the nurse said to me. "Soon his breathing will stop and simply not start. Say good-by to him now."

And so I did, with a kiss on his bald, shiny head. I had dreaded this moment all my life, but now it had a certain beauty. We had said our good-byes. He would always be there. I smoothed his bushy eyebrows once more and let myself cry as I left the room.

Tony was waiting to drive me home. For a moment I regained the small-girl feeling Grandfather's death had wiped away. Small girls had to grow up. Most of me had, but occasionally it was nice to look back and lean.

After Grandfather's death there seemed no reason to continue living at home. I could afford my own apartment, and it would relieve the tensions created by my unpredictable schedule. Mother, even though she had Grandfather's job and salary, wanted a smaller house. With me gone, she could buy one as small as she liked.

I knew exactly what apartment I wanted. In my teens I had watched it being built—enormous windows looking out on the lake and twelve ample stories up in the sky. Somehow, some way, I would live there someday, I used to promise myself.

Irving said, "Well, the rents are what you can afford, but you'll never get in."

Why?

"The Acme Realty Company owns it and uses it as bait. When they sell a house, they let the sellers have an apartment there."

Mother was not using a realtor. They were selling the house to Uncle Bernard, so no help there. But there must be some way. I broadcast my problem as widely as I could. Someone I knew must be selling a house.

Bert Simmons, a local radio time salesman, was—and yes, he would use Acme to sell it on their promise of an apartment to me. The day that Mother and Grandmother moved from the house where Grandfather no longer lived, the new apartment was mine.

On my first night there, I sat with my feet on the windowsill, watching boats on the lake. It was as lovely as I had dreamed: big, open, soundproof rooms and a view that nothing could match.

Two weeks later I recognized the reality of dust. Where had it disappeared to in Grandmother's house? And how had the bathrooms stayed clean? I didn't think I liked the answer. Words of Mother's came back to me: "I hope you marry a man who can afford a maid. I'd hate to see your house if you don't." Well, *I* could afford a cleaning woman myself. Soon the Polish immigrant woman I met on the elevator added me to her once-a-week list.

There was little time, however, to enjoy the cleanliness or the view. Most evenings I collapsed into bed. Business was growing almost too fast, and even Jane worked nights.

"Why not?" she said, when I tried to send her home. "What else do I have to do?"

I had tried—subtly at first and then in an all-out campaign—to make the outside of Jane as attractive as she was inside. At twenty-eight, she had never dated and I was sure I knew why.

"Jane, some bright-colored dresses with softer lines would make all the difference in the world. And what's wrong with lipstick?"

"The right man," Jane said, setting her chin, "won't need that phony façade."

"But," I argued, "manufacturers spend millions on packaging. If you don't catch someone's eye, they'll never know what's inside."

The right man, Jane insisted, would.

Jane, I had noticed, carried all forms of honesty a bit too far. When our hotel client presented one of our ideas as his, she was outraged.

Back at the office she fumed to me, *"You* told him to give free suites to celebrities. *You* arranged it with the theaters and informed the press. *You* got him all that publicity absolutely free. All he did was stand there and say yes. You should have set him straight."

But, I explained, letting him have the credit didn't cost a cent. It made him feel good, and somewhere in his mind he knew we were valuable if not precisely why.

Jane had almost throttled our new Chicago client, Mr. Neuman's cousin, who manufactured shoes. When I suggested he change the name from Chicago Shoe Corporation to something like Casual Classics, he sat back in his chair. "Well, my cousin said you were two smart girls. You really do think like men."

I knew enough to grab Jane's arm like a vise and announce that we were late for our train. In the hallway I shushed her as she exploded. "He was *trying* to be nice, Jane. What does it cost? He certainly pays us as if we were men."

"And calling us 'girls,' " Jane blustered again. "I'm hardly sixteen. I'm a woman, not a girl."

During the ninety-minute train ride back to Milwaukee, Jane sulked while I teased. "Next time I'll say, 'Thanks, Mr. Bashkin, you think like a woman' and embarrass the poor man to death."

Jane's sulk turned to horror the next morning when the newspapers came. Big, bold headlines featured one of our clients. "Medville Chocolate Company in Bankruptcy," it read. A small local bank, the article stated, might go down with the melting chocolate because of unsecured loans.

And we might go down with them. Agencies bought and paid for space for clients. Our profit was the 15 percent commission. Meanwhile, $10,000 of our money was tied up in Medville— $1,500 was profit; the rest was our operating cash.

Sally, Joe, Jane, and I sat in my office, as shocked and helpless as if we had been robbed. I wondered where we would all get jobs and how much I could get for the furniture.

The mail clunked through the door slot. Sally went listlessly to get it. She waved an envelope from Medville. A notice to creditors, no doubt.

Sally screamed, "Hey! It's a certified check. The whole amount!"

I lunged for the phone to thank Mr. Medville. Then, triumphantly, I told Jane what he had said: "I couldn't let nice girls like you take a beating."

He, too, I reminded Jane, had said we thought like men, but the last check he wrote was a chivalrous gesture that kept "nice girls" in business.

With the hair-raising brush with bankruptcy over and our Chicago account doing well, life for me felt secure and serene. I was having some interesting dates—dates who did not mind waiting until I finished my work, who had interesting work of their own— a criminal lawyer, a contractor's heir, a salesman for heavy machines. It was fun to compare goals and problems, to have late-evening snacks, or to dance. It was fun to show off the expensive clothes I could now afford.

But on evenings when the world seemed too much, there was always Tony. He knew, without my telling him, that things were going well for me. He enjoyed his new teaching job, and I knew some lucky students enjoyed him.

But one evening when he picked me up at my apartment, I knew there was something wrong. We went to our favorite place for dinner. Tony played with the silver until he finally spoke.

"I need to ask you a question, honey, and I don't think I'll like the answer."

I waited. Tony would ask.

"I want to be married, Lois, preferably to you. I'll wait as long as I think there's a chance. But if there isn't—if you know—there's a teacher at school. I could be happy with her if your answer is no."

I took a slow sip of my drink. Oh, Lord, I did not want to grow up this fast. I had just lost Grandpa. Not Tony, too. It would be, I knew, so easy to say, "Wait for me, Tony. Maybe next year."

Tony said, "Don't answer now. Just give it some thought."

But I knew if I did I'd be lost. It would be so easy to keep Tony waiting, and so wrong. I owed him a lot, and grownups paid their debts.

When I spoke, my office voice came out, the sure-of-myself voice I had never used with Tony. I *could* free Tony for the kind of marriage he deserved, if I did it fast and didn't stop to think how much I'd miss his undemanding love.

"Marry her, Tony. Don't wait for me. I may not be the marrying kind at all."

We reminisced during dinner—how scared I was at the first college dances, how scared he was when I first drove that car.

When he took me home—in that same crazy car I had been determined to drive—he said, "But we'll still see each other. This isn't good-by."

Oh, yes, it was. "Give your attention to her. It wouldn't be fair otherwise." And, I said silently, I'm not sure I can be this strong twice.

One quick kiss and I ran inside. Part of my past drove away.

I knew that for the rest of my life I would often miss the childlike feeling Tony's love had given me. But could anyone stay a child forever without tremendous cost? It was better to move ahead, to deal with what was real. Cee Cee Porter, a client, called from Chicago. She had an idea for a new product her father's chemical company was about to introduce. I took the train.

As the sleek silver train swayed on its way to Chicago, I wondered if Cee Cee knew how much I envied her. Not for the maids who took care of her clothes or for the chauffeur who drove her around town or for the beautiful lakefront apartment where she lived with her parents. I envied Cee Cee for her parents—her vibrant mother who seemed to run every charity event in town, and her internationally successful father who left the most vital conferences if Cee Cee needed to see him.

And he had unlimited confidence in her. He had given her a division of his chemical company to run as her own. She had made the cleaning-compound division into a profitable business for the first time in its history. Her mother was as proud of her accomplishments as was her father. To me, Cee Cee had everything a young woman could possibly want.

Envy, I decided as the train sped along, was too strong a word. Cee Cee was too likable to envy—unaffected, bright, sensitive, and direct. It was actually pleasant to know someone who had what seemed to be so many lovely things in life.

It was, therefore, a surprise to see Cee Cee's pert face looking sad when I met her in the lobby of the Drake Hotel for our planned lunch-conference. As we talked of her idea—reusable containers of the new miracle, plastic—a wistfulness kept encroaching on her usual enthusiasm.

Over coffee she turned to me. "I doubt you have any idea how much I envy you."

Me? Whatever for? It was I who envied her.

"You have something, Lois, that I can never get: recognition for what you accomplish. No matter how successful I am, no matter what I do, people—like the woman Mother had to brunch today— can always say, 'Well, of course, look who her father is.' "

"But, Cee Cee, you're one of the brightest people I know. You could have done all this without your father."

"Perhaps. But that's something no one—including me—will ever know. You're very fortunate, Lois. You *know* you did it on your own. If you had to start over, you know you could do it again. That's something I'll never have." Her blue eyes showed a brief twinge of pain.

Cee Cee changed the subject as she slipped into her mink coat. I was glad she did. Cee Cee, I realized, was absolutely right. Recognition from others was not important to me, but my own sense of accomplishment was. I had taken it for granted until Cee Cee made it clear. But even more important, I *had* started from scratch. I *could* do it again. Suddenly, that felt like the best insurance policy in the world. Being born rich, with wonderful, supportive parents, had seemed idyllic, but fortunes can be lost and parents die. Practice in "starting from scratch" could never be lost.

I shrugged into my cloth coat. Cee Cee had made me feel very rich indeed.

The months moved quickly. Business increased. A tall, exceedingly thin young man walked into the office just as Jane and I were discussing increasing our staff. Andy Volnik had just graduated from the journalism school at Marquette and was making the rounds of agencies in search of a job. His degree, he said, was opening no doors. Would it open one here?

Jane and I held a hurried conference. To me, he seemed smart and trainable. Jane wondered how he would feel about working for women. What was the problem? I had worked for *men*.

Andy proved to be smart, willing—and thoroughly unprepared for the functions of a small agency. "Studying General Motors's advertising," he apologized, "didn't prepare me for Mr. Neuman's hand cleaner!"

At last I found myself saying to someone else, "Don't worry. You'll learn." Gradually, he did.

When, as Andy's employer, I got a follow-up letter from Marquette, it struck me as an excellent idea. They wanted to know how well they had prepared their graduates. They deserved the truth: "Not very well."

Professor Stanner called. Would I be willing to come in and explain their inadequacies in detail? Yes, of course. On my way to the Journalism Department, I had a thought. Just as medical schools had laboratory courses, why not use the college paper as a lab for journalism students? They could sell space, prepare the ads, and be responsible to real clients for results. Few graduates, I explained to Professor Stanner, were likely to be hired to direct advertising for General Motors. Most would start in small agencies like mine. Working on the newspaper would prepare them.

Professor Stanner, a short, rumpled man, beamed. "A fine idea. Would you be willing to teach the course?"

I laughed. I had never even gone to college, I explained.

No problem. "We tend to get isolated. Genuine experience would be much more important than a list of degrees.

My high-school principal, I reflected, would never believe this;

his view of my future had included jail, not teaching in college. But challenging as the idea was, I simply did not have the time. Perhaps someday, I told Dr. Stanner, but not now.

Well, then, could I at least participate in a research project? It would take only five morning hours. Marquette was compiling "psychological profiles" of "successful professionals" to be matched with the tests of aspiring students.

For five mornings I took written tests in the office of Marquette's guidance counselor. The following week another rumpled professor discussed the results. "Rather surprising," he said. "The expected motivations of money and prestige are, in your case, extremely low. Social welfare and religion are by far the highest." He looked at me with a puzzled frown as if I could explain.

Hardly. I had not attended church since my confirmation and I was not at all sure what "social welfare" meant. Marquette University was an innovative, concerned institution, but it apparently had a wire or two crossed.

Jane, when I told her, decided that "religion" could only mean "ethics." She was baffled by "social welfare" too. We settled down to continue Andy's training.

On a Sunday, just before my twenty-fifth birthday, the telephone rang in my apartment.

It was Mother. "Lois, I have some terrible news for you."

I held my breath while she paused. Bobby? Grandmother? Her own health?

"Lois, your father was killed last night."

Oddly, I felt no emotions at all. While Mother explained ("A freak accident. His car rolled down a slope and pinned him against a fence. Aunt Josey just called"), I held the phone, waiting to know whom to mourn—the father who had ignored me all those long, lonely years or the gregarious, generous man I had only begun to know. I could not combine them, and each seemed to cancel out the other.

I phoned Aunt Josey to tell her I would be responsible for burial costs. Ironically, I was just about to repay Father's loan. Had I put it off to maintain a tie between us? Or out of revenge?

My father's funeral was held on my twenty-fifth birthday. As the priest droned on, I looked up at Bobby beside me, wondering if it was any easier for him. He looked detached. When I had taken Bobby to meet Father, two totally different men had shaken hands and ignored each other for the weekend. College was making Bobby into someone who valued proprieties. Father had never even known the word.

Father's body was lowered into the ground. When Grandfather died, my emotions were simple—the clear loss of a man I had loved all my life. Saying good-by to Tony was also clear-cut. This was not. Perhaps, a long time from now, I would understand all the contradictions. At present, all I could do was walk away.

Chapter 9

IN THE YEAR AFTER Father's death, Grandfather's death, and my good-by to Tony, my center of gravity seemed to shift, if indeed it existed at all. I had accomplished more than I had expected in my career. The question was: what now?

Irving said, laughingly, "Well, you could always try getting rich and famous. Or you could try falling in love."

Falling in love was not something you planned, but "rich" might be something to try. We had increased our accounts in Chicago and could expand them even more.

"Famous," however, was not attractive to me. I had been meeting famous people, and fame did strange things. A new account, the state distributor for Columbia Records, required my handling local publicity when stars came to town. I had watched singer Johnny Ray work himself into exhaustion, trying to please every fan in sight. By contrast, young Rosemary Clooney treated record-store owners with haughty disdain. When Eugene Ormandy came to town, I arranged a reception of high-school music students, all thrilled to come so close to their idol. At the last minute, someone phoned to say he had made other plans.

When Adolph Menjou appeared at the store to autograph his book, I pitied the young woman the publisher had sent. On his arrogant commands, she opened doors, fetched coffee, hauled suits to be pressed. At noon, she explained nervously, she had to leave.

Could I shepherd him through his afternoon dates? Yes, but he would probably miss her tender, loving care.

At the first closed door that Menjou and I encountered alone, he stopped, his waxed gray mustache twitching with impatience.

"If you," I told him, "are waiting for *me* to open doors for *you*, we'll stand here until I'm as old as you are."

Only President Truman's "veep," craggy, gallant Alben Barkley, gave the lie to my belief that fame turned personality awry. I had done volunteer work for the charity that Barkley was in town to support. The head of the local committee asked if I would like to meet the vice-president. Yes, I thought, standing in line to shake his hand would certainly be worth the time.

Instead, I arrived as requested at a suite at the Shroeder Hotel, where two enormous Secret Service man looked at me closely and waved me inside. No receiving line at all; just the committee head and a smiling, gracious Barkley. He rose and came toward me with his hand outstretched. "Well, Miss Mark, I've heard so much about you."

My knees almost buckled, but there was only one reply: "And I've heard a lot about you, Mr. Vice-President."

During the next five minutes, I realized that this expert politician had asked the chairman who I was. He talked about *me*. So that's how it worked. For interested, flattering Alben Barkley, I *would* have opened doors, picking their locks if need be.

On my now-frequent trips between Milwaukee and Chicago, I tried to sort out the experiences that were flashing through my life as fast as the scenery outside. I had not been able to fall in love, but I was dating several young men I liked.

Zack Munn, a criminal lawyer, was fun. His hours were as unpredictable as mine and his clients were fascinating. Criminals, I learned, were very polite. Often, over late suppers, I would find myself chatting with a convicted burglar, a brothel owner, or the men who controlled gambling in town. If an off-color word slipped out, it was followed by blushes and apologies. An "innocent" counterfeiter even instructed me on how to age bogus bills —bury them in coffee grounds for a period of time I promptly forgot.

Don Wendt was fun too—too much so for romance. With his unique sense of humor and brilliant mind, he was headed, I knew, for the top. "We'd make a great team," he said often, "if I could get you to respond to my kisses as you do to my jokes." He was right. I continued to laugh.

For a while, Lou Seely looked likely. He would stride into my office and haul me away. During dinner and dancing, he told me his plans. He was leaving the store to start his own firm. His bronzed, blond good looks and his gaiety made me care if he phoned.

Then gradually, his gaiety faded. His new business was not going well. "But, Lou, it will. All companies lose money at first."

To lift his mood, I suggested a weekend at Aunt May's in the peaceful north woods. Lou hated to drive. All right, I would take my car, and I would do the driving.

Lou sulked for two hundred miles. "If you've seen one pine tree, you've seen them all." When we arrived at Aunt May's, he was barely polite. His business, I decided, must be in worse shape than I thought. Aunt May's charm, Uncle Gus's homely wit, the pines, the sparkling river, seemed to please him about as much as a traffic ticket.

That evening he began sniping at women in business. His sniping shots, like the sparks in the fireplace, turned into a roar. Women should not *be* in business; it was distracting to men. With Aunt May listening, open-mouthed (Uncle Gus had escaped to his store in disgust), Lou turned on me. *"You* are successful only because you're attractive. Men feel protective toward you. If you were a man, you'd never have made it."

All right. Lou was the type to blame someone or something else for his failures. This weekend, I was apparently it. Too bad, but I should have noticed sooner the petulant twist to his mouth and the sometimes petty remarks that slipped out. My handsome blond giant had shrunk.

Aunt May whispered to me in the kitchen, "Are you going to let him say things like that?" Yes, for now. He was, after all, my guest.

By Sunday his rude behavior toward Aunt May and Uncle Gus enraged me far more than his silly jabs at me. It was finally time to leave, and I knew exactly what I was going to do.

Through Shawano, Wisconsin, he whined about his luck. In Neenah-Menasha he decided that all women should stay at home. In Fond du Lac his fuming went on, but so did my smile. At Menomonee Falls I knew that justice lay just ahead.

When the Milwaukee County sign came into view, I stopped my car, reached over Lou, and opened the door.

"Out," I said cheerily, my duty discharged.

He looked around at the sprawling countryside. "Here?"

"Absolutely."

I never even wondered how he got home.

In contrast to Lou, there was Morey Wells. Morey sold syndicated radio shows to local stations. "With me behind you, Lois, there's nothing you can't do," he said on our third—and last—date.

Falling in love, I told Irving, was not all that easy to do.

Neither Irving nor I mentioned Wes Spreckles. The week after my father's death, I had fallen unwillingly and helplessly in love with this more-or-less married restaurateur, twenty years older than I. Everyone in town knew that Wes was as unreliable as a weather forecast, married in name only and prone to showing up for two o'clock appointments at about five, if ever. But after an evening of pacing the floor, I melted when Wes walked through the door, usually bearing some frivolous, extravagant gift—a twenty-five-year-old bottle of Scotch, a silk blouse, a gold bottle opener.

After the first week of our romance, Wes announced he was getting a divorce. "We never divorced before because neither of us wanted to remarry. It'll just be routine, baby-face." I believed every word.

Irving's amused gray eyes were now filled with concern as he tried to deter me. "He's put five women I know through this. God knows how many I don't know. He'll never get a divorce."

This time, I was certain, was different. I loved him, he loved me, and he had, he said, moved out of his house.

On New Year's Eve, Wes had not come at seven—or at eight, or at nine. There was no answer in his room at the hotel. At ten he phoned. "Jesus Christ, baby, I've been trying to get away. Son of a bitch, I'm leaving right now." I sat at the window for another hour, watching for a bright-red Buick that never came. For the first time in five months of *fearing* he was dead, I found myself *hoping* he was. It now seemed the only way out of this inexplicable net. At two o'clock I fell asleep, exhausted by tears, still dressed in clothes I never wanted to see again.

Jane phoned at ten. I had called her in agony several times the night before. All during those awful months, Jane had said, "If this is love, give me tomato soup." Now she suggested a drive in the country—"what you need to clear your head." Her brother, Joe, would drive and take us to lunch.

Joe drove directly past what I believed was Wes's *former* home. The red Buick was in the driveway. Under Jane's prodding, Joe confessed he had been with Wes at a party the night before, and Wes had been with his wife. At the table during lunch, I could feel hysteria rising. In the well-appointed women's room, I sobbed out an ending.

The next day I considered suicide, realized I had no idea how to go about it—and plunged desperately into work.

When Irving and I teased about my falling in love, he never mentioned Wes. Nor did I. Somewhere in my mind, I could put pieces together—my father's death, my inability to care for the nice men I dated. But I could not pick too much at a slow-healing wound.

Irving had suggested, laughing, that I try to fall in love with him.

"What? And lose my best friend?"

Irving was the only person I felt I could talk to at all. Still, even he could not be expected to understand the confusion that bubbled up during the rare quiet periods at work. New clients, new projects, were always a challenge, but sometimes I wondered, "What now?" Luck had moved me ahead too fast. Even Irving could hardly relate to my vague and unjustified discontent.

I could not discuss my life with Mother, although sometimes I tried. Her vague "That's nice, dear" or "That's too bad" actually hurt. But, I reminded myself, there were a lot of people who wished for a mother who never interfered.

It was, I knew, impossible to confide in Jenny, Jean, or Martha, my friends from high school with whom I kept in touch. Their lives were totally different from mine. Jean had once said quietly, "I envy your exciting life, but then you always were different." I felt I was not. Jean remained stubbornly unconvinced. I wanted to say, but held back, that she could have pursued her artistic talent before she married. I had urged her to submit samples to the store. "Oh, I'm not that good" had been her reply. Now she made beautiful, elaborate cards her children would cherish some-day. Who was I to say her choice was wrong? Or Jenny's. She was helping her husband establish a car-repair shop, raising her chil-dren, and keeping his books. Martha seemed the least content, cross with her children and surly with Jim. But she never com-plained directly. Nor could I—with the "glamorous" life my friends insisted was mine.

It was, I had to admit, often a great deal of fun. Our corset ac-count needed a memorable splash during market week in New York. We would, I decided, have a drawing for buyers. The prize would be a John-Fredericks hat made of corset lace. John-Fredericks agreed. And why not, to attract a crowd, display a $250,000 version of the girdle? Their newly hired public-relations woman in New York could easily figure that one out—borrow diamonds from Harry Winston, something like that.

Betty Lou Long, the PR woman in New York, assured me in her Texas accent that "y'all can sure count on me, honey." I did—and got to New York to find nothing done.

I planned to murder ol' Betty Lou if I had a moment. Meanwhile the ads had run and the buyers were arriving the next day. I got Harry Winston on the phone. (How? My desperate tone of voice may have helped.) He was sweet and apologetic. His show diamonds were in Dallas, but why not use zircons instead? Only an expert could tell.

And only an expert, I figured, could tell that the girdle was not "gold-plated," merely sprayed with gilt in a baffled car body shop. To complete the charade, I rented a display case and hired a guard —and raced to the gem center where Harry Winston's call got me a packet of zircons. That night, with a penknife, I "set" my "diamonds." I could, I figured, carry off the bluff. Ken Kafsky, my client, had better not know. After all, we were not planning to *sell* the darn thing.

The press came. So did the buyers. The most important buyer won the hat. Ken may have had secrets of his own. At the end of a day of record-breaking orders, I told Ken I was dismissing the guard. He had been impressive, hand on his gun, steely eyes watching the crowds.

Ken said, "Sure he should go? That's a quarter of a million in diamonds he's watching."

"Two thousand dollars in zircons, but I kept them under my pillow anyway and I will again tonight."

Ken said, "Hot damn," shook with laughter, and went back to recording the orders.

Later he decided I deserved a night on the town, a super night of the best of New York. At "21" I thought of Jean, Martha, and Jenny. It *was* a glamorous life. A musical, the famous Stork Club, and, at the Blue Angel, sharing a women's room mirror with movie star Linda Darnell. Renewing my lipstick near her flawless face depressed me slightly, but not for long. My Pollyanna side emerged: in the years ahead, she would have more to lose than I. On to a nightcap at the bar at Toots Shor's.

Between the glamour and the challenging crises, I had time to reflect. Perhaps no one's life was all that he or she wished. My "What now?" feeling was silly and thankless, considering all the good breaks that I had gotten over the years. The Marquette test was crazy—"religiously motivated" indeed! I enjoyed the money I was making, the clothes I could buy, the gifts I could give. Grandmother now had the first television set on her block.

Still, I avoided looking ahead. Jane looked forward to years and years of more of the same. Somehow I could not. Years and years of helping sell girdles or hand cleaner or records? But what did I want instead? The idea of children scared me. I knew nothing about mothering at all. What if I "That's nice, deared" when they needed me, or yelled as Grandmother had done? Perhaps it was best for me—and those unlikely children—that I did not look too far ahead.

And what was wrong with making money? Everyone seemed to try. Bobby had abandoned counseling work to go into fund-raising. "Much more money to be made," he said. Irving used the money from his profitable law practice to test his theories on stocks. When they worked, he bought antiques. When he lost, he shrugged. All the men I dated talked about making money—a bit more income and they would open larger offices, or buy a boat, or feel they could relax. If, as the silly test at Marquette claimed to show, I was not motivated by money, it might be a flaw I should cure.

Some of these reflections took place on the train as I traveled to see Chicago clients. Sometimes I talked with people and had no time to think. A soft-spoken Negro professor chided me for not loving math, a radiant girl was on her way to marry the man of her dreams, a fiftyish woman was just as radiant—she was leaving *her* man now that her children were grown. I left my question unasked: If she had survived a marriage for twenty years, why would she want to leave now? Talks on trains were like unfinished articles in dentists' office magazines.

The day I talked with the woman who was triumphantly leaving her husband, I was whisked by cab to my favorite account. The Chez Paree night club did not bring too much profit, but the fringe benefits were nice. Mr. Pignelli, one of the owners, and I would discuss his radio ads over steak and try out new ideas as the floor show went on. But that night Mr. Pignelli was eager to show off his new Key Club which had just opened.

This room, lavishly appointed and off to the side, was open only to those who paid the sizable membership fee. It was hard for me to understand its appeal. Why sit in here when Martin and Lewis or Jimmy Durante were performing outside?

The room was crowded, however. I admired the paneling, the leather chairs, the solid walnut tables . . . and the guests. "The biggest big shots in Chicago," Mr. Pignelli said, "are sittin' right in here." He puffed his cigar and beamed.

A square-faced, red-haired man waved us over to join his corner table. I was introduced. Bill Veeck, it developed, owned a baseball team. Jerry Fairbanks had something to do with the movies. I missed the other names.

Conversation swirled around me. The short, bald man with the pungent cigar could not decide whether to sue "Joe" for the half million he had lost. The thin man with the sharp little nose was angry at "Mack" who was "killing a deal." Yachts were described and Rolls-Royces disparaged—"takes a year to get the damned parts."

At first I was intrigued. Millions of dollars were being discussed. These big shots were indeed big. Then gradually I began to notice the worry, the tension, the discontent. So money did not buy happiness. But what struck me hardest was that, except for the sums involved, the talk sounded exactly like what I had heard as a child. Uncle Carl worried about taking a loan for a new car with the same anxiety the thin-faced man expressed about a loan for a building. The bald man could not hide his wish to own a baseball team—his expression was exactly like Uncle Bernard's when his neighbor bought a ten-foot boat.

I was not sure I wanted to learn this at all, but the talk and the drinks flowed on. I sipped on a Coke and watched all the faces. No one looked relaxed.

Those middle-aged men must have struggled for years. They had not stopped struggling yet. Sons were discussed: "The bum won't work." Wives were "ungrateful and bitchy." The "biggest big shots in Chicago" were not happier, it seemed, than the men in some blue-collar bar. Maybe less so. The men in the bar could at least dream of how they might someday get rich.

On the late train home, I knew I had just learned an important secret, but I doubted anyone would believe me.

In May of 1953, on a windy corner near his office, Irving introduced me to Jerry Webster. Jerry looked a lot like Tony: the athlete's stance, the bulldog features. He was, Irving said, sales manager for an industrial company.

"Nice enough guy. Just got left at the altar by some gal from New York. Seems to be recovering though. Looked at you as if he is."

That night Jerry phoned. Would I like to see the Milwaukee Braves play New York? Why not? I had been dancing a lot with Zack and Don. A change could be healthy.

Healthy, but boring. I was glad when someone finally won.

Jerry, however, over a late-night snack, seemed charming, bright, and sweet. At the door he kissed my nose as Tony used to do. "I don't want to move too fast, but I'm going to marry you soon." I laughed, but agreed to go to his country-club dance.

Jerry was a terrible dancer, but so eager to please. He introduced me to friends with beaming pride. Marge and Bill Sewell, Ellen and Jack Curtis, all said I was "good for Jerry. He's been through a lot." Invitations came for dinner at Marge and Bill's, Ellen and Jack's. Their homes were lovely, their children polite. Maids served dinner. Jerry roughhoused with the little boys and told the girls how pretty they were.

"This could be our life," Jerry said as we left the Sewells' one night. "Just say yes. I own a great strip of land right on the lake. We could build a house that would make the Sewells' look like a shack."

Now, as I kissed his bulldog face good night, I wondered if it might after all work out. Unlike Wes, Jerry was as reliable as a calendar. He had worked himself up from the bottom. He was successful, but not ruthlessly ambitious—the kind of man who would stay at home, play with children, help them grow.

Jane said, "Do you love him?" Well, I liked him a lot. The kind of love I had felt for Wes was, I told Jane, closer to temporary insanity. Maybe "deep liking" was love after all.

At the end of May, I said yes. Jerry couldn't wait to tell his friends. He had, he said, an enormous diamond—"barely used." I said no thanks.

Mother said, "That's nice, dear." Jane was enthralled. Irving said, "You could do worse."

And then mysterious moods began. For no reason I knew, I would burst into tears. At baseball games and movies no one noticed, but at bridge games they certainly did.

Ellen Curtis comforted me. "Just prebridal jitters. You'll see.

They'll pass. Jerry loves you so. And you'll make him a wonderful wife."

Not if I kept leaking tears on the aces and spades.

"The problem, honey, is that we haven't made love. Women can feel sexual frustrations too," Jerry said.

Five minutes into the "experiment," I knew that was not the solution. I wanted to weep more than ever. Jerry believed that condoms should be used only at orgasm. I felt too despondent to argue with him. He promptly fell asleep.

I sat up and smoked. Whatever was wrong, it was not going to change. Something inside me rebelled at marrying Jerry, something I could not understand or overcome. I had tried my best. It felt good to stop. I would tell him gently, the next day at lunch.

Jerry was, to my surprise, more argumentative than crushed: "But I've told *everyone*" and "You *promised* you would."

"Jerry, it's better to break a promise than to ruin two lives."

As my disgruntled ex-fiancé abruptly left, I paid the luncheon check.

Life went back, I believed, to normal. Jane understood. "It might have been those baseball games or maybe the golf. And any man who adores 'What's My Line' can't be all good."

My laughter stopped in late June. I had missed a period and my breasts felt tender. A gynecologist confirmed what I feared.

A block from the doctor's office I groped into a coffee shop. I ordered a cola, then, forgetting it was there, ordered a coffee too. The two beverages in front of me, I thought as I stared at them, were like the decisions seesawing in my mind. I could have an abortion. They were illegal, but perhaps I could find some safe abortionist. Or I could have the baby alone. Or I could marry Jerry. Whatever had caused my tears over the marriage was unimportant now compared to the small human being inside me. I left the coffee shop without touching either beverage.

Jerry treated my announcement as if I had come down with some rare disease. At what was once our favorite restaurant, he rearranged the silverware, repositioned the water glass, and said, looking down, "Don't worry about it."

"Jerry, do you still want to get married?"

He moved the forks two inches apart. "I guess so. I don't know. Let's forget it for tonight."

We began seeing each other again. Jerry, I reminded myself, loved me, had wanted to marry me. I had hurt him. It would take time. But not too much time, please. Pregnancies did not wait while people decided. I approached the subject; Jerry changed it.

One evening I asked the question directly: "What do you want to do: get married or have me have an abortion?"

"Why do you ruin an evening by bringing *that* up?" was his irritated reply.

Alone in my apartment, I realized it was time to face what I had tried to avoid. Jerry did not want to marry me—he also did not want the responsibility of choosing an abortion. Once he had wanted marriage—but not necessarily to me, *for* me. Anyone would have served his purpose—to wipe out the stigma of having been jilted. Perhaps my tears came from an instinct that I was being used. Yet I may have been using Jerry too—as an escape from my mysterious discontent. Those were two lousy reasons for marriage, but that was now beside the point. A pregnant bride would not ease Jerry's ego—with himself or with his friends. There would be no marriage.

A long, deep sigh felt refreshing. At least I could stop considering an alternative that didn't really exist. The decision had to be mine alone, and it had to be made soon. I was almost three months pregnant. Abortions had to be done early or not at all.

Suddenly, the person inside me seemed very, very real. I would have to decide for the tiny him or her. "What's best for you?" I asked through flooding tears. Did this child want to grow up without a father, as I had, with that constant ache of feeling unwanted? Did it want to grow up with parents who were not his or hers—to wonder always "why?" Could I endure bearing a child and then letting it go to some fate I would forever worry about? If, someday, I had other children, how would my lost child affect them? Those future children, the planned, hoped-for, wanted children, needed a whole mother, undivided and unscarred.

I pressed my hand against the place where the baby was growing. I could no longer speak, but I sent it my thoughts. "I'm so sorry, so sorry. But I have to decide for you what seems to be best." Huddled, sobbing, in the corner of the sofa, I told it good-by.

I had to think of it as an unplanned union of sperm and egg—one of a million sperm, a dozen eggs, that happened to meet, something with no more humanity than the eggs and sperm that did not meet. Only then could I try to remember the name Ella had mentioned so long ago at the store.

The phone book showed that Dr. Calvin Wenton was still in practice, but I would make a visit to my own Dr. Simon before I called.

At Dr. Simon's office I chose my words carefully. "I know you can't *recommend* an abortionist, but can you warn me if Dr. Wenton is bad?"

Dr. Simon's kind gray eyes looked at me across his desk. "Oh, Lois, I'm sorry. Don't worry. Dr. Wenton is good. Have it done, but call me immediately if there's the slightest problem—and come for a checkup that week." He rose from his desk, patted my shoulder, and gave me a tissue.

Dr. Wenton answered his own phone. Yes, he could see me at two o'clock and then "discuss any future appointment." It was reassuring that his office was in the center of town—no run-down building in some decaying area. But the two blocks I walked from my office seemed long.

The frosted glass door had large letters: "By Appointment Only." Inside, Dr. Wenton sat at a desk, a round-faced, rosy-cheeked, middle-aged man. I glanced at the open door on the right—an examining table, cupboards, and lights. There was no sound from the small room. Whatever either of us said could never be proved.

"I'm pregnant. I need an abortion. Dr. Simon says you're good." I now felt incredibly calm; it was shock perhaps, but I needed my wits. I was risking my body, perhaps my life. One wrong impression about him and I would be out the door.

Dr. Wenton nodded. "Will *you* be paying for this? Or the gentleman?"

"I will pay." It was my decision, my self-respect.

"Three hundred dollars, then. In cash, of course." Then his rosy face turned firm. "And you have to know that I do this without anesthetic—for your good and mine. I can't have a nurse here, and anesthesia can be dangerous. And I can't keep you here long enough for it to wear off. The procedure hurts like hell, but if you want to get rid of the problem enough, you can stand the pain. If you yell, I stop."

Yes, I was going to pay all right.

We set a time for the following day. I left. Jane was in Chicago, but perhaps Irving could drive me home after the abortion was done. His secretary told me he had been called to New York. Ella had moved, long ago, to Cleveland. I could not involve Jenny or Martha or Jean. Sally had to run the office.

I telephoned Mother and blurted it all out. "Oh, that's too bad, dear." I waited for more. Only silence.

"Mother, do you want me to call you so you'll know I'm all right?"

"Yes, dear, do that. I'd like to know."

There was then only Jerry. "Really, Lois, why did you choose Friday—"

I hung up. At least there was no need ever to speak to him again.

That evening I sat by my window, looking out over the lake. Tomorrow, Fate had decreed, I would be all alone and, strangely, that seemed familiar and best. I watched the lights of a boat cross the vast black expanse of the lake. I had wanted, badly, for someone to be there for me. Yet when you survived alone, it gave you strength—a strength that was better than hopes or wishes or disappointments, something you owned that no one could take away.

I slept. And the next morning I put one foot firmly in front of the other as I walked among shoppers, workers, and strollers. Few, I suspected, were on errands like mine. I was able to smile. A street photographer snapped my picture and I took the order card. Yes, appropriate. A day to record.

When I was strapped to Dr. Wenton's table, the pain began. I gasped, but carefully, softly, so that he would not stop. But there surely could not be this much pain, this aching fire that spread to fingertips, toes, the back of my eyes. I turned my head—careful, do not move, do not scream—turned it back. With every scrape of the curette, I knew that this kind of pain could leave no one unchanged. It invaded every cell, every pore, every part of my mind.

Carefully, with my neck muscles hard, I could only keep turning my head—to the window, to the door. If I screamed, he would stop; if I screamed, *I* would never stop.

Yet as pain moved my head back and forth, I understood its value. This kind of unbelievable torment was cleansing the guilt. It was setting a standard for what I could bear. Nothing ever again could be like this. I was paying, and I was free from wondering how much I could survive—*if*, for as long as this lasted, I could survive at all.

The pain ended like a battle—gradually. It took minutes to realize that the tearing bullets of torment had stopped, that the need to fight it was over.

Dr. Wenton helped me from the table to a chair. "Sit here

you can walk. Then walk around the room until you're all right."

He talked. I walked. He chatted. I hardly listened at all. .thing more than a pregnancy had been destroyed inside me and I wanted to know what it was. If only he would stop talking, perhaps I could hear.

Where the pain had been, there was only a faraway soreness. I was walking easily now.

He said, "You handled it well. You're ready to leave." And then, "But you'll be back. They always are."

I could feel a wonderful lightness in my heart and in my smile as I told him, "Oh, no. You're wrong." I walked through the frosted glass door. There were many things I did not know yet, but that one I *knew*.

In the taxi that took me home, in the bed as I went off to sleep, I knew there were *many* places I would never be again. In the morning, I was quite sure, it would be easy to sort them out.

Chapter 10

THE MORNING AFTER the abortion, the telephone woke me. It was a client. He was flying to Texas. He was so sorry to bother me, but the advertising campaign we talked about—could I possibly put it on paper and leave it with his watchman so that he could pick it up that night?

As he talked, I tested my body. I felt all right. Yes, I would go to the office and write a proposal.

It didn't take long. Soon the big manila envelope was sealed and ready for delivery. But I sat, staring across my desk toward the big Chagall print on my burnt-orange wall. Suddenly I could not imagine why I had chosen that color. Or the bulky beige lamp. I wandered through the rest of the empty offices. Joe's production office was drowning in page proofs, yet in the seven years he had worked for me, he could always find things fast. Jane's office was neat as always. Sally's plants were thriving. But had our reception room always been this ugly shade of blue? I went back to my own office, to sit in the burnt-orange chair where visitors sat.

The day before, I believed I had pieces to sort out. The first one to work its way up—like a small piece of shrapnel perhaps—was the realization that I did not want to be here. Not today or any other day.

Ridiculous. No one walked away from a business built with a lot of hard work over many years—away from clients, employees.

Even Jerry had expected me to continue to work. It was a business I had built—not exactly out of choice, but it had been a success, and you did not, as I wanted to do at that moment, lock the door and leave.

From where I sat, I could see in the windows across the way reflections of the street below. A trolley passed, committed forever to its steel path. And Grandfather was committed to those trolleys for most of his life—the 7:20 that took him to work and the 5:23 that brought him home. Mother still took the same trolleys every day.

Perhaps that was how life was supposed to be, after all. You found the best track you could and kept on it. I should have no complaints. I could do largely as I pleased, and it had been—largely—fun.

But not anymore. Did everything in the world eventually become routine? Television shows, new campaigns, new clients, trips that my housewife friends thought "exciting," were borderline boring by now. Perhaps even lion tamers and acrobats flinched at the same old growls, the same old trapeze.

I had obligations—to Jane, Sally, Joe, and Andy, to the clients. I had worked hard to help them build their businesses too. I probably also had an obligation to the people who had helped me learn. No, you did not walk away from a business and close the door.

What did you do instead? Stay stoically where you did not want to be until life was gone? I had just decided for an unborn baby what its life was *not* to be. Could I not do as well with my own?

A trolley clanged in the street below and I suddenly sat up straight. Once an "impossible" decision has surfaced, I had already discovered, the *can't*s begin to disappear.

My employees? Jane had had an excellent offer from a utility company and was loyally turning it down. Sally's husband was doing well and I knew she was eager to leave. Andy dreamed of his own agency "someday." It could be sooner. He was already older than I had been when I started out. Joe Santos had experience now and a fine reputation. He would have no trouble finding a job.

And, glory be, our lease was almost up.

The clients—what about them? David Cohen, who had split with Murray and was now running his agency alone, had once suggested we merge. That was out. David was now using his considerable talents without the distraction of our ill-starred romance. But there were other agencies in town to whom I could confidently take, and gradually turn over, my accounts.

And then I would be free. For what? It was too soon to tell. I stood at the window, looking down. What big and small things did I really want? Go ahead. Pick three. Well, to go to Europe, to have a baby, and to write a book—if I ever had something to say.

I walked around the office again. A lot of good things had happened within these walls, and I would not forget them. But it was time to move on. As another trolley clanged, I locked the door.

Two months later, I was glad I had had lessons in starving during the army days with Tony. Lovett and Wynn advertising agency was the perfect choice for my clients, but not particularly for me. White-haired, rosily benevolent Abner Lovett looked as if he came down chimneys at Christmas; Kurt Wynn looked as if he swept them out. Both men had impeccable reputations for ethics, but, unfortunately for me, some of our accounts clashed. L and W could not handle two candy companies, two dairies, or two brands of shoes. I passed these accounts to Andy. My one-third of the remaining profits barely covered the rent.

But I found I was more content than I expected. Jane, pleased with her new job and staff at the utility company, had nonetheless said, "Maybe now you'll understand about men's attitudes toward women. Those other account executives might give you problems."

I didn't see how they could. Our arrangement was clear. Lloyd, Cameron, Frank, and I each handled our own accounts. Each of us got our third of what we grossed. They were all nice men, all older than I, but friendly and helpful and even gallant. At our monthly meetings they held my chair, brought me coffee, and appeared to enjoy their masculine courtesies as much as I did.

Jane, now happily heading the advertising department at the utility company, looked at me thoughtfully when I described my new associates. "I think I've finally figured it out. You *expect* people to act right—then their egos won't let them disappoint you. I've got to admit it works."

Jane, I thought, made it all too complex. These were simply nice people—good at their jobs and certainly not envious of me.

My only problem those first months was eating. Thank heavens for dinner dates with Hal, Don, and Irving. Hal and Don may have wondered at my newly voracious appetite. Irving knew.

He said, "It wouldn't be so terrible, would it, if you married me?"

I gave him a sisterly hug. His sympathy, I knew, was overcoming his excellent judgment. I could envision his meticulous, antique-furnished bachelor apartment—and my hopeless clutter messing it up in less than a day.

"People," I said as I hugged him, "should not get married out of sympathy or malnutrition. But thanks a lot."

"Yes, I guess it's better if I just bring you a case of soup."

"I'll always love you. Make it vegetable."

Hungry though I often was, I was free, I realized, to concentrate on the creative side of my accounts. I had not known how much I disliked the business side of business until balance sheets, payroll, and billing were no longer my problems. Almost without my being aware, old clients spent more, new clients developed, and my monthly commissions increased.

After six months, chubby, bald Cam said one day, "Do you know you made more than anyone else last month?" He smiled. "Happened to see the figures."

"Cam, does anyone mind?" All the men had families to support. I had merely banked big checks without paying attention.

Cam patted my hand and looked concerned. "No, of course we don't mind. Everyone sees how hard you work. In fact, Lloyd and I were talking. It's been good for the agency to have your viewpoint. We hope you never leave."

It wouldn't be easy, but it had been part of my plan. I would stay a year, until my clients knew and trusted Cam or Lloyd or Frank. Abner Lovett had volunteered, "And, on the accounts that stay with us, I'll pay you a sliding percentage for, let's say, five years. But I hope you'll stay around."

It was tempting. Especially with people as generous as they. And then came Hal's telephone call. I had been working late and was not nearly done. Hal's enthusiastic voice said, "Hey, come on. Play hooky. There's a new band at the Tic Toc Club." Sorry, not tonight.

My hand stayed on the phone after I hung it up. Hal was charming, handsome, and a genuine millionaire—but not someone I felt I could love. But what kind of woman turned down millionaires to figure out how to sell more pretzels?

The kind of woman, possibly, who was scared stiff of getting married.

I had dodged that idea for some time, but a lot of the symptoms were present: a serious attachment to a married man, inability to take eligible men seriously, devotion to work.

Yes, I could admit I was scared, and possibly with legitimate reason. This time if I married it would have to be for keeps—as it would have been with Tony if we had had a child. More and more I was aware of how impossible it would be for me to take a child from its father. If I had married Jerry, I would have stayed, no matter what.

But why must I marry at all? I might be a terrible mother; I might be a terrible wife. Heaven knows, I could support myself very well indeed. And I didn't know what *lonely* meant—there were always men friends to take me dancing, to talk with. There would probably always be. Perhaps I was simply not the kind who should be married. Did people have to pair off in eternal twos as if they were boarding the Ark?

Lights flashed on and off around the city. Come on, get back to work. Instead, I watched the light of a plane crossing the sky.

I might indeed choose not to get married, but damn it, not out of fear. How much had fear caused me to erect the life I was leading? If someone I liked got too close, I could find good reasons for a new client campaign that would keep me "too busy," "too tired," or "out of town."

The lights of Milwaukee below me appeared almost to dim. I had lived here all my twenty-eight-year life and perhaps that was wrong. Perhaps the way to make the choices best was to go somewhere else. Hometowns were safe and familiar and habit-forming. Yes, somewhere else would be best. I would decide where after the pretzel campaign was launched and my new paper-company account was organized. I went back to work.

Three months later, in May of 1954, Betty Speece, a former part-time employee of mine, phoned from Chicago. Did I know of anyone, she had asked, who could take over her job at short notice? A chronic illness was flaring up and she had to have surgery fast. If possible, she wanted to replace herself at McCann-Erickson, the big Chicago agency where she wrote radio and TV ads.

I hung up the phone and went for a walk. It was hard to think in the noontime crowd, but at least I was undisturbed. There it was. If I took Betty's job, I would have what I knew I should have —nine to five, time to date, a new town to explore. The job paid less than one-third of what I was making—$10,000 to my $36,000. I could use the cut in income as an excuse, or I could go ahead.

At three o'clock the next afternoon, I was talking with Con Matthews, the radio-TV director at McCann-Erickson. I liked him. In his late thirties, curly-haired, frantic, but open, he grinned at me. "What can I offer? Flowers? Champagne? I can't match what you probably make now, but, wow, do I need you!"

I had walked through the busy, buzzing office on Michigan Avenue. Maybe I needed McCann-Erickson. No matter what I decided about my personal future, it would be good to learn how an enormous international agency functioned. Easy, too, to be as small a cog as I wanted in this presumably well-oiled machine.

Con waited, searching my face as I flipped quickly through all possible reasons for saying no. Cam, Lloyd, and Frank were well acquainted now with my accounts; I had stayed with Lovett and Wynn for more than a year. And my apartment lease was almost up.

"When do I start?"

"Bless the Lord. Yesterday?"

It took a week—a week of quick arrangements that gave me little time to think. My clients, I knew, would be well taken care of by Lovett and Wynn. I could commute to Chicago until my lease was up. Still, as I rode the train to my first day at my new job, I looked over my shoulder for a formal good-by. I was leaving a lot behind in my hometown.

As the train raced along, I watched Milwaukee recede. Odd, for the first time since that day in high school when I read about writing in that blue book, I had no clear-cut goals in mind. The flat landscape stretched as far as I could see, yet I felt as if I were holding a rather tattered map. Once I had chosen a route and followed it, making better time than I had expected. The trip had been exciting, but somehow I had stayed at my destination a bit too long. Now I was moving, but only a short way. Chicago could be a resting-place.

For a few weeks it appeared that I had found exactly what I wanted for the time being—a pleasant, easy job, time to make new friends, and time to think about where I had been, where I was, and where I might want to go.

Mostly, I wrote scripts for Swift's "Martha Logan" segment of "Don McNeil's Breakfast Club." Women wrote in questions and a marvelous woman, Beth McLean, head of Swift's home-economics department, sent the questions and their answers to me. I put them in the proper form for radio—and learned how to cook. Or learned about gasoline, canned cream, or Swift's Meats for Babies as I wrote for all of them.

Meg Gamble, the agency's home economist, was my first—and I suspected would be my best—friend. She had introduced herself the first day. "And don't let Beth McLean scare you. Everyone here trembles when she speaks. She founded Swift's home-ec department before we were born and runs it with an iron hand, but she's also a fine lady."

It seemed to me that many people there trembled when others spoke. I asked Meg. Her blue eyes flashed laughter above her crisp white uniform. "Funny, isn't it? The junior account executives are afraid of their bosses. The account execs are afraid of the supervisor, and *everyone's* afraid of the clients! And have you been to a meeting yet?" Meg held her ash-blond head.

Yes, my day had started with one. Everyone appeared to be trying to guess what the client wanted. "They spent a *hour*," I said, "arguing about *crispy-fresh* versus *snappy-smooth*."

Meg laughed again. "Those endless meetings! I always end up doing exactly what I planned to do anyway. Come on up to my kitchen for coffee."

Meg's job was developing recipes using clients' products. While we nibbled—and compared—two different recipes for oatmeal cookies, I learned that Meg was working only until Howard, her husband, had his architectural practice well underway. "Won't be long now. We've started building our house. Soon I'll be home spooning Pablum into someone instead of testing it."

Often, after talking with Meg, I would spend the train ride home staring at my reflection in the window. Meg was so glowingly content—talking about progress on their house, the baby she hoped to have ("at home, with only Howard and the Christian Science practitioner there"), and the stay-at-home life she planned to lead. Why did the idea of marriage frighten me so much?

So far, I had good excuses to avoid dates. No dating co-workers— that was still out. But Irving's cousin lived in Chicago, and he was eager to introduce me to "some young men I know." Instead I was spending my evenings on trains. I looked back at the woman in the window. All right. No tricks. I would find an apartment tomorrow.

Irving's cousin, Gene, suggested the Near North Side, where he lived. "Convenient—and lots of young people around. Bartlett Realty is converting a building to smaller units. Might be just right. I've been watching the work."

It was right enough. A wall of bookcases, a view of the lake (if you stood on tiptoes), a fireplace that did not work; but the rooms were large and the rent was all right. I would be the first tenant. My apartment was the only finished one. Well, no noisy neighbors —at least for a while. I signed the lease.

Gene, a tall distinguished, white-haired man, was eager to show me around. At a cocktail party in his apartment two blocks away, I met John, Glenn, and Bob. Very soon my new apartment was a place to sleep and to change for dates—often with a sigh. I was getting the new-girl-in-town rush, I told myself, a teen-ager's dream, but at twenty-eight I felt it was often more like a chore. John danced well but talked mostly of electronics—"They'll change the world." Glenn was pleasant when I managed to forget he was a pathologist who cut up bodies all day. It was hard to find anything wrong with witty, charming Bob, but I knew I would keep trying.

Meg teased me. "Don't look so bored at the idea of dinner at the Pump Room 'again.' " By now, Meg knew what I was fighting and she understood. "I was lucky. My parents have a happy marriage. If they didn't, I'd probably be as scared as you."

There was always the possibility, I reminded her, that I might simply not be the marrying type. "Well"—Meg smiled—"we'll see."

On Saturday evening, as Bob and I drank after-dinner coffee at the Drake, two young men waved from across the room. "Marty and Les. O.K. if I ask them to join us?"

Les looked like a full-size Pinocchio: slim, with puppet-bright eyes, and limbs on strings. Marty looked familiar: tall, husky, and blond. Like whom? Bob, more a buddy now than a date, smiled indulgently when Les asked me to dance. While I danced with him—or tried to follow his loosely strung legs—Bob and Marty were in deep conversation.

Later, Bob said, "Marty asked if he could phone you. I said I wished him better luck than mine. He's a good guy. Legal counsel for a real estate firm—not happy there, never was. Anyway, I told him I'd trust him with you."

When Marty Gross stepped over the construction materials strewn near my front door to pick me up for our first date, I liked his off-center smile, and his shy sense of humor, and more things about him than I wanted to like. He talked fondly of his parents, retired now in Florida, and of his married sister ("older than I—busy raising kids in Wilmette"). Dinner, a concert, and "I'll call you soon." I hoped he would.

He did call—nearly every day that week. More concerts, more dinners, and long walks along Oak Street Beach. Talk about himself (he *was* discontent with his job; he shared an apartment with Les and felt he should have his own), questions of me: Did I like my job? (Well, yes.) What were my goals? (None at the moment.)

Meg grinned at my reports. "You do like him, don't you?"

Yes, but on general principles I continued to accept dates with John and Glenn. Bob had moved on, to some girl who did not see him as only a friend.

I was thinking about Marty on a Saturday morning when I had planned to wash my hair and read. Outside my door I heard a clunk and a muttered curse. In the street I could see a packed-up car waiting to be unloaded. Great! I would no longer be alone in the building. A husky young man with receding sandy hair emerged to collect another box.

As the clunks continued, I tried to ignore them. I did not want to meet another young man. On the other hand, it might be wise. In case of burglary or fire, at least I should know what name to scream. It was, I decided, worth the effort of getting—leisurely—dressed on my lazy Saturday morning.

An hour later I walked across the hall. Through his open door I saw him bending over a carton, mumbling more curses. I cleared my throat and asked, "Would you like to borrow a knife?"

The face that turned to me, first with a glower and then with a smile, was boyish, but his premature baldness and square jaw reminded me strongly of Grandfather. "Yes, I sure would. Do you have a vacuum cleaner I can borrow too? But would you like a cup of coffee first?"

I had not planned to get that involved, but I said yes. He had done, I noticed, a remarkable job of getting settled. The kettle, cups, and instant coffee were already in the cabinets. His closet door was open. Suits, slacks and shirts hung in a precise row over shoes in shoe trees lined up on the floor. Except for a few unopened boxes, his small apartment was neater than my large one after all those weeks. He had my admiration.

Over coffee I began to suspect that this young man could be the friend I had lost in Bob. We were, in many ways, as alike as brother and sister. We were born the oldest in our families, each with a younger brother. His parents were middle-class: his father a foreman, his mother a secretary. And he was in advertising too.

"I was with an agency back home—Cleveland. Then this job as ad manager for Crown Foods came up. Let's hope I made the right choice."

Yes, I thought, he had. He was unlike the wheeling-and-dealing young men at my agency, less glib and more organized. Yes, distinctly Grandfather's type.

We finished our coffee. He rinsed our cups and I took him to my messy place to get the vacuum cleaner and knife. As he left, I realized I had forgotten my original mission. "Hey, I don't know your name."

"George Stalvey. I'm sure I told you."

Well, maybe he had. It was a hard name to remember, Stalvey— but a good friend to have across the hall. I went back to my book. And my thoughts about Marty.

That night Marty mentioned the word *marriage* for the first time. His parents were concerned that, at thirty-two, he had not married and "settled down." There was plenty of time, I told him. My favorite uncle had married Aunt May when he was forty-five. Marty looked at me oddly and talked of his job. And did not phone for a week.

At the office Meg tried to look stern. "You idiot, Lois. You really squelched his hopes. You're still using your old tricks."

Perhaps I was, and if so I was sorry, but how could I conquer this fear?

Meg set aside the concoction she was mixing and looked directly at me. "You have to remember you're not your mother—or your grandmother. You're you. And Marty is not any of the men in your childhood. It's as easy, and difficult, as that."

Through the day's endless meetings I thought about what she had said. In one way she was wrong. I had finally realized whom Marty reminded me of—Uncle Irv, who had died when I was four. They had the same big build, blue eyes, and blond hair, the same off-center smile. Well, later for that. Marty might never call.

George helped some evenings pass. He did, I thought, an incredible amount of vacuuming. My vacuum got three times more use in his place than it did in mine. He used it as an excuse to visit, I knew, but I enjoyed our talks. George had the ambition I had put aside.

At the agency it was increasingly strange to pull back instead of advance. Perhaps, I told myself, it was simply because a large agency was no place I wanted to be. At first I had expected to learn things I had not known when I ran my own business. Here, at least, there were dozens of "experts" and world-wide resources to use. But the interminable meetings continued. In my own agency I had talked with my clients, executed the ideas, and that was that. Here, communication was stretched so thin that it was amazing when anything got done at all. A few times I opened my mouth to speak—and shut it again. I had too many ideas they might use, and then I'd be back in a job that stretched beyond five o'clock. Better to give my ideas to George.

Marty finally called. He had been, he said, out of town. More dinners, more movies and concerts and plays. One night he took me home and, a ritual now, went up to the corner to get the Sunday papers—one for him and one for me. But the usual five minutes stretched into ten—to twenty—to twenty-five.

I found myself actually pacing the floor, gripped by some terrible ache. This was the agony of waiting for Wes—but—I stopped. It was something more. Meg's words came back with a shock. "He is not your father." No, he wasn't, but the waiting felt the same.

In minutes Marty was at the door. The usual newsstand had been sold out. He had walked six blocks and back. And I had learned how long and deeply old scars could hurt.

All right, I was slowly learning—if not at work, at least in my personal life. But not fast enough. I was, as I had planned, "parked," but my discontent with my own agency had made me vulnerable to Jerry Webster. My discontent now might make me vulnerable too.

Meg said, "Don't laugh, but have you ever thought of a hobby? Lots of everyday problems melt as we work on our house."

"Model airplanes?" But during a meeting on a new show about babies that I had been assigned to write, I played with Meg's idea. Anything was worth a try. Energy, apparently, could not be blocked, and I was not using much at work. My attention came back to the meeting when a tall, full-figured woman started to speak. Pete Gregg, who owned the baby show, had introduced her as Ruth Crowley—mother of five, trained nurse, editor of a household magazine, and creator of the Ann Landers advice column. She would be doing the baby show too. *Her* energies were jolly well *not* blocked. A hobby, then. But what? Well, Meg sewed—suits, coats, dresses. All right, why not? My eighth-grade sewing class had been a disaster, but now that I *wanted* to sew, perhaps I could do it.

The gamble on buying a sewing machine was only money, I reminded myself. My choice of a Vogue Easy-To-Make pattern was wise—no point in asking for frustration. I bought good fabric, though, or I might not respect it enough to take pains. Marty was out of town, so I would have a quiet weekend to puzzle over instructions on how the machine worked, and then how to cut and sew.

On Monday morning Meg looked at my face and gasped, "What on earth happened? You look radiant. Did Marty propose?"

I hugged Meg hard, then twirled around. "No! I made this dress *myself!*" I could hardly believe the crazy sense of accomplishment I got from that one simple act. Here I was, immeasurably proud of my beige wool dress. In my super-rich days, no costly Oleg Cassini or Adele Simpson creation had thrilled me like that.

Meg admired my work. "Hah! Domesticity rears its inevitable head."

"Not a bit! But now I can *sew* what I want instead of hunting for it in stores. I think I'll try a cocktail dress next."

My excitement abated enough to notice Meg's own radiance. "What happened to *you?*"

Meg's heart-shaped face looked different, not excited but softly glowing. "We found out Friday night. I'm pregnant, Lois. I didn't think it would work out this well. The house will be done before the baby is born. Timed it on the nose."

I had no idea I could be so happy for somebody else. Another hug, this time for her triumph. "But, Meg, shouldn't you sit down or something? Are you quitting work? Are you throwing up yet?"

"Lois, you idiot. I never felt better. My mother didn't have morning sickness and neither will I. And I'm going to work through my seventh month. By then the house will be done and the bedroom will be ready to have the baby in."

Christian Science, I thought, must be a marvelous religion. If I ever had a child, it would be in the best hospital I could find and use every anesthetic developed by then.

But to Meg I said, "Wonderful! I'd hate to have you leave soon." I would miss her terribly when she really did leave. Our confidences, her understanding, had made her the big sister I had never had. What would I do when she left? "Well, honey, you'll have to come visit that baby show I'm writing. Meg, I'm so happy for you."

That night George returned my vacuum cleaner and admired my dress. Marty felt it "deserved the best restaurant in town." Both men tried, I could see, to share with me my exuberant joy for Meg. George said, "That's nice." Marty said, "A birth at home?" And "The concert is early tonight."

In Chicago's Orchestra Hall, Mahler's Seventh Symphony flooded around me. It had been quite a day—my dress, Meg's news. The music flowed through me and the hundreds of people in Orchestra Hall. Then, abrupt as a change in the musical theme, I was aware of the *women* around me—not as people, but as women. Strange, but up until then I had thought of myself vaguely as a *person*—one part of the large mass of human beings, each with different talents, different tastes, different temperaments—but never so acutely, so suddenly, as a special half of the human race. I sat, not looking around, but feeling a new tie with the females in the large, dim hall. We were different from the men who sat beside us. We had bodies, viewpoints, and feelings only women could know— like Meg's joy in her pregnancy. As the music surged on, I felt wonder at how long it had taken me to feel so thoroughly a woman.

Pete Gregg, producer of the "All about Baby" show, phoned a few days later. When I heard his voice, I was ready for our usual banter or his avuncular advice. Pete felt I was "hiding" myself at McCann, that I should "unleash my talent" and write a book. I always laughed that I had nothing yet to say. I was already smiling when I heard the strain in Pete's voice.

"Lois, Ruth Crowley died."

No. Impossible. I had read her Ann Landers column that morning. The film of the baby show had run the night before. No one that vital could die.

"An embolism. Very quick. We're canceling the show."

Of course. No one could replace Ruth. At her funeral I looked at her children. Who could replace her for them? But her college-age son and her teen-age daughter held and comforted the younger ones. Ruth would have prepared them to go on alone. Her son was supporting his weeping father. A wonderful mother had passed on her strength—to her children and to many others.

I was still mourning privately when Pete Gregg called again. The *Sun-Times,* which published and syndicated Ruth's column, felt it had to continue. "Lois, I recommended you. Ruth would have approved. The editor wants you to call."

Pete could not see me shaking my head. Ruth could not be replaced. Pete said, "Someone has to. Give it some thought."

I still shook my head as I sat on the bus going home through Chicago's teeming Loop. These were the people who turned to "Ann Landers." Did I perhaps have an obligation to try? The bus stopped, started, and lumbered on.

As I walked the few blocks to my apartment, I wondered again. If I did it for Ruth, it might be also for me—to replace the goals I had put aside. George's door was open. I talked to him as I had talked to myself. "It probably pays a lot, Lois, and you'd be great. There's nothing you can't do well." George was sweet. I went home to continue to think.

In the morning I phoned the editor. "Let me write a sample and then we'll both see." In his office he stuffed a large manila envelope with handfuls of letters from bulging sacks. I carried it back to my office.

Then I began to read. After the fourth letter I put on my coat. Perhaps, as a nurse, Ruth had learned to cope with suffering. I had not. Each letter had been such a searing, personal cry for help, it had literally wrung my heart. Yes, I knew that Ruth had doctors, ministers, lawyers to consult for her private replies. Yet to me it seemed that no words on paper could be enough. I wanted to hold the woman who had lost a child, hold the child whose mother had left, hold the hand of the old man who was dying alone—and since all that was impossible, I wanted to get rid of that envelope with its pieces of suffering that infected the world.

I ran up Michigan Avenue, knowing what a coward I was. It was almost a relief to see the extent of my cowardice, I thought, to know exactly where my courage stopped.

After I had thrust the envelope into the editor's hand, I walked back slowly. Shop windows blurred, bodies propelled me along. Back at the office I was expected to write words about bacon and gas. And I would do it. There was nothing better to do. Someone with more strength than I had would write Ruth's column, some-one with the maturity I did not have, with a wisdom I had yet to earn, and with an immunity to suffering I might never achieve.

I sewed more dresses in the months that followed. Cutting, stitch-ing, weaving a needle in and out gave me something to do. Marty talked more of marriage. George talked of his work. Meg's body enlarged. As I sewed, my mind drifted like a rudderless boat, but maybe that was all right. I had learned what I did not want, what I could not do, and what I feared. Perhaps, between stitches, the rest would work itself out.

And I would be thirty years old the next summer. The "young" would then officially be removed from my name—no more "young executive," no more status for early achievement. At thirty it was time for me to accept the responsibility of being as grown-up as I would ever be.

In the first week of January 1955, Meg announced that their house was ready. The baby was due the following month. "Lois, do you want our apartment? It would be perfect for you. The fireplace really works."

Why not? My own patched-up, remodeled apartment suddenly seemed too small. Maybe sitting before a fire while I sewed would help me sort things out at a faster rate. George Stalvey looked dismayed. Well, George would just have to buy his own vacuum cleaner.

Chapter 11

AS THE DAY APPROACHED, I had an interesting—but not crucial, I thought—moving decision to make. George had offered to help. "If you rent a truck, I can handle your things. And I'll get boxes and help you pack." Marty had grinned. "There's only one civilized way to move. Give the moving company the two addresses. Then I'll take you to lunch at the Pump Room. By the time we're done, they'll have everything set up at your new place."

George's plan, of course, was thrifty, practical, and what I "should" do. But Marty's idea sounded like much more fun. More expensive, true, but why not use the money I had earned to buy convenience?

I felt wickedly frivolous lunching with Marty while the moving men took charge—and immensely relaxed to arrive at my new apartment to find almost everything in place. Only a few boxes remained for me to unpack when I decided where things should go —on shelves, in cupboards, or into the trash.

Marty left, and I walked through the rooms that were to be home. The move, I decided, had been a good idea. The marble-faced fireplace would be delightful. The big bay window was the perfect place to sit and watch the leaves. I might even cook dinners in the large, bright kitchen. Yes, good things had happened here for Meg and her husband. I had a feeling they would happen for me.

George phoned to ask if he could help me unpack.

"There's not much to do, but you can come visit if you like."

It was always pleasant to talk to George—no flirting, no tension at all. When Meg teased me about marriage, she had occasionally said, "What about George?" Heavens, no. George was my *friend*—a buddy I talked to almost as if to myself.

George did look different to me when he sat that night next to the fire I had built in my new fireplace. As the logs crackled, he seemed no longer "the boy next door" who borrowed my vacuum, to whom I waved when I went out with others. He was, I realized, quite an attractive man—good square chin, well-formed nose, light-blue eyes.

I blinked and poked the fire. Come on, it's only George. Yet, for no reason I knew, I began to talk about my past—about Tony, my youthful ambitions, the abortion, my leaving Milwaukee. The fire burned down. George simply listened. At the door he looked as if he wanted to kiss me. Oh, why not? He *had* been a good friend. With his arms around me, George was taller than I thought.

Marty phoned moments after George left. Was I comfortably settled? I said yes, and thought, unfairly, with no thanks to you. No, Marty was not the domestic type at all. I tried to picture him mowing a lawn as Grandpa had done. Not Marty; he would pay someone to do it.

I expected a restless night in a brand-new home, but after I had sifted casually through a box of old letters, my diaries, long-paid bills, I did not expect to toss quite so restlessly in bed. Stupid decisions seemed monumental—repaint the apartment (yes, no), buy a new chair (why, why not), a dining-room table? Light peeked through the lovely new shutter-blinds before I fell asleep.

It was Meg's last week at the office. In the seven months we had known each other, our chats between chores had become important to me. The agency, with its endless, frantic rush to nowhere, would now be harder to bear. Yet it was impossible not to share her immeasurable joy. Despite what she called her "enormous front," she emptied drawers, polished pots and pans for her successor, and straightened files with amazing energy.

That was not the way I remembered pregnancies at all. Aunt May had sat, sending Uncle Irv on urgent errands for pillows, footstools, and lemon drops. Mother had talked of her aching legs and other details I had chosen until now to forget: "The doctor said he had never seen anyone torn like me when you were born. And that long, awful labor! He finally pulled you out with forceps or we'd both have been dead.''

Yet Meg moved lightly around the room, stopping to grin and pat her "little passenger inside" when he or she moved.

"Meg, are you scared?"

She sat on the chair next to me and took my hands. "Lois, you nut! What on earth is there to be scared about? Our bodies were *made* to bear children. Oh, I guess if a woman is really scared, she tightens her muscles and it could hurt then. But according to my mother, the worst contractions feel like the kind of stomach cramps we've all had at times. They don't even last as long."

Meg put her hands on her round front. "Honey, I just hope you know the wonderful feeling soon. I can't wait until I hold this little person in my arms instead of my body. And until Howard can hold our baby too. Someday—you'll see—all husbands will be allowed to be there for the birth the way it ought to be."

Looking at Meg's face was like looking at a masterful stained-glass window with sun pouring through. Joy, pride, love, confidence, and generosity were like glowing colors radiating from inside. It was a happiness I had never realized existed before.

Meg left. Days passed. I sewed between dates with Marty—and now George. I made a blue brocade dress to wear to a party Marty's sister was giving. George sat with me while I chattered and sewed up the hem. I tried it on.

George said, "That dress should go dancing at the Pump Room. May I take you Saturday night?"

His invitation was touching. His salary was hardly half of mine, one-fourth of Marty's. The Pump Room would cost what he made in a week. Yet I could hardly say no and remind him of that. George's ego, I knew, was a fragile thing. We made the date. I ordered the least expensive thing on the menu and bravely danced with George. My toes were stomped, my ankles nicked, while George danced to some rhythm only he heard.

The blue-brocade went out again with Marty to his sister's suburban home. Maids passed food, a white-jacketed man mixed drinks, and children were displayed and dismissed. Marty never left my side, and I found myself wishing he would. It was, I decided as we drove home that night, my fear of marriage rearing its head. At least I knew the source. But I pleaded a headache and said good night at my door.

It was still early enough to unpack the boxes that had stood too long in the hall. And to light a fire to enjoy alone. A handful of old useless papers went into the flames. When I reached into a box to grab some more, I saw the layer of diaries I had kept since my teens. I opened one. Such a silly child, playing at growing up. Suddenly, I never wanted to see those diaries again. With no idea why it seemed so right, I tossed them, one after another, into the flames. The half-empty box still stood in the hall when I went, quite relaxed, to sleep.

In Chicago, March came in like a lion off the lake. Sleet pelted me on my way to the bus and as I hurried to get home—to unpack that damn box, to wash my hair, at least to be inside.

George's call got me out of the shower. "There's something important I want to talk to you about. Is it O.K. if I come over?"

Sure. George had seen me in curlers often enough, and his voice was strained. Some worry at work, no doubt. George wanted so badly to succeed. He worried far too much about any criticism his boss made. Like Mother, really. Well, whatever his problem was, it must seem serious to George if he was willing to walk through the sleet to discuss it.

While George talked, I scoured a skillet—couldn't leave *that* all week for the cleaning woman. The problem, George said, was that his boss had *told* him to send ad proofs to Pittsburgh—and was now denying he'd given the order. "George, can't you just phone the guy in Pittsburgh and tell him to mail them back? Who cares who said what?"

George looked relieved, but not relaxed. "There's something else. Could you sit down?" I put my half-cleaned skillet aside.

"Lois, I was just wondering if you'd marry me."

I bit off my laughing answer. Just a minute, now. As I looked at his serious, familiar face across the table, I held my breath. Why did I feel as if I were at the top of a roller coaster about to plunge? Because, I realized, I was looking at George, but also straight at myself. This fine man had asked me to marry him. One more laughing refusal and I would have to admit I was too cowardly to think about it at all. Suddenly George looked very dear, waiting across my kitchen table, his heart in his eyes.

Funny, but for the first time I could feel how strong my fear was. And I had a choice: I could let it hold me forever or try to push through. I took a breath. I closed my eyes. The roller coaster plunged.

George was saying, "You don't have to answer now. I just wanted to know if I'm the *kind* of man you'd think of marrying." Then he said, "I think I'd be very lucky if you would."

I was whizzing down a slope a million miles a minute, and, to my surprise, I was keeping my head. I never had thought about the *kind* of man I would want to marry. I was much too busy fighting my fear. What kind of man did I really want to father my children?

George talked on, filling the silence. "I don't make as much money as you do now, but someday I will. With college and the army, I figure I'm six years behind. But I *will* catch up."

Now I could speak. "George, money doesn't matter. How do you feel about kids?"

An hour later I had learned that, like the proverbial plunge into a cold lake, it wasn't so bad once you got used to it. We talked about "if"—and I was surprised at how much George and I agreed. Three children, a house in the suburbs, a lawn for him to cut—and no more career for me. George had said, "You can work if you want. My mother did." Absolutely not. Marriage was for children and children needed mothers at home.

"George, if we did marry, I'd rather find ways to live on your salary than leave my children even for a day." Then, "just in case," we named them—"George Stalvey, Junior, for you—and Christina *Lois* for me." Christina was the name of one of my father's sisters. I wondered why it came into my mind.

It was late. George kissed me on the forehead and said, "I want you so much to say yes, but not until you're sure. I'll wait until you know." I watched him, bent against the sleet, from my window—then sat on the sofa and wept.

Just plain emotional exhaustion, I told myself. I had pushed through an old, deep fear. Naturally I was drained. No, it was something more than that. But what? A double-edged feeling, really—sadness *and* serenity—as if I were sadly giving up a precious illusion for a more important truth.

I thought of George. Was love something quite different from what I had thought it was? I could see him as a *husband,* diligently taking care of me and the children I wanted to have, doing all those daily unexciting things that made families survive. I felt respect for him, admiration, and a deep, unquestioning trust.

But not the feelings promised by the love songs. Love had not "walked right in and chased the gloom of the past." I did not *feel* gloomy about my past. I did not need "someone to watch over me." The romantic lyrics we had all grown up with still held their illusory promises, but—I found I could smile now—those "icy fingers up and down my spine" might be more a symptom of flu than the kind of love you married on. The "longing for you follows wherever I go" and the "yearning, both day and night, for you" could be a form of temporary insanity, the insanity I had felt for Wes, not something on which you build a home.

Dancing in Marty's arms to "Lover Come Back to Me" had indeed been romantic. Marty looked so much like the beloved uncle I had lost, and Marty was romantic—impractical, fun, endearing. But Marty had said at his sister's party, "That's the civilized way with kids. Have someone else dress them up, show them off and get them offstage." The thought of Marty reading a bedtime story was like imagining Humphrey Bogart baking bread.

The thought of Marty caused another wave of weeping to break over me. I would miss him very much. (Miss him! Supposedly I was only *considering* George's proposal!) Marty was the possibility of those Sinatra love songs coming true—all the songs that promised eternal passion.

A gust of sleet struck the window. You did not, I realized suddenly, sing love songs to children; you sang lullabies. And when you married the man who would be their father, you chose someone who put them first, who would be there always—someone like George.

How odd it was that when I let myself think of George now, signals I had missed so long were clear. George wanted to marry *me*—not the person who dressed up and made sophisticated conversation on dates. George had seen me in my messy apartment, my hair in pin curls, with colds, cramps, and in crotchety moods. And we were *friends*. Maybe that was what love was after all—a deep, undramatic affection—not zooming fireworks, but a fireplace where the warmth grew and lasted.

George, I reminded myself, would never be an "overnight success." Living on his $6,000 salary would be no problem though. The army days and the other pull-in-your-belt times I had known had given me practice. George *was* six years behind me as he had said. It would even feel good to help him catch up. All I had learned would not go to waste. He might do much, much better than I. His patient persistence rather than my crazy jumps might be like his Tortoise to my retired Hare.

But, for tonight, I instructed myself firmly, time to put aside lovely fantasies of George holding our child or trimming Christmas trees as Grandfather had done. I had agreed only to think. George was taking a two-week vacation to visit his parents in Ohio. While he was gone I could try to decide, soberly, sensibly. Because if I married, it would truly be "till death do us part."

I thought of Mother. It was early enough to phone before I went to sleep. The news, the decision I had to make, was something I wanted to share. When she answered, I burst out with all my feelings. "That's nice, dear," she said, as I had half expected. "I always liked George."

George left for Ohio. I telephoned Meg. Her baby was almost due. I told her my news. "But if I decide to marry George, I don't know how I can bear to hurt Marty."

Meg's low laugh came comfortingly over the phone. "Lois, honey, I think both you and Marty worked out your fears of marriage on each other. Now you're free to marry George. Bet you anything Marty will marry inside a year. I've seen it work before."

"But when should I tell him?"

Meg laughed maternally. "When you *decide*. I thought you were just thinking it over."

I was. Yet on a date with Marty, I felt detached and disloyal. And a poignant pity for someone I used to know. Best, I decided, to plead fatigue, stay home, and sew for the weekend.

As I spread the blue lining on the floor, placed the pattern, and pinned it down, I glanced at the lace. Yes, the match was fine. There would be enough fabric left for a small cap with a short veil. Such a pretty blue. White would be inappropriate for a second marriage.

Wait! I looked down at what I was doing. Completely unaware, I had shopped for—and was now cutting out—my wedding dress. Some part of me had decided and was very, very sure.

Finally George returned. "I'll be right over, if that's O.K." Yes, it certainly was. I watched from the window. He came in sight, tall and familiar and dear. At the door, when I saw his face, one love song *did* seem to come true—"Our Love Is Here to Stay"—and with this quiet, persistent man I would be "going a long, long way." It was, suddenly, very clear.

All during the weeks of excited planning for "the most perfect June wedding ever," my decision seemed more and more to be the right one. I loved the look on George's face as I bubbled with plans. Loving, sometimes amused, he agreed with even my worst offbeat ideas.

"George, I want to give us a big, terrific reception for all our relatives and friends, but, honey, I don't want to stand in front of a big crowd when we take those important wedding vows. It's so personal. Would it be O.K. if we got married in the clergyman's parlor with just my family and yours there?"

"Sure, darling, whatever you want."

The reception, I had decided, would be "perfect." No commercial hotel for us. I knew of a beautiful house on the lake in Milwaukee that one could rent for weddings and parties. It would be almost like being married at home. Grandmother had died just before I left Milwaukee and Mother lived in a tiny apartment; there was hardly room for me to visit, let alone marry from there. But in this old-fashioned, enormous house on the lake, I could pretend. The woman who owned it handled all the details—the food, the cake—and there was even a beautiful stairway on which to stand and throw my bouquet.

"And, of course," I told George, "we must have only imported champagne." Mother could not pay for my wedding. I could, easily, and have plenty left over for a down payment on a house, appliances, and all the practical things. But for my last, my perfect, wedding, I wanted everything to be the best—engraved invitations, an enormous cake, and a lot of champagne from France.

George's strong, rugged face showed a quiet pride. "Well, honey, at least I can get the champagne for you wholesale. One of the secretaries at the office knows a liquor distributor."

Good. George would take care of that.

Meg phoned in the midst of my happiness with some of her own. "Guess what! It's a girl! Lois, no one can ever describe what it feels like to hold your baby for the first time. I hope it's soon for you too. And my mother was right. The worst contractions felt like stomach cramps. The delivery was beautiful with Howard right there. And I'm so *happy!*"

I could share Meg's happiness just as my friends shared mine. Jane, still pleased with her job at the utility company, said, "As soon as you got bored with your agency, I kind of figured this was what you really wanted." Only Pete Gregg expressed doubts.

Pete had understood why I could not do the Ann Landers column, but not why I intended to end my career. "How can you stay home, waxing floors and furniture, after all you've accomplished? You'll be bored blue."

I felt indignant, then forgiving. Pete had no idea of what staying at home meant to me. Bored? I was taking on the most important challenge of my life. I knew, firsthand, what George went through every day, and I wanted to create a comfortable, serene home where he could be recharged. Building a family was far more important and long-lasting than creating a million commercials for Swift's ham. I only hoped I would have the luck and stamina for this new career as I had had for the old one. I had a feeling it would be much more demanding.

At the end of April, George and I drove to Ohio so that I could meet his parents. Theirs had been, he told me, a stormy marriage, but they were happy now. His father had been the high-school football star in a small Georgia town where his mother had been the town beauty. They had married when they were fifteen and seventeen, which was not uncommon in the South, George said. George was born when his mother was sixteen. His brother, Wayne, was born the next year. George could remember terrible times—lack of money during the Depression, other women, physical fights. The family moved to Ohio when George was eight.

"They're happy now," George had said, "and I'm grateful that they stayed together." So was I. I was marrying a family at last.

It was no problem at all loving John Stalvey on sight—hearty, warm, and welcoming. Alice, George's mother, was more reserved, and I wondered at the bitter lines around her mouth. But she had raised the man I loved, and for that alone I would love her. John Stalvey told wonderful stories of hunting and fishing while George talked quietly with his mother. George, I realized, was nothing like his father at all. It was amusing to see how they differed. John hunted, fished, bowled, and golfed, told jokes with near-professional ease. He was president or founder, I learned, of nearly all the organizations in town. George forgot punch lines, guttered bowling balls, and refused to touch a gun. I looked fondly at George across the room. No hunting, fishing, or evening meetings —George would be home with his family. No other women, either. George still bore scars from the agony his mother had confided to him.

Yet, as we drove home after I had been welcomed into the family, I could not help feeling some discomfort. It was unfair, but I wasn't surprised. I had just taken another step toward marriage, and the old, old fears were not easily laid to rest. They were com-ing up through silly critical reactions to the perfectly normal imperfections I saw in George. I looked across at his rather im-passive face—even his smiles were reserved. On the other hand, he had shown a surprising temper with his landlord over some minor thing, and according to George's angry report, they had almost come to blows. On the *other* hand, he agreed too much with me. And, I noticed, as a car near us angrily honked its horn, his mind wandered when he drove.

As the lights of Chicago came in sight, I took myself in hand. How silly could I get? What did I want, a man who mugged like Milton Berle, let landlords scare him, and argued with *me?* Of course his driving was distracted. He too was taking the most im-portant step of his life—he was handling his prenuptial doubts as I must handle mine. I reached for his hand.

But, as the weeks passed, I could not make the silly fears sub-side.

"George, honey, I've been through times like this before, but this time I don't *want* to get scared and run. How would you feel if we went down *soon* to City Hall and got the whole thing done?"

"But the reception. You put down a lot of money in deposits. And the invitations are out."

"We just won't tell anyone we're already married. It might be kind of nice to be married and relaxed and enjoy the party. The minister seems like a nice guy. He'd play along. I don't want to run this time. I want to marry *you*. Next week. As soon as we can do it."

George held my shoulders, looked at me, and smiled. "O.K., darling, if that's what you want."

The blood tests and licenses were arranged by Saturday, May 14. I had quickly worked in a gynecological exam. If I were in-capable of having children, that *would* be reason to call it off—not fair to George. The doctor pronounced me fine, fitted a new diaphragm and reminded me about the "fertile fourteenth day." (Funny, I had always thought it was in the middle of my peculiar thirty-six-day cycle.) All that was left now was to telephone Jane. She would be my maid of honor at City Hall and a man from his office would be best man for George.

Jane came in on the Milwaukee train early and straight to my door. At noon she asked, "Are you planning to get married in your housecoat?" Oh, yes, married. I had spent the morning in shock. But, yes, I must get dressed. Jane interrupted what I thought was my well-thought-out plan. When George and Bert, his friend from the office, were at the door, she asked again, "Had you planned to put on shoes?"

Then a tall, gray-haired man was speaking while I looked up at George in a small, book-lined room. George looked straight ahead. I looked at his chin. This was the man I would look at for the rest of my life.

I felt Jane poke me. "Oh. Yes. I do." I had just heard "till death do us part." I was married. And for longer than death if need be.

That night I lay next to George as he slept. I was glad we had waited in the old-fashioned way. It had been what lovemaking ought to be—all the trust and love had flowed through my body again and again. Any child conceived in a moment like that would come into the finest of lives.

The plans for the "formal" wedding went on. I had been right. With the legal part over, I was relaxed and looking forward to the "public" wedding. It would indeed be beautiful and perfect: the big, antique-filled, homelike house where my friends could toast us with champagne, my lovely blue-lace dress, the cake, the honeymoon—a beautiful time to remember for life.

And while I planned it all, I was already a wife. George had moved in with me. I jumped up each morning and cooked breakfast for both of us before we parted for work. George was impressed. "George, dear, writing all those scripts on cooking had to rub off." Cooking was fun. Dishes were not, but I could no longer leave them until my cleaning woman came. My brand-new husband's eyebrows lifted at dishes stacked in the sink. They also lifted at the sight of the clutter on *my* side of the bathroom shelves.

George's neatness, I decided, was good for me. It might be contagious. George left no shirts or socks or towels for me to pick up. Everything he owned or used was carefully, consistently put away. Lucky for me I had married a man like George. I would try to become as neat.

The week before the wedding in Milwaukee, George brought home the wine he had ordered for me through his friend at the office. The boxes were labeled "Asti Spumante." "But, George," I said, near tears, "I wanted imported *champagne!*"

This, George insisted, *was* imported and it *was* champagne. Nothing—the dictionary or my tears—persuaded him. Finally, it seemed foolish to have our first fight over something so small. George, I realized, hated being wrong. Most people did. "George, let's stop arguing. Open a bottle." It sprayed the ceiling. Drenched in wine, I kissed him and we made love.

At the wedding, no one but me knew that it was not champagne the waiters served in the napkin-wrapped bottles. I forgot it myself as all the beauty I had planned unfolded. The ceremony in the clergyman's parlor was like being married at home. He even made his special joke for us: "You are taking vows you have already taken . . . in your heart." At the reception I looked around the big beautiful house. How wonderful it would be to live in a house like this—mellowed by age, by families who had lived in and loved it, by brides who had stood on its graceful staircase and thrown bouquets.

When I threw mine, I aimed for Jane. And missed.

Jane, Meg, Irving, and Pete had remembered the rice. George and I ran through its rain to his car and on to the honeymoon for which George had so carefully saved to surprise me. Mackinaw Island, with its carriages instead of cars, was delightful. On the boat ride over, I learned that George could not swim. I reviewed my lifesaving techniques, crossed my fingers, and we made it to shore. And then back home. It had been a wonderful wedding; it would be a wonderful life.

By the end of July, I knew I was pregnant. The doctor disagreed. No matter, he would find out in time. My breasts were tender, my period was two weeks late, and I had an insane desire to smile.

George said, "The doctor must be right."

I smiled some more and waited. The doctor, it seemed, had confidence in the diaphragm he had fitted. But he had never asked me about my menstrual cycle. I had been "careful" on *his* "fourteenth day"—but not on my eighteenth. I had, I knew, neatly arranged an accident I wanted very much.

George was, at first, just a bit concerned. "Can we really live on what I make?"

Of course we could. It seemed that I had gone from riches to rags so often, it had almost become routine. Now, while George got his much-prized eight hours' sleep, I often sat up late, looking around my expensive apartment and telling it good-by. It belonged to someone who was no longer me. That fireplace had consumed my old diaries, and the closet held clothes I did not care to wear.

It was too soon to buy patterns for maternity clothes, I said to myself with a grin, but not too soon to dream. A house in the suburbs with a lawn for George to tend, where a child could play. My bank account was still full of money I had earned all those years, enough for a down payment and for all the modern appliances. No bleeding hands like Grandmother's from hanging out wash. No greasy dishwater and dripping garbage. I had—I laughed quietly—timed it just right. Medical progress had been made too. For me, and for the baby I was sure was inside me, childbirth would be different from what Mother had described.

In the middle of August, Dr. Kelly's frog confirmed what I had known all along. From his office lobby I telephoned George. "It's true! It's true!"

As I headed back toward my office on the bus, I sat unwillingly still. I wanted to run, jump, dance. I was not, I told myself, the first pregnant woman in the world, but, damn, it felt that way. People now looked different. The unshaven man, the big woman with the closed-up face—they had grown inside someone's body as my baby was growing in mine. The intoxicating miracle had obviously gone on for centuries. Why had no one ever told me how wildly ecstatic it would make one feel?

This time.

For just a moment I thought of the times I had been pregnant before. If Tony's child had not miscarried, what would my life be like now? And if I had not had the abortion? I felt a sting of sadness for unwillingly pregnant women, and a new surge of joy for the child who was—and would always be—so very much wanted and loved, by its mother and by a father who would always be there.

I swung down the block to my office, my stride matching some special music inside. In the elevator Con Matthews said, *"What happened to you? You look like your horse came in!"* In a way, I guessed it had.

That evening I cooked dinner and waited for George. He would arrive, I knew, at almost exactly 6:15. Love for George was stirred in with the gravy. Dear, punctual, reliable George would be beside me in this new life ahead. Like a new country, with different customs, a different terrain, George and I would explore it, learn its ways, and feel at home. I stopped my stirring and glanced at my watch. It was 6:15 and George was at the door. Tonight when he hugged me, he would officially be hugging two.

His first words were: "Do you want to quit work?"

Of course not. If Meg had worked through her seventh month, so could I. "Besides," I said, "we'll need money. Honey, I'd like to talk about buying a house."

I knew nothing about neighborhoods, prices, or how to tell if a house was silently being eaten by termites and about to collapse. Whatever George chose, I told him, was fine with me—the price, the amount of the mortgage, the interest to be paid.

George confessed he knew as little as I. What if we were tied down for years and years, I worried, by our innocent mistake?

Then I remembered some office jokes about Park Forest. All the houses looked alike. Someone had said, disparagingly, that husbands came home to the wrong house.

"George, honey, if all the Park Forest houses *are* alike, then it would be hard to make a serious mistake in buying one, wouldn't it?" I didn't mind living in a look-alike house. It might, in fact, be rather nice. There was so much I needed to learn; perhaps I could learn it from women who lived as I did.

George said, "Sure, honey. If that's what you want, we'll drive out on Saturday."

The acre upon acre of small ranch houses did not all look alike, I thought as we explored the winding streets. The young couples I glimpsed had painted them different colors and landscaped the yards in different ways. Some had evergreens, some had tiny trees that would someday be tall, and nearly all the yards had children's toys strewn around or being used.

It looked like the most wonderful place I had ever seen. If we owned one of those neat little houses, I could fit in like a piece of a jigsaw puzzle—pushing a carriage, then a stroller, rocking my babies to sleep. I squeezed George's hand. Could we look for the real estate office?

There were several houses for sale. Two hours later, George and I sat in the car. The houses we had seen were well within our budget. I now remembered having read that a house should cost twice the family income. But I could pay cash for nearly half of what these houses cost. George's salary and the commissions I would get for four more years from Lovett and Wynn made a

$13,000 to $14,000 house a conservative buy for us. The one I really wanted was $13,500—a three-bedroom house on a large lot. George, I was sure, would agree now that we could discuss it privately.

"George, the fourteen-thousand-dollar house has carpeting I don't want and draperies I can't stand. The cheapest one has such a tiny yard. I vote for the one on Shabbona Drive."

To my surprise, George preferred a two-bedroom house I had immediately dismissed. "It's got that nice breezeway."

"George, with a baby on the way and two sets of parents from out of town, we need three bedrooms."

"Well, guests could sleep in the breezeway."

I thought of his parents, lightly covered with an Illinois snow, or Mother, digging her way inside. I had thought *George* was the practical one in the family. "Honey, we need the bedrooms. We can always add a breezeway later. You can build it between the house and the garage."

The idea appealed to George. We went back inside the real estate office and then back to 108 Shabbona Drive. In my mind I decorated its empty rooms—wooden shutter-blinds, a swinging louvered door to the kitchen, and, for the big, sunny, quiet bedroom at the back, all the enchantment a baby's room could hold.

George had to pull me down the driveway. I wanted to stay. Here, at last, was where I would make a home. It was hard to wait even weeks to start.

Chapter 12

THE ARRANGEMENTS FOR MOVING into our new house would be completed by October. Until then I had nothing much to do except enjoy the marvelous feeling of being pregnant. How did other women have the self-control to keep from grinning all the time?

Of course, I realized, I was lucky. When we telephoned Mother to give her the news, her first words were: "Is the morning sickness very bad?" I had almost forgotten women had it. It was apparently skipping me.

Dr. Kelly had said, "Don't worry. Many women of thirty have no trouble at all." The thought had never crossed my mind. Meg was three years older than I. She had had, she said, a "lovely delivery" in the bedroom of her home. She had brought her tiny, perfect little daughter to the office—nursed her, in fact, in my office when Jennifer cried.

Until I watched Meg's tiny baby nestled at her breast, I had no idea how very much I hoped to breast-feed my own child. Meg had said, "It's cheaper, easier, and a lot healthier for the baby." She had looked down at her daughter with that stained-glass Madonna expression. "And it makes you feel so close."

But Meg was busy at home now and her wonderful example began to erode. Much as I was reveling in pregnancy, there was the problem of getting the baby out. To Meg, childbirth was a natural, painless process, but Meg was a Christian Scientist. She devoutly believed that God protected His well-made bodies. My spirit cringed hopelessly even at the thought of a dentist's drill.

Suddenly, scripts on gasoline, bacon, and ham sat unfinished in my typewriter while other thoughts intruded. All right, I could discount Mother's gory tales, but Mother had not produced the movies I now tried hard to forget—all those movies of women clutching bedposts or biting bullets while people boiled water to the sound of their moans.

If anyone but Mother had discussed childbirth with me, I had carefully tuned it out. I tried now to tune back in. My friends from high school had casually said, "You forget the pains." What scared me now was exactly what I was supposed to forget. Mother had remembered every lurid detail, it seemed.

I tried to discuss labor with Dr. Kelly. He said, "Just let me worry about that." How could he? I was the one having the baby.

There was no need to worry George more. He had already told me his mother had nearly died giving birth to him. But, I reminded us both, she was only sixteen years old and he weighed ten pounds.

I sat at my desk, trying to concentrate on the marvels of Swift's Premium ham, but I stared at the telephone. It wouldn't be right to disturb Meg. She was so busy. But maybe just the briefest chat.

Jennifer was fine—sleeping through the night now. Then, "Lois, you sound scared." Well, maybe, just a little.

"I've got a terrific book you've got to read."

"Meg, it's too late to make me a Christian Scientist *now*."

"You dope! It's not a religious book. It's on natural childbirth, by Dr. Grantly Dick Read. *Childbirth without Fear.*"

I wrote down the name. Anything that might reduce the fear a tiny bit was worth a try. Meg insisted it would do just that. I went to the bookstore at noon.

That night, when George was asleep, I opened the book. There was no way on earth I would have natural childbirth. I wanted all the painkillers that had been developed or would be in the next six months. I scanned the contents page. Ah, Chapter 11, "The Relief of Pain in Labor." Since Mother's day, surely something better than chloroform had been developed.

As I read, my fingers tightened on the book. "No anesthetic is free from danger to mother or child." "All narcotic agents are injurious to babies during birth; they are all more or less severe respiratory depressants."

In that moment I wondered if there had ever been a quicker or more reluctant conversion to natural childbirth. There was now no way on earth I could knowingly expose my baby to even the slightest risk. With an enormous sigh, I turned to the beginning of the book. Natural childbirth had been, to me, a fad among women who wove their own fabrics, ate health foods, and did push-ups three times a day. My exercises consisted of turning pages in a book. Too bad, but for the safety of my baby, I intended to follow every rule in this and any similar books around.

By one in the morning, I was relieved to find, Dr. Read's theory made a great deal of sense. By 1:30 I was doing the exercises on the floor.

"Are you sure?" George asked the next morning. Absolutely. And sure that Dr. Kelly had to go. Too much "Don't you worry, Lois" and no discussion of how childbirth worked. He had even winced when I returned his "Lois" by calling him "Ben." Pete Gregg's sister had just had a baby. Maybe he knew an obstetrician I would like.

Pete recommended Dr. Sol De Lee. I would, I decided, interview him. "Where do you stand on natural childbirth?"

This lanky doctor with the crisp, black, curly hair grinned.

The next day Pete called back. He had done some checking, and Dr. Sol De Lee was the foremost natural-childbirth obstetrician in town. "Dr. Read dedicated his book to Dr. Lee's uncle." My goodness, he had. So the crazy luck of my old career was following me to my new one!

On October 1, George and a friend from his office loaded my furniture onto a rented truck. No casually handing out two addresses and going to lunch this time. But George was right. We would need money for other things. I admired the way he checked off items on his lists, numbered the boxes, and loaded the van. I drove ahead in our car. The appliances should be in place—the washer, the drier, all the needed conveniences paid for in cash. There was no need to burden George with installment payments. The money I had accumulated was now buying the best kind of gift for the husband I loved.

I leaned against my beautiful portable dishwasher and tested my waistband again. It *still* was not tight. Well, it would be soon, and I had already bought some patterns for maternity clothes. I knew just which corner of the guest room I could make my place to sew.

Our newly installed telephone rang. It was Mrs. Balka, the cleaning woman I had had in the city. She could not get out to Park Forest—no car—but her sister could. I wanted to start out cleaning my own house all by myself, but until I quit work it was best to have someone.

Then the doorbell rang. Two smiling young women stood outside.

"I'm Emily Smith and this is Betty Grau. And welcome to Picture Window Town." Betty held a tray with coffee, cups, and a plate of cookies.

We sat on the floor. I learned they each had three children and lots of advice for me. As we sat on the bare tiles in my bare new house, I looked happily at both of them, wondering if they had any idea how much I wanted to be just like them. In only six months I would be.

Emily asked where I worked. "At McCann-Erickson," I said.

"Oh, did you know Ann Meadows? She was a secretary there too."

No, I had not known Ann. I let Emily's misconception ride.

For the next two months, my daily train rides to the office were interruptions. Each morning I made breakfast for George and watched him drive off in the car. His office could not be as easily reached by train as mine. I dressed, always hopeful my clothes would not fit. My maternity wardrobe hung waiting. By now a friendly bus driver stopped in front of my door instead of down the street. I went off to catch the train, put in my time, and then went back to where life really was.

Finally, one morning my waistband felt tight. Well, tight enough to change into the brown wool Empire dress I had made. Later I would go with George to buy our first Thanksgiving turkey. After writing all those scripts on how to cook a turkey, I could finally cook my own. And after we shopped, George could put together the enchanting "ice-cream chairs" that had arrived unassembled that day.

From the kitchen where I was copying recipes onto cards, I heard a thump and George's mumbled curse. Then he was at the kitchen door, waving a paper. "These instructions are wrong. Or there are parts missing or something. Just send the damned things back."

O.K. Then would he pick up the platter Emily was lending

me? George looked happy to go. He put the slightly crumpled instruction sheet on the table. I winced as the door slammed, then glanced idly at the paper.

The instruction sheet looked clear enough to me. I went to the scattered parts on the living-room floor to look for "Bolt A." With an odd sadness I connected E, F, and G. I would have to lie to George. He would feel bad if I put the chairs together from the instructions he said were wrong. Best to say I had once had some like this. It was a loving lie. George needed to feel he could do things well.

The turkey was perfect—brown, juicy, and rich. I had cooked all day, and after dinner I decided to rest before tackling the roasting pans. Stretched out on the bed, I felt a twinge deep inside me. Had I eaten too fast? I closed my eyes. Another small movement just below my navel. Another!

George put down his paper as I rushed, no longer tired, into the room. "I felt the baby, George! It really moved!"

He smiled. "That's nice, dear." In that moment I realized that there were some things no couple could truly share. The small person inside me had just flexed his/her muscles—surely not a history-changing event, except for me. But I would try to keep George involved in the birth of our child as much as a husband could be. He was attending classes with me at Chicago Lying-In Hospital, would be there during my labor if not during the delivery. It would, I assured myself, make him feel part of it.

Mother had said, "I hope it's a girl. They're easier to raise." Was I? But I knew I wanted a boy. The daughter I would have someday should not be an older sister with all the obligations that entailed. Better to give her an older brother.

By New Year's I decided it had *better* be a boy—preferably just one. The twitches were now interior somersaults, punches, and kicks. "That's a real tiger we've got in there," I told George, "unless he's invited friends in to play." The small renter inside me was now named "Tige," and I was surprised at how I could love someone I had not yet seen.

By February I was counting the days at work. The baby was due at the end of March, and my arms were already stretching past my expanding front to reach the typewriter keys. In twenty-eight days—then ten, then five—I could officially start my career as full-time wife and soon-to-be full-time mother. Mrs. Hughes, my cleaning woman, knew that on the first of March I would be gloriously on my own. No more riding the trains or writing of Swift's Meats for Babies. Like Meg, I would soon be spooning them out.

March 1 finally arrived. I made George's breakfast and kissed him good-by. Now, exactly what did housewives do? I looked out the window. No clues there. Draperies and blinds were still tightly drawn at my neighbors' houses.

While I had a second cup of coffee, I pushed a feeling of ineptness away. I wished I had watched Grandma more closely. What *had* she done when I was off at school? What had my cleaning women done while I was at work?

It was, I told myself, reassuring to know I had done improbable things before—driven that car coast to coast the day after I first touched a clutch, written radio shows, television shows, with no training, run an advertising agency on nothing but lucky guesses. And I had done those things when I was very young, very immature. Surely at thirty I could do the wonderfully womanly task of cleaning a house. Everything else had turned out better than I had a right to expect. Now, with all the appliances money could buy, this would too.

Four hours later, I sat on the bathroom floor, rested my head on the tub, and sobbed. I had tried to mop the kitchen, with a bucket and the roasting pan (one for soap, one for rinse), and managed, like an idiot, to mop myself into a corner. To protect the body that was only half mine now, I had crossed the slippery floor, grabbing windowsill, cabinet, table, and chair. Slamming a swinging door in frustration was no satisfaction. It had swung back and hit me on the nose.

Still, I had gone on to tackle the bathroom. My back ached from scrubbing the bottom of the tub while bending across the soap bucket and rinse-water pan. I had just learned that my clean tub bottom got streaked with dirt when I scrubbed its sides. I looked up. Even the bathroom mirror was streaked. Soap and water had not worked.

But my sobbing was not for the floor, the mirror, the tub. All through the house, dust was standing waiting to be removed. I would remove it. It would return. So would the ring in the tub, the spots on the mirror, and the footprints on the kitchen floor. I would fight them *forever,* and if I stopped, even briefly, they would win. Other women seemed to join the battle happily. On TV, women mopped and glowed. A spic-and-span house apparently delighted many. And I had hated every suds-rinsed, wiped-and-polished moment. In time I could probably learn to mop a floor and clean a bathtub right, but I knew it would never seem more than a temporary skirmish in a battle I was expected to fight for the rest of my life.

There was something terribly wrong with me as a woman. I had married with such naïve high hopes. If I could not clean a house, how could I rear a baby? My sobs increased. Kitchens, bathrooms, and a house full of dust would survive my ineptness and distaste, but not a baby. I had believed, somehow, that I would know the things that women did. Hah! I even made a lumpy bed. Beds didn't matter, but if I did something terribly wrong with my baby, it might suffer all its life. I had read Dr. Spock. His sentence "You know more than you think you do" was designed to comfort. But Dr. Spock had never met me.

Inside me, Tige kicked. Maybe it was his way of saying what I needed so badly to hear: "Don't worry. You'll learn." At the moment it seemed unlikely, but the thought of my baby at least got me up off the floor. I already loved Tige so much. "Poor kid," I told him as he somersaulted inside. "You should have picked a better mother, but for you, my love, I'll try." Make the bed, dust the tables, and, most important, finish the draperies for his room so that the light would never disturb his naps.

Midway through the dusting, I thought of George. He would say out loud and clearly, "Don't worry. You'll learn." I was not, after all, in this alone. He would realize—and remind me—that I had taken on a brand-new profession, totally different from the one I had just left behind. When he raised his sandy eyebrows at the state of my closet, he probably forgot that I could hardly equal his mother's standards overnight. He would comfort me as I comforted him when he worried about his job. He would tell me the things that I needed to hear—that somehow I would make it all right.

It was time to start dinner. At least, I could cook, no matter where else I had failed. Chicken Cacciatore, Italian spinach, and turmeric rice, cooked with love for a husband who would be home at exactly 6:35 and who would understand all my fears.

While I washed the spinach, the mail clunked through its slot. A letter from Mother, who always—I smiled—reported on funerals and food, and a check from Lovett and Wynn. Quite a large check. My former clients must be doing well. I thought of them fondly, and went back to the spinach.

At 6:35 George came through the door, kissed me, and, as always, went to change. I was making his drink when I heard the splash. The roasting pan/rinse pail was still in front of the sink.

The entire day came back to hit me. Yes, George should have put on the light, but the pan should have been put away. While George wiped off his shoes, I sobbed out apologies and my report of the stupid things I had done all day.

George looked up from removing sodden socks. "Other women manage."

He would, I decided, feel better after dinner. During coffee I nestled close to him and poured out my doubts. Tears returned. I wanted so badly to have him say it would be all right.

Instead, George looked bored. "You did so well in business. Housework should be easy. By the way, did the cleaner deliver my suit?"

On the sofa I moved away from George. Why did the strong features I had admired now seem made of stone? Alone in the corner of the sofa, I sobbed out my need for him to understand my confusion at my change in occupations, to help me fight the fear that I might fail our baby too.

George listened silently, then cut me off in mid-sentence. "Oh, come on, Lois. It's only housework. Say, would you mind separating my black socks from the navy blue? They look alike in the mornings." He looked at his watch. "Almost ten. Coming to bed?"

I shook my head and dried my eyes. Something had changed. Let George get his sleep while I figured it out. I picked up a book as a prop. George yawned and went to bed.

George had been right; it was "only housework." But his problems at work often seemed minor to me, yet I never dismissed them. If they bothered George, I cared. I could not force him to care about mine.

But I felt a sudden, familiar sense of loss. Where it came from was unclear, but I felt agonizingly alone. All right, I would have to handle this new life without comfort from George, learn how to keep house—and, most important, how to care for my child.

I would also, I began to suspect, have to take care of George. Small incidents, now that I faced them, did not bode well. The Asti Spumante episode had unaccountably stayed in my mind. Now I knew why. What people drank at our wedding was not important, but George's inability to face a mistake was. Other things passed through my head. The instruction sheet for the chairs was "wrong." George never "dropped things"—the many things from my single days "fell" (by themselves?) from his hands. His problems at work were the mistakes of others—a secretary who mislaid a file, a "hostile" colleague, a boss who didn't explain things well.

The French have a saying, "He who cannot admit a mistake doubles it." Well, that was George. I had tried many times to get him to *think* about the other person's side in some problem at work, to feel the excitement of correcting a mistake. I had stopped. Someone, in a childhood he rarely discussed, had punished him badly for being wrong. Perhaps he was too internally involved in defending himself to give comfort to somebody else.

I closed the unread book on my lap. All right, I could not expect comfort from George or encouragement or change. It was an unexpected relief to realize I was on my own. Tige kicked, a big one that knocked my book to the floor. "Well, honey," I whispered to him, "I haven't done terribly badly in picking you a father." There were a lot of things George did *not* do—he didn't drink or lose his paycheck gambling or see other women. He was, instead, seeding the lawn and building a fence so that our baby would have a safe place to play. No matter if the fence was spaced too wide to contain a toddling child. I would work it out in some face-saving way.

Tige kicked again. "Darling," I assured him, "we'll work it out." I had meant that "till death do us part." No child of mine would grow up without a father. That, at least, I could provide—and would to the point of death. "You'll have a father, honey, all your life."

Suddenly the other problems dissolved. So housework completely depressed me. What did cleaning women cost? Eight dollars a day now. If I worked a few nights a week at some local store, I could easily make that much. Luckily, I didn't have to. I fondled the check from Lovett and Wynn. When they stopped coming, I would find some other way. That left meals, laundry, making the bed, and straightening up. Some woman author I had seen on TV talked about time-motion studies. That might take the drudgery out of routine jobs—I could try to beat my record every day, work out how to save time and steps.

Tige kicked again. "But not with you, darling. You come first. I promise that."

With Mrs. Hughes's phone number on my mind, I finally went to bed. In the morning I would ask her to come back. Tonight I would look across to my snoring, not-so-perfect husband and dream the dreams of a not-so-perfect wife.

Dr. De Lee put his stethoscope to my round and active belly. "You're a week overdue. But I don't like inducing labor." Neither did I. Since we were doing "natural," we should be consistent. I was feeling great. It was a little hard turning over in bed at night, but I might even miss this handy bulging shelf on which I propped books and rested my arms.

"The only problem," Dr. De Lee continued, "is that I have to go out of town. But Dr. James will fill in for me. He's a fine doctor."

By now I felt I hardly needed a doctor. I could easily have the baby all by myself anywhere I chose. It would be at Chicago Lying-In, of course, on the off chance some special help was needed, but I had read everything about what was supposed to happen. I had even made George read the chapter in Goodrich's *Natural Childbirth* on how to help deliver babies if they arrived in the car. "Any baby that comes *that* fast," Dr. De Lee had said during one of the classes George and I attended, "doesn't really need me around." In the car I had put newspapers, twine to tie the cord, and an extra blanket. I planned to grab the book. If George forgot anything, I could read it to him while the baby came.

That day I reminded Dr. De Lee that I had been born two weeks late, but to be sure to tell Dr. James I expected a seven-and-a-half-pound boy—big enough to thrive but not too big to arrive without exit problems.

On the morning of April 6, George was still shaving when my stomach muscles tightened. Odd sensation. I wondered what it meant. I turned the bacon. It happened again. Hmm, five minutes apart. The books said to leave for the hospital when the contractions were *ten* minutes apart. Should I wait until then? Probably not. I quietly phoned Dr. De Lee's nurse. She said, "Leave!"

The onset of labor, the books had said, releases something in the bloodstream that causes euphoria. The books were dead right. Everything seemed delightful, funny, and a jolly adventure.

"George, dear, phone your office. You're taking your wife to have a baby today." George, misbuttoning his shirt, looked hilarious. As he rushed out the door with my suitcase, I giggled. "Hey, don't forget me!"

On the drive to the hospital I found that the breathing exercises worked just fine. I breathed my way through contractions that felt like mild menstrual cramps. In the middle of one, George invariably asked how I felt. I held up a finger for patience and breathed them through. At a railroad crossing, I breathed and giggled through a slapstick situation involving a long, long freight train. George lit a cigarette, took one puff, threw it out the window, and lit another—all with distraught looks in my direction. "Don't worry." I giggled. "I'm staying right here."

At the hospital I realized why our classes had included a tour. It was great to come waddling into a place that was familiar. In a sunny private labor room, I was prodded and probed—and asked to explain my breathing. Not everyone there, I learned, was involved in natural childbirth. George left the room and returned in a short white coat marked "Father." His job now, the book had said, was to time the contractions and massage my back.

I didn't need my back massaged. I was too excited to lie there. Happily, the hospital encouraged walking. While George followed me with pencil, paper, and stopwatch, I strolled the halls. Some doors were closed, some stood open to show sleeping women. Just inside one open door, a baby in a glassed-in crib was being admired by its parents. I looked at it closely. Someone that big was going to come out of me?

Gradually, as we walked, my mood changed. Euphoria gave way to a feeling of seriousness. There was a job ahead and I was ready for it. Dr. James, short, sandy-haired, chubby, visited me in my room. Did I want scopolamine? Demerol? No, thank you, I could handle it with the breathing. Meg had been right. The contractions did feel like a combination of menstrual cramps and the kind I might get after eating pickles and ice cream. They rose in a peak—to a count, now, of ten—and then subsided. The slow breathing kept my muscles relaxed. What *was* all this talk about the horrors of labor? Perhaps frightened women who didn't know what to expect tightened up in fear, worked against what their bodies were trying to do, and did feel not only pain, but fear and pain mixed. Some woman down the hall was certainly feeling *something*. George winced each time she yelled.

The contractions were abruptly replaced by a powerful urge to have a bowel movement. Aha! I knew what that meant—the last stage of labor. "George, dear, please call a nurse." A very young, very nervous nurse responded.

"Breathe like a dog," she instructed uncertainly.

Huh? Oh, she must mean to pant.

While I panted patiently, people lifted me onto a cart. I looked at my watch before they took it away. Just ten hours of labor—the *average* time. How nice.

George walked next to the cart as it was pushed down the hall. Looking up, I could see his worried face. Poor George, he would have to wait, while I would be where the action was. The euphoria had returned. "Listen"—I grinned—"don't go away. I'll be right back." And I was whooshed through a swinging door.

Dr. James's face was above me. I noticed the laugh lines around his eyes. "Just tell me when I'm allowed to push," I said. Pushing was going to feel awfully good.

I heard Dr. James say, "Anesthesia ready?"

As I took a breath to say, "No anesthesia, thanks," someone put a rubbery-smelling mask on my face. The people, the room, the world disappeared while I was thinking, "Oh, damn."

In what seemed like a second, I noticed that everyone had left the room. Not very polite. They could have told me where they were going and when they would be back to help me finish this project. At least they had taken my legs out of the stirrups. I flexed my knees—and from somewhere across the room I heard a baby cry. Mine? Had I missed the whole thing? It had been stupid of me to assume that Dr. James knew I didn't want to be knocked out.

A woman's voice above my head said, "Are you awake?"

Completely. "Is that *my* baby crying?"

"Yes, it is, dear. A healthy baby boy. Do you want to hold him?"

More than anything in the world.

In a moment Tige was nestled in the curve of my arm. I would have known him anywhere—those little arms and legs flailed as they had inside me. I kissed his tiny hairless head.

"Hello, honey. I'm your mother!" And a kind of love I never knew existed flooded out—warm, glowing, and, I knew, eternal. This tiny person had grown inside my body. He was truly a part of me, to be loved freely and fully for the rest of my life. I had never before cried from happiness. I did now, wiping away the tears that splashed on my wonderful baby as I examined him from his miraculously tiny toes to his pink head with glints of golden hair.

The nurse said, "Do you want to see your husband now?"

Of course! George must be chewing the furniture in anxiety.

I asked, as she brought the little glassed-in cart close to me and put Tige in, "Don't all women want to see their husbands right away?"

"Dearie, you'd be surprised."

It was only a storage room just outside Delivery with sheets and towels stacked along its walls, but George, Tige, and I were given a moment of privacy together.

"Meet George Stalvey, Junior!" I said to George as I lounged on the hospital cart. George could only look at Tige, could not hold him as I had done. I felt a spasm of pity just then. George would hold him later, but he would never know the pride, the closeness, the physical satisfaction that I felt. Only a woman could. How did men feel? Barren? Unfinished? Left out of the miracle only women knew?

In a little while I would know whether I could complete the last part of the miracle—whether my body could nourish the baby my body had produced. I felt my breasts through the hospital gown. Please, please provide milk! While George admired Tige, I sat up to do the exercises the book said would increase my milk. Elbows at my sides, wrists crossed, reach up slowly, then arms out and down.

Dr. James stuck his head into the linen closet. "Ah, you're the athletic type, huh?" Not really; just for now.

I was in my new room on the maternity floor, counting the minutes until Mother would be home from work. Perhaps we would be closer now. We had an experience to share. She must have felt as I did when she first held me. Now I felt a surge of love for her. Did having a baby make you love the whole world?

It was hard to wait while the hospital operator put through the call. Finally Mother answered.

"Mother, I just had the baby. It's a very healthy boy."

"Lois, please don't tease me. I'm worried enough."

Why would she think I was teasing? "Mother, I really did."

"Don't be silly. If you'd just had a baby, you wouldn't be talking to me right now."

I felt close to tears. "Mother, I had the baby at a quarter to five. Call me back at the hospital if you don't believe me."

She still sounded dubious. "Was it very bad, dear? Oh, well, your ordeal was worth it if your baby's all right."

"It wasn't an ordeal and the baby's fine. How does it feel to be a grandmother?"

"Don't talk now, dear. Rest or you'll lose your milk. You can call me tomorrow."

I did try to sleep. Not a chance. I was much too excited. A nurse strode in, but with a needle, not with Tige.

"What's this injection for?"

"Just to dry up your milk."

Good heavens, no! She checked her chart, shrugged, and left.

Finally another nurse walked in briskly carrying Tige. She put him in my arms, mumbled, "Ten minutes each side," and walked out before I could speak. Hey! Wasn't anyone going to give me instructions? I had never done this before.

Tige was red-faced with urgent demands. What if I did something wrong? I unbuttoned my gown. There could not be, I decided, too many different ways to do this. Tige's thrashing around did not leave much time to reflect. I moved him close to my breast.

"O.K., darling, let's see how two amateurs make out."

Tige, to my delighted astonishment, was no amateur. His frantically thrashing little head found the target immediately. With enormous enthusiasm, he nursed as if he had been doing it for months. Ten minutes later, one small fist banged against my breast, as if to tell me the right-hand "well" was dry. I shifted him to the left breast. Ten more minutes of ferocious, efficient nursing and my tiny professional turned his head and slept with a smile. It was only gas, I told myself, but it looked like a smile. My baby had found me satisfactory and maybe delicious. I had entered a special new world. I was now me—plus. And I would never be only me again.

Chapter 13

ON MY FIRST NIGHT HOME from the hospital I wondered
—frantically—why the myths of childbirth were dramatized while
the real horror was ignored. I had felt so comfortable and competent with my baby in the hospital; now, at home, I had never felt
so clumsy, ignorant, and terrified before.

Mother had volunteered to be there when we came home. I had
wanted one private evening with just George, the baby, and me.
Now I bitterly regretted my sentimentality. Mother, at least, might
know if the baby was too warm, too cold, too wet, or whatever.
She had said only, "Watch his little face. Babies do smother in
blankets."

Tige could not smother in the zip-up blanket suit I had bought
months before. I had also bought a scale. Dr. Freeman, our new
pediatrician, had, half-jokingly, suggested it.

"You're the only nursing mother I have," he had said. "But in
hospitals they do weigh the babies before and after they've nursed.
Don't change his diapers or clothes or anything. That way you can
tell how much milk he gets." "Of course"—he grinned—"we could
weigh *you* instead."

George had brought Tige and me home to the rented baby scale,
the safe zip-up blanket, and the sturdy crib. But where was the
rocker? I had talked for weeks about my fantasy of singing and
rocking my baby to sleep.

George had forgotten the rocker, but there was a furniture store nearby. While he went off, my neighbors descended.

Emily said, "We knew you had it in you." Pat said, "Anything you need? Got a sterilizer? Bottles?"

"No," I said proudly, "I'm breast-feeding." My 34A was now 36C. It would be, I knew, only temporary, but it was great to look like Sophia Loren instead of Katharine Hepburn, if only for a while.

Each woman said, wistfully I thought, that their doctors had discouraged breast-feeding. Pat's doctor had said that "modern women can't." Emily said she felt she would have been tied to the house, and "Aren't you afraid of drooping breasts?"

Ordinarily, I confessed, I did not have that much to droop, but those old wives' tales had been proved untrue. As for "tied to the house," Dr. Freeman had suggested I give Tige an occasional bottle to let him know milk came in different containers. "Then if I want to get a sitter and go out, I can." Meanwhile, at the flick of a blouse button, my baby could eat. I had joined some ancient rank of mothers and felt tremendously proud.

My feeling of pride and expertise lasted until my neighbors went home. George arrived with the rocking chair, an odd modern design molded of plastic. But at least it rocked.

Brand-new or not, Tige knew a lousy voice when he heard one. His yells—perhaps altruistic—drowned out my attempts at a lullaby.

George hovered nervously. "Do you think he's all right?"

"I think he's just got a musical ear." He nursed with his usual ferocity and went promptly to sleep. But why did he look so much more fragile than he had looked before? He had gotten, the scale said, a full eight ounces out of me. I had never realized how reassuring it was to have doctors and nurses nearby. This very small and very precious person was now totally in my inexperienced care.

George, as usual, went to bed and immediately to sleep. I lay in the dark, wide awake. Tige was safe in his blanket suit, I told myself; no possibility of smothering. Try to sleep. He would wake for his two o'clock feeding, maybe before. And I could not ask George to nurse him for me.

My eyes closed as briefly as a camera shutter. Tige's bedroom seemed terribly far away. A solid wall separated our room from his. What if he did stop breathing? What if he caught his head in the crib bars? What if he burped and choked? George's snoring blocked out any sound Tige might make.

I nudged George. "Honey, the baby is so far away. Maybe it would be better to have him in our room."

The second time I explained my worries, George stumbled up, into Tige's room, and, while I held Tige and made apologies, disassembled the crib. He reassembled it in the bedroom and, if he had been awake at all, went back to sleep.

I closed my eyes. Then opened them. Tige had taken an awfully long time between breaths. Some book said, "The breathing of the newborn is irregular." *That* irregular? I held my breath every time Tige delayed his.

An hour later I knew this was not going to work. Tige had breathed successfully every night in the hospital, and I could not lie here all night, counting the seconds between his breaths. I felt choked with tears of frustration. I was getting upset; I would lose my milk. I had not slept a minute. Everything had seemed so easy in the hospital. I had felt confident that I could care for my baby. Now I couldn't even decide where he should sleep.

I hated to nudge George again. All I could hope was that he would not remember any of this in the morning. In the morning I would phone Dr. Freeman. Meanwhile, George, a stark-naked zombie, moved the crib back into the nursery. It was almost two o'clock. I nursed Tige, put him into his crib, and finally fell asleep. I didn't introduce the subject at breakfast.

Later, on the phone, I poured out all my indecisions of the night before to Dr. Freeman. "In the nursery I can't hear him breathe. In our bedroom I count every breath." I almost wailed, "I don't know *what* to do!"

Dr. Freeman paused as if in deep deliberation. "Well, Mrs. Stalvey, have you considered the garage?"

My laughter broke the tension—and Dr. Freeman reassured me that Tige would be quite all right in his own room. He was coming by the next day, he said, to give Tige his first checkup at home.

Mother arrived in the morning. As I waited for George to bring her from the station, I felt the affection I had always hoped to feel. The guest room—courtesy of my cleaning woman—was spotless, but I added a few spring flowers and the quilted Bonwit Teller hangers I had bought in my "other life." Most important, I had given her a grandchild—a child I loved as she had loved me. With Tige snoozing in my arms, I waited in the April sunshine.

"Oh, Lois, get back from the door. He'll catch cold in the draft."

"Mother, do you want to hold him?"

"Oh, I don't know. I haven't held a baby in so many years. But I'd love to watch you bathe him."

Bathe him! At that moment I would have gladly walked a tight-rope over a pit of vipers rather than handle my precious baby—wet. Again I thought of all those Westerns with Bessie biting a bullet in the back of the wagon while her baby was born. That part had been easy. Why had no one dramatized the terror of the first days at home? Tige, however, could hardly remain unbathed until he could bathe himself. After all, what could happen? Plenty. I could drop him, drown him, get soap in his eyes—or simply faint at the thought of hurting this irreplaceable being.

Mother and George played Greek chorus to my fearful dunking of Tige into his Bathinette. "Don't let him slip." "Watch out for the soft spot on his head." Mother said, "Wash him 'down there.' That's where infections start." George said, "The water must be cooling. He'll catch a cold." Mother voted for pneumonia. Tige survived the bath a great deal better than I.

Still, as I placed clean, rosy Tige in the arms of my mother, who sat securely in a corner of the sofa, it was a special moment for me. Love did make the world go 'round. Mother's bad marriage had not ended the chain. Someday I would look adoringly at a child of Tige's as she looked at him.

Mother said, "He looks so thin. Is he getting enough to eat?"

The scales said eight ounces at every feeding.

"Do your nipples hurt a lot? I had abscesses in both breasts."

At that moment I realized that to survive the week I would have to see the humor in Mother's eternal predictions of disaster. This was the same woman who had predicted that I would fall out of trees, break my neck skating, and fail at all my improbable jobs. "Mother, Dr. Freeman will be here soon. If the baby's not perfect, I'll just send him back. O.K.?"

Dr. Freeman arrived almost on cue. Mother, to my surprise, was aggressive with questions. Dr. Freeman answered each one patiently: "No, the baby is not too thin." "Belly bands are no longer used." "Feeding times are more flexible now—it's not good to let a baby cry until the clock says 'Go.'" "We don't put shoes on babies now until they start to walk."

While Mother asked her stream of questions, he examined Tige.

"Going to be tall and lean. Growing fine. Don't change the formula."

"Dr. Freeman, I'm breast-feeding."

"Ah, yes. Well, you're doing it well." As he spoke, he scribbled a prescription while he answered several more of Mother's questions. She looked over his shoulder while he wrote. He handed it to me.

"Phenobarbital?" I asked. "A sedative for the baby?"

He patted my shoulder as he went to the door. "No, my dear, for you."

When my mother left at last, George's arrived. Alice Stalvey had had George's brother's child to practice on. I decided I adored her and her what's-all-the-fuss-about attitude. When she left, I felt ready to handle my precious baby without fear of breaking off a tiny toe, arm, or foot. I could settle down and enjoy my son alone.

And get back, more or less, to the routine I had organized before Tige's arrival. It *did* work when I figured out how to cut steps out of boring chores. The intellectual challenge of finding the easiest way to make a bed was actually stimulating. I now walked around the bed only once. Cooking two pot roasts instead of one allowed me to "bank" quick meals in the freezer. Separating George's black and navy-blue socks was still a problem. Very well; a mesh sock bag at each end of the closet so that George could separate them when he took them off.

It had gradually occurred to me that George would like a lot more service than I expected to give. I *did* know how hard he worked at the office—and I was learning how much harder, emotionally and physically, I was working at home.

I didn't blame George a bit for *wanting* the services Grandpa had demanded, or, for that matter, the deference George's mother almost thrust at George's father—"his" special chair, the untouched newspaper, fetching (literally) pipe and slippers. If George had slaved in a factory or hoisted loads on a dock as other generations of men had done, fine. But I knew about the office coffee breaks, the lounging at desks, the long lunch hours that no baby's cry cut short (if, indeed, I remembered to eat lunch at all).

For the first time in my life, I was learning how hard a homemaker works. Unlike deadlines I had faced in business, life now had two daily, immutable deadlines—breakfast and dinner—and the day was paced around them. In an office your task is never interrupted by door-to-door salesmen or machines that suddenly leak, clank, or refuse to work. Work at home was both physical and mental, like running from the kitchen to Tige a thousand times a day while thinking about what to cook that was nutritious, tasty, and cheap. And there was none of the exhilarating satisfaction one got from a job completed; the same laundry would have to be washed again, the dinner and its dishes would be repeated seven days a week. You could not let a dinner or a load of dirty clothes sit on a desk while you chatted with a colleague to relax. You could chat only with the walls or the washing machine. There was no way to get ahead on your work—to diaper a baby twenty times in one day so that you could rest a bit the next, or to make the bed twice to avoid it on weekends.

The TV women, dancing and singing with their newly waxed floors or their whiter-than-white laundry, were as much a myth as Bessie in labor biting her bullet. So why did generation after generation of women take on the housekeeper's chores? Grandmother had done it, probably because she believed she couldn't support herself. Mother had, only briefly, tried to keep a house. She had returned to her job and added Bobby and me to Grandmother's chores. So why was I here, trying to do the hardest job I had ever taken on in my life?

As I folded a tiny shirt of Tige's, I knew exactly why. This child of mine was forcing me to grow. For him—and for the brother and sister who would come after him—I was stretching myself. Perhaps, I thought as I smoothed the shirt on the pile in front of me, the strange discontent I had felt in my career was a signal that growth had stopped. Well, it had started again, taking a new direction. Just pulling myself from the warm narcotic of exhausted sleep to nurse Tige at night required an effort of will I had never exercised before. There would be many, many other times when I would have to stretch myself far more. Somewhere, way up ahead, was the grown-up, whole human being I hoped to be. And no one but my child could lead me there.

I heard Tige begin to cry. I felt a surge of milk in my breasts. In a moment he was cuddled in my arms, my body feeding his. Yes, this is what kept women close to the cave, the cabin, and now the washing machine.

Breast-feeding Tige was not without its moments of confusion. The following week he had a long bout of hiccups. I called Dr. Freeman.

"Sounds as if he's getting too much air. Just enlarge the holes in the nipples."

"Dr. Freeman, how do I *do* that?"

"Very simple. Heat a needle red-hot and enlarge them."

I clutched my breast and winced. "Well, if it helps the baby, I guess I can stand the pain."

"Pain? Oh, good Lord, I forgot. No, just try burping him longer."

A month later Tige seemed to be having mild diarrhea. Dr. Freeman said, "I just checked him yesterday; have you been sterilizing the nipples well?"

Washing carefully, but not sterilizing. How do I do that?

Dr. Freeman sighed. "Very simple. You boil them a full ten minutes."

While I wondered which pot to use, I tried my last hope. "I'm breast-feeding, remember?"

"Oh, honey, I'm so sorry. I just have so damn few nursing mothers."

Summer of 1956 came and went. George planted trees and tried for a lawn that would look like a putting green. President Eisenhower played golf and a woman named Rosa Parks refused to give up her bus seat to a white man in Montgomery, Alabama. The world, I had decided, would have to whirl around without me; still, I was rather proud of Mrs. Parks's courage and proud that no discrimination existed up North. Tige was now happily eating his Swift's Meats for Babies and George no longer came home and sat reading the paper while I continued my work.

These were modern times, I told myself, and George had not pushed a plow all day. He could easily bathe Tige after dinner and, I told him, "become closer to his son." He could also, please, carry the dishes from the table so that I could scrape and put them into the dishwasher. Then, with Tige off to sleep, we could talk about his day.

My neighbor, Emily, had said, "Jack never tells me anything about his work—and how do you get George to bathe the baby?"

I explained my theories on the nature of work in the modern world and the customs women had continued too long. "I know George would *like* to be handed his pipe and slippers, but if I did that, I'd want to hand him a cyanide cocktail too. He knows *I know* what he does all day. This way we both feel better."

Out of loyalty, I did not tell her how I envied her Jack's reticence. George told me *everything* that happened at work. It was only fair, I persuaded myself. I still had a long way to go in matching George's neatness. My side of the closet was always a mess, and my side of the dresser was heaped with books and magazines I hoped to read *someday*. When George's sandy eyebrows dipped at the clutter, I reminded myself that I did help him figure out problems at work.

Some were insoluble. Like Mother, George was sure his job would not last. Yet I knew that someone as reliable, dependable, and conscientious as George was a rarity as an advertising manager. "Just wait, honey," I said over and over. "They know you're worth a dozen fast-talking, hot-shot types." Maybe that was what marriages were all about—supportiveness at home to take out into the world. Sometimes I gave the support half-asleep, but no matter; it seemed to help.

Jane came from Milwaukee to visit. "Does it ever bother you," she asked, "to know you could be out making six times what George makes and spending whatever you like?"

Not for a minute. It was rather fun stretching a budget, but most important, I had not missed a moment of Tige's growing up. His first smile, his first laugh, were given to *me*. Hamburger instead of steak was quite all right if it meant I could watch his personality unfold day after day—happy, active, and, I was sure, with a very unbabylike sense of humor.

Now, at six months, he was showing too much sense of humor while he nursed. I phoned Dr. Freeman. "He only nurses for a few minutes. Then he wants to sit up and play."

"Is he eating his solid foods?"

"Like a truck driver. And he can drink water by himself from his spouted cup."

Dr. Freeman chuckled. "He's telling us he's through with nursing. See if he tolerates whole milk. If so, *you* stay off liquids for twenty-four hours so that your milk can dry up."

I held the phone while something inside me hit bottom. Silly. Had I expected to nurse him until he was married? No, but I had never thought of the day when our final physical tie would be broken. Silly, but tears were streaming down my face.

I remembered Mother talking about "weaning." "No matter how hard you cried, I didn't give in. In two days you took a bottle." Tige would happily drink from his cup, but weaning the *mother* was going to hurt. He had grown inside me all those months. Our bodies were connected for six months more. Now we had to separate. I was not prepared for the feeling of loss.

Three hours later, physical pain joined the emotional. My breasts, I felt certain, would burst. And, added to that, I was experiencing a raging thirst. I wondered if Dr. Freeman had ever considered graduality—and if *he* had ever gone twenty-four hours without liquids.

I looked longingly at Tige as he chortled and kicked in his playpen. Dr. Freeman, we could assume, had never nursed a baby. I said to Tige, "Come here, pal. I need a favor."

And to relieve my bursting breasts, I nursed my first baby for the last time and wiped my tears off the top of his head.

By January, Tige was thriving on milk from some impersonal cow. I thought of Jane the day Tige let go of the coffee table—not to walk, but to run. If I had been off at work, no description could have replaced the delight for Tige and me when he began careening around.

By April, I had learned only too well that he was likely to be into, on top of, or under whatever he could find, and that George's beautiful fence would not hold him.

"George, how about a big area snow-fenced in?" It would ruin the beauty of George's yard, but I had gotten a phone call the day before. "I have a nice little visitor," a woman's voice said, "and I think he might be your son."

Somewhat grimly, George put up the unattractive but secure fence. I watched from the window as he attached the gate while Tige played around his feet. George was a good father. He came home every night to Tige and me. Now he was looking down at Tige with a face that glowed with love. He would always be there. Tige would remember these years—and all the years that followed.

George, who seemed so happy to be a father, was still unhappy at work. His boss, Mr. Bixby, was, according to George, arbitrary, inflexible, and unfair. During our long talks at the end of the day, I had made suggestions on handling him. George said they had not worked. What else could he try?

He could, I suggested, try another job. No, not through the want ads. There were executive-recruitment offices in Chicago. He could see one of them.

While George began job interviews, my housekeeping, child-tending routine finally allowed for a bit more afternoon socializing. Tige could now go on visits with me and play with the other children while I talked with their mothers. Emily, Pat, Florence, and Betty all had children much older than Tige. He was safe in the yard while I had—or made—coffee inside. As a housekeeper, I decided, I fell more or less in the middle—Betty's house always smelled of fresh polish, Pat's windows sparkled. But their children were off at school all day. Florence's decorating scheme, she said, was "wall-to-wall children, Early American finger smudges, and the latest in broken toys." Emily, I noticed, was inclined to chat on the phone until some unignorable crisis tore her away.

We talked of toilet training, diets, and new ways with hamburger. No one complained about husbands. If I wished that George would decide more things for himself, I never said so. If Emily noticed that Jack's hands tried to pat every available female rear, she was silent too. A woman in the next block ran off for a week with a lover. A woman whose backyard adjoined ours simply ran off, leaving three children behind. I tried to imagine what had gone on to make a mother leave that way. Whatever it was, it had gone on behind the picture windows over which we all drew draperies at dusk.

By summer Tige was almost sixteen months old and I was thirty-two. It was time to think about producing a sibling, to be born ideally when Tige was two. Born, I decided, in May with the warm weather ahead. At the beginning of August we made our attempt. By mid-September I learned it had worked. Conceiving babies was obviously a talent of mine.

At the end of September I was on a plane, unexpectedly scared out of my wits—not of flying, but of what waited ahead. One of George's interviews had gone well. A representative of a large firm in Omaha had talked to him twice about a job as advertising director. The next step was his meeting the men at the home office—but they wanted to meet me too!

Movies and novels had described this new interest in the Corporate Wife. *My* suitability was being considered along with my husband's. While George met with the executives at the plant, I would be "entertained"—and evaluated—by the vice-president's wife. To my surprise, I was terrified.

As the plane zoomed toward Omaha, I made jokes about my fear ("Maybe it would be best if I just jumped out here"), hoping to relax George and, for heaven's sake, me. My terror was inexplicable. Since my first trembling interview at fourteen, when I had told J.D. my idea for a column, job interviews had been easy, even fun. With no qualms at all, I had gaily gotten my USO job knowing I could hardly type. Most of my life I had had often unjustified confidence. Why the trembling hands and churning stomach now?

I had even gone into a panic about what to wear. Best not, I decided, to wear my career-days clothes. I might outdress an Omaha vice-president's wife and ruin George's chances. I quickly sewed up something modest and matronly. The sewing itself had kept me calm. Now my panic seemed to fill the plane.

George's face looked white around the nose and mouth. Of course! That was why I was so scared. In my own job interviews my actions involved only me. This time I had a piece of George's future in my hands. It was like carrying a fragile, valuable piece of china. If I owned it and dropped it, too bad. If it belonged to someone else, that was different.

Well, I had to carry it—and to try to live up to someone's concept of a Proper Wife, whatever that was. Perhaps if I just said little and smiled a lot . . . I tried to make my own hands stop trembling so that I could hold one of George's. No point wishing the plane would crash. Tige was staying at Emily's. I could not make him an orphan. I patted George's hand and lied: "I know it will all go well."

At the Omaha airport, a short gray-haired man and a tall redhaired woman in her fifties greeted us. George had met Herbert Prentiss in Chicago. Gertrude Prentiss took my arm and led me to her car.

Under ordinary circumstances I would have liked her immediately. She appeared open and friendly, and she chatted companionably. "Cassie, Fay, Hilda, and Lorrie are meeting us at my house. I thought you'd feel better, though, if I met the plane." Thoughtful of her—the thoughtfulness of the priest who walks to the door with the condemned man, or the friendly policeman who gets the criminal's trust.

So—I would be meeting a *lot* of corporate wives, probably to see if I fit in. My feet had swelled in my brand-new shoes during the plane ride. Don't limp, I told myself as we parked in her driveway.

Cassie, Fay, Hilda, and Lorrie were already in the Prentiss living room when we arrived. They looked as strained as I felt. Ah, yes, Gertrude Prentiss was their husbands' boss's wife.

The first crisis, I realized, was about to start immediately. The

Prentisses' maid was approaching with a tray of cocktail glasses. In dearly beloved, safe, serene Park Forest, one cocktail muddled my head. Now, with no breakfast and under this incredible strain, one cocktail would surely land me flat on Gertrude Prentiss's Oriental rug. Yet saying no might give the wrong impression. "A teetotaling prude" or, worse, "a secret alcoholic. Can't risk even one drink." The maid and the tray came nearer.

Then I heard my voice say, "I'm not sure if I should. I'm pregnant."

Pregnant was apparently something a corporate wife should be. I was instantly the center of attention. Cassie, Fay, and Hilda offered names of Omaha obstetricians. Gertrude Prentiss smiled when I said I had never had morning sickness. Neither had she. Lorrie Brent said that her New York obstetrician knew my Dr. Sol De Lee well. "You won't find anyone like him *here,* of course." She glanced at Gertrude Prentiss and added, "But Omaha doctors are good in *different* ways."

By the end of the luncheon, I knew the details of the pregnancies and deliveries of all of Cassie's, Hilda's, Fay's and Lorrie's children. Childbirth, I learned gratefully, was a favorite topic of women. I kept my mouth shut about natural childbirth after Cassie condemned it as "that Communist method." The corporation, I assumed, would not check out my progress in labor if, indeed, George got the job.

At the airport Gertrude Prentiss returned me to George and said good-by with a hug. She whispered, "Take good care of yourself. I hope to be your new baby's first visitor."

On the plane George still frowned. He was sure he had somehow failed. Well, whatever happened, the ordeal was over. Hands steady now, I could smile and reassure him: "You probably did fine. Now let's wait and see."

Herb Prentiss phoned George at home three days later. I watched George's usually immobile face as he held the phone. Then he smiled.

Almost exactly two years from the day we had moved to Park Forest, I stood outside the big moving van as it finished loading. Tige, George, and I—and the new baby inside me—would follow it west in the car. Emily, Florence, Betty, and Pat were there to say good-by. I would miss them very much, but moving vans were a common sight in Park Forest. Young husbands worked to get better jobs and to leave—sometimes to "better" neighborhoods, sometimes, as we were doing, to other towns.

This was, I told myself, part of my job. Packing, moving, making new friends was the cost of George's advancement. The new job paid $10,000—a big step up for George. It also meant a bigger, better house for me and the children.

I thought of the woman way down the block; hers was one of the few two-career families I knew. She had been offered a promotion to another town. She had accepted, taking her children, leaving her husband behind. She had made her choices—and I had made mine.

They were not such bad choices after all. I looked around at the look-alike houses. These two years had been an important part of my education. Here, among young couples just like us, I had won some of the most vital battles of my life. With a lot less aptitude than I might have wished for, I had taken on a new kind of life. The life ahead could only be better. George might develop confidence in his new job, might learn to make friends. But no matter what, the children would have a fine place to grow. And, I expected, so would I.

The moving van pulled away from the curb. The car was packed. While Tige nestled comfortably in his back-seat bed, I sat next to George and checked the map. Omaha—and a new kind of life—was not that far away.

Chapter 14

WHEN GEORGE, TIGE, AND I drove up to our new house and parked just behind the moving van, I had the pleasant feeling that life in Omaha was going to be different. I had enjoyed being a jigsaw-puzzle piece in Park Forest. I had, I felt, learned the basics. In Omaha we had chosen a neighborhood where the houses were not all alike. Some were bigger and more elaborate, some smaller. In the last two years I had acquired the confidence to be at least a little different.

It had taken confidence to buy the house we were about to enter. The realtor had looked hesitant, and George's eyebrows had dipped on our first inspection. The realtor's descriptive card was well thumbed and creased. The house in Omaha's Rockbrook suburb had been on the market a long time, and I could see why. The living room was painted a dark blood-red; the master bedroom was a green that was close to black. So was the second bedroom. The third was an odd shade of rust. Apparently the owners shopped for paint at close-out sales.

But the ceilings were high, and wall-to-wall windows looked out over a golf course. The spotted beige carpeting could be cleaned. Built into a hill there was a lower floor with a bedroom, an extra living room (with a fireplace), and a large area that could be tiled for a playroom. The yard was enormous; it would keep George happy growing grass forever.

It took no imagination to visualize the God-awful walls painted white, the wild shrubbery pruned, and the muddy-green kitchen linoleum replaced.

George had still looked dubious.

"George, honey, there's over an acre of land. You could plant a terrific vegetable garden. And, Lord knows, the price is right."

The blood walls, filthy carpeting, and eggplant color of the exterior had brought about a desperation price of only $25,000.

George's new job, I reminded him, paid $10,000. With the large down-payment I had made on our first house and the modest profit we had made when we sold it, we could afford the new house. And I could look out its wide kitchen windows to watch Tige in the yard.

George finally agreed. I could begin planning: Tige would have the front bedroom near ours. The sunny back bedroom would be for the new baby.

I felt rather smug about having conceived the new baby exactly on schedule. Tige would be two years old when it was born. He needed another baby in the house and so did I. There was such a thing, I discovered, as too much fierce mother love. Without my wanting it to, my love focused on Tige as if it were a blinding spotlight. I watched other little boys and translated them into Tige at four, at ten, at fourteeen years old. At twenty-four?

I looked down at Tige, sleeping soundly in his just-assembled bed. Someday he *would* be twenty-four—living, perhaps, in Seattle or some other distant place, sending me a postcard once a month. That was a time to prepare for, to expect. For now, he was the focus of my life, as I was for his. A bit less focus would be healthier for both of us. Another baby in the house would split the blinding spotlight.

The first night in our new house, I sat up late while George slept. Poor George. His selection by the Omaha corporation had not increased his confidence. He was certain they would believe they had made a mistake. I sat on the sofa. No, it should be nearer the window. I tried to drag it quietly so as not to wake George. Ah, much better. I could look out over the golf course down below and across to the lights on the hill opposite.

At times George's forebodings were almost contagious. Earlier that evening I had felt my spirits lurch at his predictions of disaster, which were a lot like my mother's. She was living now with newly widowed Aunt May, continuing some ancient sibling rivalry

that Mother was certain to lose. But I had survived Mother's predictions of doom. I would survive George's. Every husband, I
suspected, had some quality that required forbearance.

I patted the place where the new baby lay. Mothers had a head
start at loving children. In a month or two, this one would have a
personality of its own and I would know it as I had known Tige's
before he was born. I felt a wave of love for whoever it was. The
news occasionally reported mothers running into burning buildings to try to rescue a child, sometimes not merely risking but losing their lives—possibly, I decided, not thinking about it at all—
just doing it. I wondered if my own mother love was that strong
. . . and hoped I would never have to find out.

It was too disturbing to think about on the first night in a happy
new home. The lights across the valley were going out. Think of
putting the house in beautiful order and, better still, think of going to sleep.

At breakfast George reiterated his fears, doubts, and tension. I
tried not to sound too impatient. "George, the president of General Motors was probably tense on his first day. It will work out
fine."

He left, came back. "The damn car wouldn't start." I knew he
had flooded the motor. He always did when he was upset. Well, if
my new neighbors wondered at my running outside in my robe,
so be it. I started the car and smiled George on his way.

Tige was happily crowing in his crib, "Mommy! Eat now!" Yes,
and while he ate breakfast, I would check our new house for any
dangers a toddler might find. I got a slide bolt on the basement
door before Tige finished his eggs. Now he could "help" me unpack his boxes of toys.

By noon I was feeling my typical early-pregnancy sleepiness. No
nap yet. Lunch for Tige, his nap, and then mine. But just for five
minutes, I thought, I would kick off my shoes and rest my feet.
From the guest-room bed I watched Tige using his push-toy to
pretend to vacuum. I wiggled my tired bare toes and, in the mirror propped against the wall, watched Tige's pink face in fierce
concentration.

One energetic shove of Tige's push-toy against the bottom edge
of the heavy mirror and, suddenly, the mirror was shattering on
top of my child.

Time stretched as I jumped up. I could already visualize blood
spurting out of his small, still body. Please let me know what to

do and to do it quickly. I ran across the glass-covered floor and pulled the mirror up.

Tige looked surprised, but he was conscious. I picked him up to carry him to the kitchen. There would be cloths there for tourniquets, to stanch the blood that I was sure would begin flowing. I looked him over carefully, checked the pupils of his eyes for brain damage. By now Tige was laughing as if we had played a new game. Miraculously, he was completely unhurt. The mirror must have shattered on his push-toy instead of his body. I put him in his playpen and went back to close the guest-room door. I would clean it up later when I recovered from the knowledge of his miracle.

At the door I stopped, momentarily hypnotized. Big, dagger-like shards of glass were scattered between the bed where I had been lying, the place where I had picked up Tige, and the door through which I had carried him. To reach him and to carry him out, *I had run barefoot through glass.* I looked across the room. There was no path at all to reach my shoes. I waited for the pain in my bare feet. Nothing. When I looked, there were no cuts.

For the rest of the day I unpacked boxes, stopping often while holding a book or a spice jar or a shoe dazedly in my hand, trying to understand our eerie experience. Several times I went back to look into the room. Yes, it was as I remembered. And, no, I would never understand it—except that there were apparently depths of love that produce miracles when needed.

When George came home, I told him breathlessly about what had happened. He said, "That's nice, dear. Glad no one was hurt." His first day at his job, he said, had been awful: too many people with too many names, and he had felt like a dunce.

"Well, of course, George! Everyone does the first day."

"But what if they decide it was a mistake to hire me? We've bought a house. You're pregnant. Ben Bright, the president, acts as if he can't stand me."

As I reached into the stewpot to put some on George's plate, I felt as if I did not have one more encouraging word to give. Well, what was the alternative? Tell George he was probably right, that on the second day they would say, "That's it. Go back to Chicago"? I felt a giggle bubbling inside. On the verge of hysteria, perhaps, I wondered what George would do if I said, "Yes, you're probably as incompetent as you think you are." Would he jump up and drown himself in the stew?

I held on tight to the plate. "George, they'll find out how good you are. You'll see."

While George bathed Tige and I listened to my son's gleeful chatter, I knew I would keep finding encouraging words somehow.

The next day, my frustrations went into wiping out my new cabinets, dreaming occasionally of how, someday, I would redo the kitchen, and thinking of how great the living room could look for parties.

At noon the doorbell rang. A tall, rangy woman with chestnut hair introduced herself as Phyllis Bordeaux. "Hi! I'm across the street and up one house. We don't want to bother you while you're unpacking, but welcome to Rockbrook. And if your little boy will go with me, he can play with my Butch this afternoon."

Tige would have happily gone with King Kong. He was already looking up at Phyllis with his what's-this-new-delight smile. Phyllis said, "I'll bring him back at five. Nap if you want to. I know how you feel."

No nap. Now I could stand on a ladder and get the top shelves organized without Tige's climbing after me. They were almost done when I felt a strange moisture between my thighs. I knew, almost immediately, what it was—the kind of bleeding that should not happen during pregnancy.

I called Phyllis. She would know the name of an obstetrician. "Call Dr. Short. And call me back as soon as you've talked to him. If necessary I can put you and the boys in the car and take you to his office. Just phone him. It'll be fine."

Bless Phyllis for being there and for being reassuring. I dialed Dr. Short. He too was reassuring to someone he had never met. "Since you have no recent history of miscarriages, it's best to just stay off your feet for now and we'll see what happens. There's a new drug for miscarriages—diethylstilbestrol—but I'd rather not use it." His voice softened. "The bleeding may simply stop. If it increases, call me immediately. And remember that a miscarriage can be nature's way of expelling an imperfect fetus. Anyway, no diethylstilbestrol. Just rest."

I hung up the phone, grateful that Dr. Short had not pushed some chancy new drug and wondering how I would manage rest with an active toddler around. I thought of phoning George. No, he had enough on his mind already.

Phyllis came through the door with Tige and a little blond boy

190

Tige's size. "Did you reach Dr. Short? If he said to stay off your feet, don't worry. Butch and Tige adore each other and I'll just keep Tige at my house during the day. Favor to me, really. Keeps Butchy out of my hair."

I said, "I'm really not the blubbery type, but I'm so damn, damn grateful." It felt extraordinary to have someone swoop up my problems and whisk them away. I wiped my eyes because Tige was looking concerned.

The bleeding stopped the next day. Dr. Short said to try some activity. In two days I was back to my normal, comfortable pregnancy—and to the beginning of our new life in Rockbrook. So far my experiences had been decidedly positive—Dr. Short's careful consideration, Phyllis's helpfulness. She gave a coffee party for me to meet the other women in the neighborhood.

Midway through the coffee party, I realized that there were differences between the women of Park Forest and the women of Rockbrook—not for better or worse, just differences. My Rockbrook neighbors—Ethel, Clarice, Zelda, Hazel—all appeared to have married right out of school, too, but for them "school" was college. Hazel Schmidt had worked for a year in the home-economics department of a food company and Phyllis had taught for a year, but all of them—except for Irene Turner and Leona Wood—now worked full-time at home.

Leona, a social worker, looked wistful when the others discussed my pregnancy. She had been trying to become pregnant for five years.

Irene was not at the party, but I was told that both she and her husband were engineers. Mrs. Matta, her housekeeper, took care of three-year-old Linda and would take care of the new baby due to arrive about the same time as mine.

"Irene," Zelda said, "has her babies 'by appointment.' You know, induced labor. I wish my doctor had offered me that."

Not me. I told my new friends about my almost-perfect natural childbirth experience with Tige, that this time I hoped to avoid any last-minute misunderstanding about anesthesia.

Clarice, a slender, impeccably groomed ash blond, said, "I could never be that brave."

Bravery had nothing to do with it, I explained. From everything I had heard, relaxed breathing really did lessen pain better than drugs.

Zelda, whose home with its muted beiges and abstract paintings, proclaimed her an art major, said, "Well, good luck with having natural childbirth here. I think they're trying to ban it along with fluoridation. Didn't you know you've moved to a cultural desert?" How could I, she asked, have left the Chicago Symphony and the art museum?

Somehow that year of going to the symphony with Marty (Meg had been right—he had married the year after I did) and spending my lunch hours at the museum seemed part of another life, one I didn't miss at all. Natural childbirth was a different matter. All I really needed, however, was Dr. Short standing by. I knew quite well how to have babies.

At my first visit, Dr. Short admitted he had never had a natural-childbirth patient. "But we can certainly do it the way you want, Mrs. Stalvey." I had visited the two hospitals where he was on the staff. Rather surprisingly, the newer had one large "labor bin" lined with beds. The older hospital had two small rooms, but at least they were private. Dr. Short said that yes, George could be with me if I chose the older hospital.

The months passed quickly. George remained unsure about himself at work, but he was happy planting trees and planning a vegetable garden for spring. We laid tiles in the big basement room for Tige—and his sister/brother—to use as a playroom. Laying tiles, I decided as I squatted, was a *productive* prenatal exercise. The new baby grew inside me—and with a personality noticeably different from Tige's.

"This one," I told George, "doesn't frisk around as Tige did. I think it sleeps and then has its periods of tremendous exercise." On cue, the new baby knocked my book off my lap—or what passed for my lap at more than eight months.

At two o'clock in the morning on May 23, the baby woke me with an enormous kick—and water gushed out onto the bed. Hmm, this *was* going to be a different delivery. The membrane had had to be broken in the delivery room before Tige was born. Better phone Dr. Short.

He agreed we should get to the hospital and ended the conversation with a formal "Thank you for calling." I wondered whether he had been *really* wide awake.

George definitely was not. I said, "George, I have to leave for the hospital." George said, "That's nice, dear," rolled over, and continued snoring.

I thought for a moment about driving myself. It might be fun to drive up to the entrance, waddle in, and announce I was in labor. Better not to give in to the early-labor euphoria. I nudged George again. "You'll have to drive me, dear."

He had his underwear and socks on before he mumbled, "Where are we going?"

This delivery, I decided as I phoned Phyllis's teen-age daughter who had agreed to stay with Tige when this event occurred, had all the elements of high comedy. I got coffee into George, let Barbie in, and off we went.

At the hospital I reminded the nurse on duty that Dr. Short was allowing George to be with me during labor.

"Oh, no. We never do that!"

I smiled cheerfully. "Better phone him. Or I'll just go out and have the baby on your front lawn."

She studied my face, dialed Dr. Short, and looked astonished.

For the next twelve hours I felt as if I were the hostess at a side show. Nurses, interns, and people I never identified all came in to see the woman who "breathed funny" and the husband who sat with a stopwatch writing contraction times on a pad.

When we were first settled in, a kind-faced nurse had instructed me: "When the pains come, just hang onto the bedpost as hard as you can." That, I told her, was not at all wise. "It tightens the muscles that should stay loose." Just then a contraction came. I breathed my way through it. She watched, shaking her head. When she came with a needle, I said, "No, thank you," and the word, apparently, was out.

Soon people came in to watch my act. Between contractions, I explained the writings of Read and the techniques of De Lee. At first it was fun. George had fallen asleep in his chair and my visitors helped pass the time. But the contractions were remaining the same and, after all those hours, I was not making much progress toward delivery. Conducting natural-childbirth demonstrations for the hospital staff was all very well, but not as a permanent career.

At eight o'clock Dr. Short sat on the edge of my bed. "Let me give you a shot of morphine. You'll get a good night's sleep and be ready to deliver in the morning."

This procedure was not discussed in the childbirth books, but perhaps Dr. Short was right. I had been awake since two in the morning. Sleep might be wise.

Thirty minutes later I understood the principles of natural

childbirth a whole lot better. The morphine had made me too dopey to catch—and breathe properly through—the contractions. I felt as if I were swimming in black water through pain I could not control. A shadowy figure stuck another needle in me while I tried to form my mouth to say no. Back under the black water where the contractions controlled me, I fought the drug with anger. Who was it who needed "a good night's sleep"—Dr. Short or me?

A pert, dark-haired nurse came in just as I saw the faint light of dawn in the window. "Do you want another shot?"

No! In fact, I had just had an idea. We were, alas, going to disturb Dr. Short's sleep. I had just remembered—although I did not feel—the symptoms of impending delivery.

"Gee," I told the nurse, "I feel exactly as if I need to have a bowel movement."

Her eyes widened. "Hang on. I'll call Dr. Short right away."

Dr. Short obviously knew at a glance that I had tricked him to the hospital, but now that I was in the delivery room, legs in the stirrups, he also knew why my labor was taking so long. I heard him say to a nurse, "See? A sunny-side-up presentation."

"What's that?" Dr. Short looked as if a forceps had just spoken. He was apparently not used to conversing with women in delivery rooms. He said, crosssly, "I'm going to push the baby back up and turn it around."

By now my relationship with Dr. Short was decidedly awry. I was, I knew, hardly in a position—legs up, body strapped down—for rational discussion. If he was going to do something as *un*-natural as shove against my muscles to turn the baby, however, a little gas might be a good idea. I suggested it.

"No, Mother. It won't hurt," he barked.

I had never felt angrier or more physically helpless in my life. Half of me was strapped up in the air. The other half was too far away to punch Dr. Short in the nose, as I dearly wanted to do. Only my mouth was workable. "Mother," indeed.

"Well, *son,* how in hell would *you* know if it hurts or not? I trust *you've* never been in labor, right?"

"Oh, just shut up."

I could feel his manipulations inside me. They were not really as uncomfortable as the night his morphine had put me through. But I fully intended to use the only available weapon I had to even up the score. I took a breath and let out yells loud enough to make the instruments rattle. And more yells. Until a nurse said into my ear that the baby was in position. I knew it was time to pant until instructed to push.

Suddenly, a rubber mask was on my face. Someone held my hands as I reached to pull it off. Oh, damn.

The delivery room was absolutely quiet when I awoke. No sound of a crying baby. For endless minutes I lay, afraid to ask. Finally I felt I had better handle bad news as soon as possible. I asked out loud of anyone who might be in the room, "Where's my baby?"

A nurse came into view. "Oh, he's in the nursery. A fine healthy little boy. You'll see him when you give him his first bottle tonight."

We were not, I decided, out of the proverbial woods yet. "I hope I have *not* been given a shot to dry up my milk."

"Oh, no, dear, that comes later."

Later, of course, I fended off the shots. George had been waiting right outside the delivery-room door. "What happened? I heard you screaming way out here!" Just a disagreement with Dr. Short. Had he seen the baby? Yes, through the window, and he looked all right.

That evening, at feeding time, I finally held Josh for the first time. He was pink, compact, and even good-natured. No screaming for his dinner as Tige had done. Josh cuddled cozily.

As he nursed, I watched his tiny, chubby hand gently patting my breast. We had survived the slapstick beginning. We could survive the rest. No first-night panic with Josh. I was an experienced mother now, raising not a child but a family.

I gently twirled Josh's not-inconsiderable hair into a Kewpie-curl as I had once done with my nearly bald grandfather. Life, I thought, was certainly a lovely river with unexpected currents. In less than three years I had left one kind of life and was sailing happily along in another. I kissed Josh's soft little forehead. I could hardly wait to take him home.

Chapter 15

THE FIRST DAY home alone with Josh and Tige it exploded in my head that although there was no "first-night panic," there was now panic enough to last all week. Somehow it had never occurred to me that I would need to be in two separate places—sometimes three—at one time.

When George left for work that first morning, I felt sure there was some logical way to adjust to two children in the house. Other women had three, four, six! By noon I wished fervently I had time to talk to those women—workers of miracles that were obviously beyond me.

Josh had begun to cry for his breakfast at the very instant Tige fell and badly skinned his knee. For a moment I was immobilized between my hungry infant and my bleeding little boy. I had never realized two children might need me at once. I stood in the hallway, a cloth to wash Tige's wound and a box of Band-Aids in my hand. Josh's cries became urgent.

Perhaps I could hold Josh while I repaired Tige. Then it was obvious that I could hold and nurse him as well. It *was* possible after all, to sit in the big chair, both hands free, to bandage and soothe Tige while Josh never missed a gulp. Breast-feeding, I realized, had more advantages than I had known.

But later, as I bathed Josh while Tige crawled around my feet, the doorbell rang. I picked up Josh the moment before Tige—now under the bath table—stood up in excitement. The bath table overturned. I was soaked from the waist down and only glad the splash had missed the clean towel on the chair. The doorbell rang again. My wet, wiggly infant was safely wrapped in the towel and plunked in the crib. While he screamed in protest, I sloshed to the door. I was not receptive to the Jehovah's Witness who stood outside. My afterlife was far less my concern, I explained, than getting through the one I lived now.

Back to mopping the floor and new water for Josh's aborted bath. Tige was whiny, not used to sharing my attention. Well, if I could bandage him while Josh nursed, I could read stories to Tige too. I had vowed he would not feel neglected—as I might have felt—with a new baby brother at home.

During the all-too-brief nap time, I managed three loads of wash and preparations for dinner. Diapers, now, were everywhere waiting to be folded. Tige's toilet training had not been top priority for either of us, but now diapers, like yeast dough, seemed to expand in the drier. When Josh cried again, I piled the wicker wash basket with a snowy heap and went to get him for his four o'clock snack. Tige, of course, woke too.

Then, during the nursing-reading time, the telephone rang. I could answer the phone without disturbing Josh's meal. It was George, asking if the cleaner had returned his suits. Just as I was saying no, the doorbell rang. For that I had to put Josh down. It was the cleaner, of course. I reported to George and went back to get Josh out of his crib.

The crib was empty! Kidnappers? No, the windows were closed. I rushed to Tige. "Where's the baby?" Not in the playpen. Not on my bed.

Then, as I ran through the kitchen, a diaper in the basket moved. Of course! I had snuggled Josh safely in the basket. He had somehow pulled a diaper over himself and gone to sleep. Tige wanted to play Hide the Baby again. I sat next to the basket and wept.

Two children were apparently beyond my ability. What if I did something *terribly* wrong and hurt one of them as a result of my ineptness? I had been so sure that I could handle having children. After all, I had managed other things. But "other things"—columns, TV shows, a business—involved only unimportant issues like money and ego. If I had failed, I could easily have walked away from any one of them. Now, when failure seemed only too

197

certain, I could *not* walk away. I could not put Tige and Josh in an envelope as I had done with those Ann Landers letters and say, "Sorry. This is something I'm not cut out to do," could not say to them, "Better get yourself another mother. This one's a lemon." There was no way out.

With Josh still sleeping in the basket while I sat and sobbed on the floor beside him, I glimpsed, through tears, Irene Turner's house next door. She'd had her babies, quickly turned them over to a housekeeper, and gone back to work. No sitting on kitchen floors and crying for her! She was more like a *father* to her children when she and her husband came home at night.

Then another wave of crashing sadness broke over me. I had apparently wanted *my* mother home all day more than I had ever realized. Just the thought of kissing Tige good-by in the morning and going off to work brought such pain I knew I could never do it. All right, I would stay here, trying my best to keep my mistakes from hurting my children too much.

Tige wandered into the kitchen. Suddenly, two little arms were around me. Then a small hand was trying to wipe my face with a diaper. "Don't cry, Mommy. We love you."

Somehow we would make it all right.

Weeks later, I had learned that it did get easier. At first I had rushed to answer Josh's every cry, Tige's every call. Now I developed "mother's ears." I knew the difference between a cry for attention and a wail of distress, knew whether silence was golden or ominous. And together, Tige, Josh, and I developed a workable routine. Up to make breakfast for George while the boys still slept, then a blur of activity dictated by the vagaries of moods, doorbells, appliances, and what needed attention most, then a nap for both boys (please!) while I had some precious time to myself to read, doze, or think. Then, refreshed, to take on dinner. George came home, precisely on time, to bathe the boys and put them to bed. I read to Tige while George bathed Josh. Then, with any luck, a quiet dinner with George—and, for the first time in our marriage, falling asleep before he did.

On Mondays Mrs. Robbins came to deep-clean the house. George's eyebrows had dipped when I hired her, but my checks from Lovett and Wynn still came each month to cover her costs. On Mondays, while the children napped, I grabbed my time to go into town, usually to visit Harriet Fischer or Sally Klein.

Sally owned a toy shop, and I had met Harriet there. They were different from my neighbors—both with grown children and both from New York. With my neighbors I enjoyed the talk of toilet training, measles, and school and learned from it too. But Monday visits with Sally or Harriet seemed to fill some other need. We talked of current events—from newspapers I never had time to read.

As Josh became two months old, then three, then four, life settled into a not-intolerable pace. I even found time to do some free-lance writing for the local department store. On Mrs. Robbins's cleaning days, I picked up assignments to write while the children napped. It was wise, I decided, to keep some work going. I hoped I would never have to go out to work, but, like an insurance policy, it was there.

Sally had said, "It's good to keep a creative outlet." But I had several others I enjoyed much more. With Tige near me in the big tiled basement playroom and Josh cooing in his playpen, I had time to sew—not clothes for Josh or Tige, who outgrew them in less time than it took to sew—but challenging Vogue Couturier clothes for myself. No advertising campaign had ever been as exciting to me as finishing a designer dress, or as impressive to me as the elaborate gourmet dinners I occasionally made for parties. There was even creative fun to be had in finding ways to trim the budget.

And, I gradually realized, I was not the world's *worst* mother. My breasts, at least, had made Josh thrive. At almost five months he was chubby and happy. Tige, I knew, would always be lean. His endless energy burned up calories, but he too was a happy, outgoing, and loving child. As a mother, I must be doing some things right.

As a wife? Well, I would fight my impatience. George did as well as he could. Sometimes after an exhausting day, I had to struggle to stay awake and listen to his problems. His style, I finally realized, was so different from mine that often he could not use the advice he asked for. And I was not (damn the phrase) "doing my duty" in bed. It was hard to feel romantic when my legs ached, and when pregnancy was always a dismaying possibility. Postmenopausal women, I read somewhere, had increased sex drives. I could understand why.

Nor was I a star as a corporate wife. Not at all like Lorrie Brent, the comptroller's wife, who entertained and socialized with the people who could do her husband, Ralph, some good. My attempt to repay her dinners had ended with a thump.

To change the formula a bit, I had invited the Kleins along too. The subject of New York came up. "Oh, I love the city," Lorrie chirped, "but the private schools are so expensive—and the public schools are crawling with Jews."

Sally, probably out of long, sad habit, changed the subject smoothly. Lorrie phoned the next day. "I did such a terrible thing," she said, and I knew I was supposed to reassure her. "Should I call the Kleins and apologize?" I gave what I knew was the wrong answer: Yes. At least there were no more Brent dinners I had to repay.

I reassured myself with the fact that I had never socialized to get ahead in business. George's conscientious work would earn him promotions, not my reluctant—and ill-conceived—dinner parties.

In October Josh showed me he was finished with nursing. Unlike Tige, Josh simply fell asleep, his tummy full with the solid foods he was taking well. Back, I realized, to the inconvenience of menstruating. The absence of periods during pregnancy and breast-feeding had been nice.

A period in November, one in December, and then none. It was impossible, I told myself, that I was pregnant so soon. My new gynecologist, Dr. Braun, had fitted me with a new diaphragm. I was using it carefully. With my eye on the calendar and my thoughts below my naval, I waited. In February I stopped waiting. Dr. Braun confirmed my fear. In October 1959, just after my thirty-fourth birthday, I would have a three-year-old, a seventeen-month-old toddler, and a brand-new baby.

In May, Jane came from Milwaukee to visit, just in time for Josh's first birthday party. If I had any guilt left from having closed my agency, her contentment with her job laid it to rest. She had had promotions, expanded departments, and the opportunity to promote the utility company exactly as she wished.

"I did learn a lot from your attitudes," she said. "But don't you ever miss the business world?" She looked at my bulging front, at Tige racing around, and at Josh in the playpen. "You sure don't do things by halves."

Jane's quite natural question startled me. I seldom thought of my career days, except when reading of Mary Wells, the young advertising woman who had opened her own extremely successful agency in New York. I had, without thinking, shuddered: a fate I had only too narrowly escaped.

Jane asked again, "Do children make up for it?"

"For me they do." I tried to project myself back into the life that Jane and I had shared. It had been exciting, challenging, different every day—like the fun of my teen-age years, which I remembered fondly but had no desire at all to relive.

Jane said, "I guess some women have more maternal feelings than others. I'm only glad I finally convinced my mother that marriage just isn't for me. Being the doting aunt to my brother's kids is just great."

It seemed to be much better than if Jane had succumbed to pressures to lead a life she did not really want.

I patted my belly. "I didn't *plan* to fill my nest quite this fast, but since this is positively my last production, I'm going to make my farewell appearance on the delivery table my best."

I told Jane about Dr. Braun. After Josh's birth I had contacted a delivery-room nurse and asked her (just in case) about the best possible natural-childbirth doctor. She had recommended Dr. Joseph Braun.

I had asked that George be allowed in the delivery room. It seemed only right that he see our last child born. Dr. Braun said he had always believed it was a good idea, "but the hospital won't allow it."

I phoned the hospital. They too said they were in sympathy, "but the doctors won't allow it."

"So I simply called Dr. Braun back to tell him it was all arranged."

Jane hooted. We reminisced about other adventures. When I drove her to the plane with Josh snuggling in her arms and Tige knocking her hat off in exuberant farewell, it seemed to me that two women were both going back to lives they had thoughtfully chosen and fully enjoyed.

By the tenth of October, Dr. Braun was obviously more weary of waiting than I was. "If I gave you *one* shot and broke the membrane, that baby would come."

Was there any *medical* reason to rush? No? Then this baby, who had decided against all odds to get conceived, should be allowed to get born in its own good time. I felt fine. Especially for a thirty-four-year-old mother. After four years of marriage, pregnancy seemed my natural state.

Eight days later, relaxing after Sunday dinner, I felt we could now relieve Dr. Braun's mind. I called him. "Well, Lois, thank goodness. I thought you were going to be my permanent pregnant patient. See you at the hospital."

At the hospital Dr. Braun said, grinning, "If you'd listened to me, Lois, you could have had this baby two weeks ago."

"Ask your wife, Joe. A baby *inside* is a lot easier to take care of than the ones that are out."

Dr. Braun admitted he had never thought of that.

In the same tiny labor room where Josh had begun to be born, George took up his stopwatch and paper again. I reminded the nurses that Dr. Braun had given permission for George to be in the delivery room. They remembered me from my very recent visit. Anything, their expressions seemed to say, could be expected from this nut.

Eventually George and I ran out of conversation. I wrote notes to friends while George napped between my contractions. Someone was moved into the labor room separated from mine by a thin sliding door. Her moans were soft at first, but I could hear her calls to the nurses, louder moans, and then a nurse's voice: "I'm sorry, dear, but I simply can't give you another shot."

Poor thing! I wondered if some very late lessons in natural childbirth would help. While George snored peacefully, I slipped out of bed to talk to the nurse. Could I go in to see the woman next door?

"Honey, you can do anything you *want* to the woman next door, short of knocking her out with a bedpan."

The moans I had heard came from a small, blond, very young girl who looked up at me with red-rimmed and terrified eyes. Her hands clutched the bedpost behind her. "Aren't you . . . shouldn't you . . . why are you walking?" she stammered. I explained natural-childbirth theories, quickly condensed. Just then a contraction of my own hit. I grinned. "Watch!" As I did my slow breathing, the contraction felt *much* more productive than before. Hmm, maybe standing up was a better posture for labor. Linda, the young woman, watched me, wide-eyed. "Try it," I said. She breathed through a contraction while I held her hand.

Her contraction over, she looked up with a sun-bright smile. "It works! Will you stay for the next one?" Sure. Apparently last-minute instruction was better than none.

Four of Linda's contractions later, four of my own, and Dr. Braun stood grinning in Linda's doorway. "Can I tear you away for a minute?" Well, Linda felt she could handle things alone.

I got back into bed. Dr. Braun examined me. "Well, kid, unless you want to have the baby on your neighbor's floor, I think we'd better go into the delivery room soon."

Where was George? Changing into delivery-room clothes. Dr. Braun was keeping his promise.

Then came the sensation that proved Dr. Braun's hurry was probably right. And this time it looked as if I would be wide awake to experience it all. The contractions no longer caused any discomfort, just a tremendous desire to push. I panted the short breaths that prevented me from pushing until the cart was wheeled into the delivery room.

This was what I had missed the times before! When Dr. Braun said, "Push," it was the most satisfying feeling on earth—physically satisfying, but intellectually and emotionally satisfying too. My muscles were helping my child on its important journey. Three, four, five wonderful orgasmic pushes—then a push that brought a sudden change. The pressure was gone. George, who had been sitting near me, watching my face, suddenly stood up. Dr. Braun held up a wet, red, wiggling, wailing body, made it bow toward George, and said, "Hi, Pop." Our baby was born. George looked as awestruck as if the walls had moved. I grinned at the expression on his face.

Dr. Braun said, "Let me clean her up a bit and you can hold your daughter."

Did he say "daughter"? I asked, "A girl?" Yes.

A wish that must have lain deep inside exploded with the force of long suppression. I had never known I wanted a daughter so much—not until this moment when the wish was granted. Some feeling inside me burst with the colors of fireworks against the sky, of cascades of flowers, of uncontainable joy. I pulled against the straps on the table, taken with a crazy urge to jump up, to dance, to hold my *daughter* and whirl around this wonderful room.

Dr. Braun said, "Let's have one more push to expel the placenta."

Sure. Anything anyone wanted, anything to have my daughter in my arms.

Then she was there. Funny, but I had thought I loved my boy-children more than anyone could love. This new feeling was different—not more love, but a love of different, overwhelming dimensions, filling places in me that I had never dreamed existed.

Much as I loved my sons, there were so many things we could never share. But this little girl and I would know and share and love each other in our special woman's way.

I looked down at her. Christina *Lois* slept in my arms. Perhaps she could feel the surging waves of love that swept from me to her and would forever.

When Tina was brought to me later to be nursed, I tried to climb down from my pinnacle of delight to do some sober thinking. Psychologists, I had read, believed that males and females develop differently because they are treated differently. Giving erector sets to boys and dolls to girls, one man had written, was only one way children were steered into roles. I could remember being given dolls as a child, but no one seemed to mind when I put them aside for my books or crayons. I had been allowed, if only because of Mother's timid temperament, to grow up in my own way. So would Tina. If she wanted to run for President of the United States, I would carry her banner. If she wanted to drive a truck, I would pack her lunch.

Yet as I looked down at my wonderful, wonderful new daughter, it was hard not to notice how different she was from my boys. Before birth, Tige had bumped, somersaulted, and romped constantly inside me. Josh had saved up energy for his enormous kicks. With Tina, I had felt only gentle flutters. Now, as she nursed, I smiled at the—well, damn it—ladylike way she *sipped*. Her tiny hands did not pummel my breast as had her brothers'. They were daintily and gracefully resting on the blanket. My imagination? Perhaps. But interesting.

Dr. Murphy, the pediatrician I had found after a long search, lumbered into the room. He was well into his seventies but far more "modern" than the pediatricians I had left behind. I was glad I had found him in time for Tina's birth.

When Josh was born, Dr. Swenson, an Ivy League type, had handed me a list of *do*'s and *don't*'s. "And I like my vitamins given right after baths." I hoped he got them. When Tige got a mosquito bite on his penis, Dr. Swenson instructed me to put an ice cube on it. "I don't think," I told him, wincing, "that he's going to like that much." Then, Dr. Swenson said, do it while he's asleep. I switched to Dr. Molt. But Dr. Molt obviously *enjoyed* sticking needles into children. When Tige got measles, Dr. Molt made a house call to give Josh a gamma globulin shot. He pushed

Josh roughly onto his stomach, muttering, "Damn it, lie still."
Two minutes later I was pushing a rather surprised Dr. Molt out
my door wondering whether he would sue me if I kicked him as
he left.

After that, for each of Josh's monthly checkups, I had simply
gone down the list in the phone book. I had stopped at the *M*'s.
Dr. Murphy talked to the babies and, I learned later, was head of
Children's Hospital. His advanced age concerned me at first.

"Dr. Murphy, I hope you don't plan to retire too soon."

"Heavens, no. I don't even plan to die until I find out how
some of these new ideas turn out."

Dr. Murphy had no trouble remembering I breast-fed. "Never
did like those bottles. Just wait. It'll be 'in' again. Women get
back to what's practical: breast-feeding and those drug-free la-
bors."

Now he stood at the foot of my hospital bed. "Well, I examined
the baby. And if I were you, I'd keep her."

Any instructions? If Dr. Murphy wanted his vitamins after his
baths, he would get them.

He turned his rosy-cheeked, white-haired head toward the ceiling in thought, then smiled down at me. "Well, maybe you ought
to remember that cows don't run—they walk."

Taking Tina home produced no panic. I had already learned I
could not be two places at once. I didn't even try for three. There
was no panic, but as the months moved along with a three-year-
old, an eighteen-month-old toddler, and an infant, there was a
creeping and deadly fatigue.

Christmas 1959 passed in a strange, shifting fog. I tried to put
Tige's new fire engine together. After years of George's insisting
the instructions were wrong, this time they were. A call to the
store's night watchman: "My little boy was promised this toy and
it's the store's mistake!" The watchman called the toy buyer at
home. The buyer dispatched two slightly tipsy fellows who, like
Santa's elves, assembled the toy. At some point they left. In the
morning Tige found me on the sofa.

By February I knew that my chores were not getting easier, nor
were they likely to for a while. The three little people I loved
passionately had constant needs and demands.

Mother came to visit. When Tige and Josh tussled over a toy,
she took it from Tige. "You must *love* your baby brother," she

said sternly to Tige. Some memory erupted out of my bone-deep exhaustion. I took the toy and put it firmly out of reach. "You don't have to love your baby brother; you just can't sock him." That was enough to ask of a less-than-four-year-old.

Mother brought up the subject of toilet training often. *She* had trained me, she said, when I was nine months old. Even George now asked why I didn't put Tige on the toilet "at regular intervals as your mother suggests."

I was astonished to find myself bursting into tears. "I don't *have* any regular intervals!" The children had not coordinated their naps for a week. What with doorbells, telephones, Josh's toddler tumbles, Tige's endless energy, and nursing Tina, I felt like a wind-up toy, turned on in the morning and barely making it until I ran completely down at night. The day before, I had even forgotten to give Tina her lunch. Her cry usually reminded me. That day she had simply played happily in her crib while the repairman fixed the washer. While making dinner, I was suddenly hit with guilt—and worry: guilt that I had forgotten to nurse my daughter, worry that my breasts were not full, and horror that my tiny daughter might have Mother's passive temperament.

Mother and George looked astonished when I ran from the room. In the bedroom I calmed myself down. What with Mother's visit, it had simply been a difficult week. It was better to see the funny side and laugh—to remember Mother chasing balls in the yard while Tige and Josh threw them. I had called from the window, "No, *you* throw the balls and let the children run." But Tige's trip to the roof had not been funny. George had left a ladder at the side of the house. Phyllis had phoned to say, "I can see Tige up on the side of your roof." I had climbed the ladder to Mother's protestations that "Tige was right here with us." Apparently not.

Still, when Mother left, nothing improved. That mechanical-doll feeling continued. Each morning I wound myself up and moved mindlessly through dishes, diapers, meals, dishes, diapers, wiping small faces, washing small hands, zipping clothes, more diapers, dishes, and meals. Most days it felt as if the machinery inside me must surely smoke, sputter, and explode from overuse. Each night I barely made it to bed, hoping that I would wake up and find those days were only nightmares. I woke to find they were all too real.

Worst of all, I was becoming cross with the children. Josh was too little to understand why "playing rain" with Tige's Tinker

Toys caused me to shriek. I worried whether Tina could feel the tension in my arms as I nursed her, my mind only on getting through the next chore. One day when, for the first time in weeks, all the children seemed settled for their naps at once, I sat down for a blessed few minutes' rest. Tige's happy little face peeked around a corner. I screamed at him to go back to bed—saw the fear in his eyes, and felt my own detestable anger. Tige went quietly back to his room. I wept, too tired even to follow and soothe him.

On a snowy day in March, the radio news told of a young mother who had turned on the gas, put her head in the oven, and died. No explanation, the announcer said, for the suicide of this mother of three. It was too frighteningly clear to me. I could understand the feeling of dreading another day, of having heedlessly brought three small people into the world without the strength to care for them as they should be cared for, of working frantically every hour—not ever getting ahead, only a bit less behind.

Tears started again. I looked at my own oven. Electric. The best I could do was *broil* myself to death.

Anyway, I didn't have time for suicide that day. Tina was due at Dr. Murphy's for immunization shots. Dress all three, into the car, and drive through piles of dirty snow.

"Dr. Murphy, my milk is dwindling fast. I have to give her more and more supplementary bottles."

Dr. Murphy smiled his kind, wrinkled smile. "Five months of nursing for a third baby is just about right. You're tired, my dear. This *is* the hardest part of a young woman's life. The only good thing is that it *does* end."

It did? I had been too exhausted to think beyond each nightmare day. Now I felt only the usual sadness of ending this physical tie with my baby. I zipped up the children and drove back home.

George came home that evening in an unusually good mood. He had, he said after dinner, gotten the final quotation for the bomb shelter. The men could start the next week. Somewhere in my fog of fatigue I remembered his talk of a bomb shelter. I had said little, sure he would dismiss the idea on the sheer basis of cost. He had, instead, arranged for a loan. The bomb-shelter builders, he told me now, would excavate beneath the garage.

George was so seldom enthusiastic about anything that I hated to dampen his excitement, but $2,000 was too much to spend for something as impractical as this.

"George, dear, even if we felt we could keep our neighbors out at gunpoint, have you ever thought about where we live? The

Strategic Air Command is only ten miles away! If the Russians *did* attack, that would be their first target. And no pilot is going to drop just *one* bomb expecting a hit."

I had long ago accepted the fact that in a nuclear war we would have no place to go. Any attack worth its kopecks would land one or two bombs right on our heads. Spending $2,000 for some fantasy protection was too expensive. From the slipping smile on George's face I could see he grasped the logic.

"Well, Lois, I was only *talking* to the bomb-shelter people."

An hour later George said crossly, "Could I have your recent receipts?"

I pulled myself out of the chair I had finally collapsed in. Receipts to George were important, and I tried to go along, not really understanding why he wanted charge receipts when they would come again later with the bills. But I was glad George was responsible for paying the bills—one less chore for me.

I dug in my handbag for the crumpled papers I usually jammed there with one eye on the kids. I was rather proud that I had improved. Shopping with children was frantic at best, but I generally remembered to keep track of receipts. "Here, I've got them all—except for the quarter or thirty cents I spent for some thread today."

George's eyebrows dipped and—unusual for him—he scowled openly. "I need *all* the receipts. How could you have lost it?"

I had lost it, I explained, because Tige was climbing a counter, Josh had wandered out of sight, and Tina was crying. Now I looked at George incredulously as he launched into a lecture on my "irresponsibility." Then I knew exactly why the twenty-five-cent receipt had become so important. It was a fact of our marriage I had lived with for years.

George swallowed anger whenever he was proved wrong. The bomb-shelter episode was coming out in his tirade on receipts. I had, this time, been too tired to be subtle. I had too clearly pointed out his mistakes—and now he was pointing out one of mine.

Until this moment, dead with my usual fatigue and gazing up at George's scowling face, I had never realized what a difficult man I was married to. All the things I had hidden away marched out relentlessly as George recited my flaws. He had several of them absolutely right, but "extravagant," no; "selfish," hardly. I had kept myself awake too many evenings listening to his problems—

and then having him change the subject if I tried to talk about mine.

It was almost relaxing to look up at George and realize that I did not like him at all. Close up, the "stability" I had once admired was a growing rigidity—those suits and shoes compulsively hung and lined up. What I had seen as healthy caution was really a deep suspicion of people—George alienated workmen and made no friends at all. Whatever was closed inside George that he would never discuss had made him ungenerous—not only with money, but with attention and sympathy as well. I had often covered for George on social occasions when his remarks showed he had heard nothing of what was being discussed.

George ranted on. I had "refused to visit his parents." True: hauling three small children to Ohio was harder than having his young, healthy parents visit us. I "didn't care about the family budget." I, who saved hundreds by sewing and devising meal-making tricks? By now I was listlessly correcting his statements, knowing that with each reply he would switch accusations.

Suddenly, I realized I wanted to leave this unpleasant man. I had once misjudged him severely, fallen in love with qualities whose dark sides were then unrevealed. Now it would feel good never to see him again. Even my bone-deep fatigue lifted at the thought of taking my children and going.

Then, just as suddenly, all my new plans collapsed. I thought of telling Tige we were leaving his daddy behind. A wave of pain way beyond my control blocked the exit I thought I had reached. I could not do to my children what had been done to me. I knew much too well how it felt. Those damn memories had never gone away. Even the thought of telling Tige brought sobs up through my throat.

I felt like an animal trapped in a corner by my own emotions. George's words now—something about "using tears as weapons"— seemed to come from a distance. I would have to endure the situation as best I could—endure the fatigue that worried me, endure a marriage that was not working out. I was not the first woman to "stay for the sake of the children." Mother had not, but I had to try.

George left the room. It must have been almost ten. Earthquakes, floods, or bomb attacks would never keep George from his eight hours' sleep. I was alone, and it seemed a familiar way to be.

Chapter 16

THE NEXT MORNING I found that facing reality had released new energy. Perhaps a person lost in a forest feels better knowing for certain he is lost. No wasteful wishing it is not true. Acceptance makes one think, assess, and act. All right, I was "lost" for the moment—lost on a treadmill of fatigue and with a difficult husband. The path to divorce was blocked. I would have to find some other.

At breakfast I could say sincerely to George, "I'm sorry." I was— sorry that we were so different, sorry for whatever made him panic at his mistakes, sorry I could no longer be totally honest with him. As I cooked his eggs, I had already decided on one solution. Benjamin Franklin had advised: "Keep your eyes wide open before marriage, half-closed after." I thought I had married with wide-open eyes. Never mind. I would close them now.

Tige was up early. Just one glance at his glowing face as he looked at George made closing my eyes worth the effort.

"George, I'll try to be better about the receipts." That was the kind of apology George liked—nothing too probing, but accepting the blame.

George said, "O.K., Lois, I know you'll try." He looked relieved and gave Tige an extra hug.

As Tige waved from the window at his daddy's car, Josh's squeals told me another day had begun. I saw Irene Turner's housekeeper arrive. No solution there. My vow never to leave my children to go out to work had been reinforced one day when Mrs. Matta, the housekeeper, brought Linda to play with Tige. Linda had been carefully taught "Eenie, meenie . . . catch a *nigger* by the toe," and had been told, when she fidgeted, that her hand would fall off if she touched herself "down there." Irene had said often that Mrs. Matta was a "gem." "Never misses a day and keeps the house spotless." Mrs. Matta clumped up Irene's driveway. Hard as it was, I preferred to be home, to mess up my children if that was inevitable, but in my own way. I went to get Josh before Tina woke too.

That day I sorted more thoughts. All right, the days with pre-school children were, according to Dr. Murphy, the most exhausting time of a woman's life. I remembered a gray-haired woman in a store who had cooed at my children and said to me, "Enjoy them while they're young. It's such a short time." I had wondered then if she had a bad memory—or a smaller family. Now I wondered if she had simply blocked out her memories of inadequacy, panic, and deadly fatigue. Labor was dramatic for women to discuss, but the days of exhaustion, impatience, and self-doubt were probably kept secret or pushed aside.

Labor was dramatized in novels, in movies, and on TV. No one wrote of or showed the deadly days of rinsing diapers, scraping Pablum off tables and walls, of zipping, pinning, buttoning children you loved into winter clothes you hated, of wiping noses and bottoms and sticky or teary faces. In movies and novels, those days had so far been ignored. On television, spotless children romped happily in spotless homes while housewives, grinning (maniacally?), praised their floor wax.

I stopped, holding a half-washed pot of oatmeal. Good Lord, had I been taken in by commercials? I had written them myself; now I knew what the realities were! Was part of my dragging exhaustion simply guilt that I couldn't dance through my days adoring waxed floors?

I looked at my oven—not with suicide in mind, but at the mess left from an apple pie. The last time I cleaned it I had felt badly depressed. No great elation at a job well done, just guilt that I hated every minute I had spent—and would have to spend again too soon.

How many great insights, I wondered, come while holding oatmeal pots? Suddenly I knew how much easier it was going to be to hate unpleasant chores freely. The only woman who could feel orgiastic over scouring a broiler pan was a well-paid actress spouting lines written by the girl I once was—a girl who had never seen a broiler pan up close. Damn, I did *not* have to love those chores. I only had to do them.

One step out of the wasteland in which I had felt terribly lost. Tina cried. Josh and Tige fought over a toy again, *one* in their room of wall-to-wall toys. Dr. Murphy's words—and the gray-haired woman's—came back again: "such a short time" and "at least it's finally over." I separated the boys, Josh in the bedroom, Tige on the sofa with his pile of picture books. Then I looked at our street in a brand-new way. At the end of this winding road stood the school. Somehow I had never realized before that life did not remain static. Someday that wonderful institution at the top of the hill would accept my children day after day. Racing on my treadmill, I had simply never realized that this would not go on forever. Perhaps those wanderers in forests felt the same. Then, even though a sign read *"Fifty* miles to town," they would feel as I felt— a long, long way, but a measurable distance. In only eighteen months Tige could start kindergarten. I could manage those eighteen months now that I had measured them. Eighteen months for Josh, eighteen months for Tina—four and one-half years and the school up the hill would welcome them, teach them, and send them home to a less frantic mother. I was not sentenced for life to Pablum, diapers, and crayons on walls. It had only seemed that way. Four years was something I could now survive.

Back to the oatmeal pot—and then to a startling memory of my business days. Yes, solving one tangle had always made another idea develop. It was happening now.

"Tige, honey, how would you like to go to nursery school?"

Tige's blue eyes widened and his face lit up. "When, Mommy?"

"As soon as you don't wear diapers anymore." That rule had kept me from seriously considering nursery school for Tige before.

In two days Tige toilet-trained himself. Three days later, he was registered and scheduled for his first morning pickup. He raced to the car. At noon he related adventures until he conked out for his nap. He had met his new world and adored it. I would have to take my turns driving, but for five glorious mornings a week I would have only two children's needs to fill.

The year 1960 moved right along. As I folded fewer diapers, I could occasionally catch a newscast on the radio. "Negro" college students in North Carolina "sat in" at a Woolworth's lunch counter to protest segregation. President Eisenhower said we had no spy planes—and was caught in the lie when a U-2 was captured in Russia. I felt disillusioned that a President would lie. Richard Nixon was preparing to run against John Kennedy, and the FDA said the new birth-control pill was safe. I would vote, I decided, for Kennedy, but not for the Pill. It was too soon to tell if that was *really* safe.

I was a bit surprised when George came out strongly for Nixon. Years before, Nixon's "Checkers" speech had aroused my distrust. Yet everyone in the neighborhood seemed to be for Nixon. But George? Well, it might be good for Tige to know that parents could disagree. He happily wore a Nixon button on one side of his coat and a Kennedy button on the other.

Although my neighbors disapproved of Kennedy, they all seemed to support the sit-ins in the South. No such cruel segregation had ever existed in Omaha as far as I knew. Phyllis said it was "primitive" to treat "Negro" people that way. At the sewing club I had organized, we all talked smugly of "southern bigotry" and let it go at that.

Politics, the Pill, and southern segregation were, however, far less a part of my life than watching my children develop. While my neighborhood friends talked of specific goals for their children, I looked at mine and grinned. How could anyone know how inborn qualities would be used? Perceptive, sensitive Tige still had his speedometer stuck at seventy miles an hour. He might set speed records as a surgeon—or use his unlimited energy wiping windshields and filling gas tanks. Josh had an irresistible way of negotiating an extra cookie. Law? Or the best con man west of the Mississippi?

As I watched Tina grow, imagining a career for her was endlessly entertaining. For a while I had felt an unreasonable concern when she merely sat in her playpen, blond curls gleaming and green eyes simply observing her brothers' antics. If she had a passive personality inherited from Mother, we might always be as inscrutable to each other as Mother and I were. Well, if it were true, perhaps I could try to understand my daughter better than I did my mother.

Then one day Tina sat in her playpen while I sewed on buttons nearby. Her graceful little hands were arranged in her lap and her green eyes studied the playpen rails. A small hand reached out to grasp a bar. She pulled herself up, let go of the rail, and bounced down on her bottom. That, I expected, would be that. No, a second try, a third, a fourth. The fifth time she managed to balance herself on her tiny feet. With a toss of her head, she lowered herself to the playpen floor and played happily with her toys. I had watched, open-mouthed. She had set a goal and determinedly accomplished it. Beneath that blond, pink exterior was a strong-willed female I could understand.

By Tina's first birthday, she was more than holding her own with her brothers. In a toy dispute her decibel level exceeded theirs. Josh, now two and a half, said, "She's turned up *real* loud." Tige tried to look down her throat to see where it was all coming from. No need to say, "Be gentle with your baby sister." She had found her own way to function.

By early 1961, so had I. Shaking off the guilt had made housework easier. Despite what I had once believed was an endless time of frantic days with tiny children, the time had passed. In five months Josh would be ready for nursery school. Four months more and Tige would start kindergarten.

With the children just a bit older, I even had time—and energy —for activities outside the house: some more free-lance copy for the department store, an occasional visit with Sally Klein or Harriet Fischer, and evenings at PTA meetings. Harriet had teased me, "Tige isn't even *in* school yet." No, but service to the community, I had decided, was an important part of life. Writing our local school newsletter I considered an advance payment to the school where Tige, Josh, and Tina would learn and grow for years.

On April 11, 1961, Harriet also teased me into attending a Brotherhood luncheon at her synagogue. Brotherhood, indeed. I had heard all those platitudes too often before. Harriet said, laughing, "Oh, come on. We could use some WASPs there."

What, I asked, was a WASP?

"A white Anglo-Saxon Protestant. The safe-from-prejudice group. Like everyone else in your neighborhood."

Oh. Yes, Harriet was right. Phyllis, Zelda, and Clarice were WASPs too, but, I told Harriet, the neighborhood was all-WASP strictly by coincidence.

Harriet smiled. I agreed to go.

That luncheon was like the dislodged pebble that begins a landslide; eventually it would take George's job and destroy my innocence as well.

A group called the Panel of American Women spoke. The moderator, a woman named Esther Brown, introduced them. "We are not professionals," they said, "simply mothers and housewives." Each woman—a Catholic, a Jew, a Negro, and a WASP—told movingly personal stories. The Catholic woman told of being ridiculed as a child when she prayed with her beads at summer camp. The pretty blond Jewish mother confessed her hurt when she discovered that certain neighborhoods were closed to her family. Of all the humiliations described by the Negro woman—a teacher—being banned from using the library somehow seemed worst.

It was the Protestant woman who affected me most. "My children will never be called the hurtful names reserved for others. For this unearned privilege I feel I must do what I can to help. If not, then I must forever wear the face of a hypocrite."

As I stood in my kitchen sometime later, packing cartons for the movers, I experienced again the chill her words produced in me. I had never before realized how many doors were automatically opened for WASPs like George and me—and for my children. My career that had gone so well would never have started if my skin had been brown instead of white. Like the panelist, I owed some debt.

After the program I had approached the slim woman with the sable-colored skin. Did she, I had wondered, prefer to be called "colored," "Negro," what? For the moment it was no problem. I simply asked, "Mrs. Jenkins, what can I do to help?" She asked if my children's school had any Negro teachers.

So *Negro* was the preferred word—and her suggestion was tailor-made—if hardly a sacrifice—for me. My children *should* learn early that people come in different colors. I talked with our district superintendent, who said he would be "happy to hire a Negro teacher if one would only apply." And then, naïvely, I phoned the Urban League to place an order.

The president of the Urban League was a Negro surgeon, and his wife was a woman I liked. As our friendship grew, I wondered about their very small house. Finally Joan Benson admitted they had been trying to find a larger one.

With a lifetime of WASP innocence behind me, I volunteered to help. Why not our neighborhood? Paul Benson asked, "How would your neighbors feel?"

George was silent as I uttered sincere—and life-changing—words: "Our neighbors are much too intelligent to be bigots."

The woman up the street did willingly show her house to Joan and me. But the next day another woman friend called. The neighbors had seen me with Joan, had held a block meeting, and threatened to "get George's job." But how silly!

Even George, usually pessimistic, laughed at the threat. Joan tried to withdraw: "The house is too small." Paul was more direct. "They'll take it out on your children." How? "Leave them out of parties, not let them come over to play, call them nigger-lovers."

Until then I had been merely indignant at neighbors who called meetings behind our backs, distressed at a silly panic I felt I could alleviate. But my neighbors avoided me. The school newsletter I wrote was mysteriously "discontinued." It was, I believed, simply a misunderstanding. I would talk to them all and explain that Paul and Joan's standards were equal to—if not much higher than —ours. My neighbors would surely understand. Paul and Joan shook their heads in wonder. It didn't work that way, and my children *could* be hurt.

I asked George what he thought. "It's you who are in the neighborhood all day," he said. "I guess it's up to you." While George slept, I sat up and thought.

In my single days, I thought as I looked out over the valley, my decisions had affected only me. Then when the corporation had wanted to meet me, I had learned with a shock that things had changed. What I did affected others—in this case my children. Why risk Tige's or Josh's or Tina's being hurt by my beliefs? They were too young to know what *nigger-lover* meant, but they would know if children had parties and they were left out.

I tried to persuade myself to forget the whole thing. Paul and Joan had asked me to. George, I suspected, would be relieved. Integration was no problem of mine, no cause I had ever espoused. In my days in the South it had been merely the *illogic* that bothered me, not the injustice. The injustice bothered me now, but I didn't have the right to hurt my children because of it. Fine. Done. Decision made. Three children, sleeping now, would never know how close they had come to being hurt by their mother's beliefs.

I got up to go to bed and then sat down again. Which would hurt my children more—names from playmates and being left out, or a mother who backed down in panic when doing what was right got rough? I had read only recently, in a woman psychiatrist's book, that unconscious feelings come through to a child. My feelings of fear would be there, saying, "Run like hell if things get tough." For the rest of my life I would know that I had. My children would know it too. If they then backed down when things got difficult—in school, in jobs, in love—they would have learned from me that it was right to run.

My choice that night seemed inevitable. Only years from now, I thought as I went to bed, will I know if it is right.

For months, everything went well. Old friends were replaced by new ones, for me and for the children. In our yard and Joan's, our children played together, looking, I felt, as the world ought to look. Our adult friends mixed too. I learned that, among the more militant, *black* was now preferred.

And then, on the first working day of the New Year, 1962, George came through the door, his features looking like melted gray wax. "I've been told I can either resign or take a demotion and transfer to Philadelphia."

Why? What had happened at work? There had been, George said bleakly, no explanation, just the choice. He looked anesthetized.

I didn't wait for George to blame me. I blamed myself. "It's all my fault. I did this to us." George just shook his head. At that moment I felt that whatever flaws he had, I owed him a lifetime of gratitude. George, who so feared his own mistakes, was not blaming me for the awful mistake that had cost him his job.

George said only, "What should we do? Take the transfer or stay here and hope I can find another job?"

To me, that decision was easy. Much as I hated to leave a house I loved, there was no future here. Who in Omaha would hire a man with a wife like me? In big, impersonal Philadelphia it would be different.

"Honey, there'll be hundreds of jobs in a big city like that." The job to which he was transferring would last a year. Meanwhile, he would have plenty of time to find something much, much better. I put on my Pollyanna optimism like a life-jacket.

In February, George left to start his new job. I stayed behind to sell the house. Paul and Joan refused my offer to sell it to them. "The corporation can still fire George in Philadelphia," Paul said.

As strangers trooped through the house and George phoned often about neighborhoods he was exploring in Philadelphia, another decision had taken shape in my mind. "George, when this house is sold, I think we ought to buy in an integrated Philadelphia neighborhood if there is one there." George was silent. I went on.

"I'd try very hard not to mess up your career again, but in an-

217

other all-WASP suburb something might happen. An already integrated neighborhood would be a lot safer." Better too for the children. Only as we were leaving Rockbrook did I realize that they would have been college age before going to school with anything but middle-class WASPs. Growing up with children *unlike* themselves would provide the kind of education they needed to function in the world. George agreed to ask realtors about neighborhoods already mixed.

In early June of 1962, as I cleared out the kitchen cupboards and prepared for our move, it seemed as if my incredible single-days' luck had returned. We had sold our Omaha house for a whopping profit. After two trips to Philadelphia, I had found our integrated neighborhood and a house I had never dreamed could be ours.

At first I had been sure there was some mistake. No enormous stone mansion on a tree-tunneled street could be bought on our $35,000 budget. Eighteen big, sunny rooms and an acre of ground; thick stone walls for easy heating and a beautiful staircase down which Tina could glide as a bride.

"George, there must be something wrong. Termites, a sinking foundation, or plans for an expressway or something." There were other "For Sale" signs up and down the quiet, luxurious street. But I had seen a black family—man, woman, and child—raking winter leaves from the lawn of a beautiful house on the corner. An integrated block was exactly right; now if only this magnificent bargain was too.

George finally agreed it was worth an architect's fee to have the house inspected before we bought or turned it down. The architect had grinned: "If you don't buy it at this price, I will. They haven't built houses like this for fifty years and never will again."

One more item to check on. "George, let's walk to the school." Three blocks away—along wide, safe sidewalks, past a small grocery, a shoe-repair shop, a candy store, the kinds of shops I had explored as a child—stood the school that our children would attend. It was closed for the summer, but I knew what was inside— the same wide stairways and big rooms I had known. I could even recall the odors of chalk dust, newly washed marble, and the pungent smell of cleaning compound that had always meant First Day of School. No walk along narrow suburban roads for my children now. They could, as I had, visit shopkeepers along the way, watch shoes being repaired and groceries sold, stand in delicious indecision in front of a candy counter.

In front of the school, I looked up at George. "Please, let's buy the house."

"It's awfully big."

"With an awfully big yard. Just think what you could plant."

I had already decided that families create x amount of dirt. It could be concentrated, as it had been, in our three-bedroom house or spread around the eight-bedroom house I wanted now. Bedrooms and baths for each of the children, a playroom, a study, a room to sew in, a den. A bit overwhelming, yes, but I had learned from the realtor that it had been built by a father as a wedding gift to a much-beloved daughter. In 1912 he had built a wonderful house in which to raise children—a perfect house in which I would raise mine. "George, you could plant a big garden. Let's buy it. I know it's right."

The dishes I now took from the shelves in Omaha would soon be housed in a *butler's pantry* in our new Philadelphia home. Paul Benson had laughed. "You didn't *know* why the house was so cheap? It's because one of *us* moved onto the block." Strange that the mixed block I had wanted had given me this magnificent house. I would miss Joan and Paul, Sally, Harriet, and other new friends. In a way I would miss my serene WASP innocence, forever destroyed. But the whole sad episode had forced a new start and given us a house in which the children—and their mother too —would have space to grow.

On June 18, our seventh wedding anniversary, I asked George to carry me across the threshold of our Westview Street house, past the huge and heavy walnut door, into the center hall. The children would grow up and someday leave, but not me. I hugged George. "The next time I'm carried through that door, I plan to be dead." I was sure I had come home to stay.

The following months were like opening gifts. The house, the neighborhood, the city were filled with delightful surprises. The children were thrilled with their "very own rooms." Tina, now two and a half, felt grown-up in her new bed without crib bars. "No more diapers," she announced. "Pink panties now." My diaper days were done. Children from the neighborhood quickly filled our yard: black, brown, white, even Oriental—and not, I learned with relief, solely middle-class.

A regal-looking woman rang my bell. She was Vangie Peters, principal of the Willis Schol, and she was so looking forward to welcoming my children. How friendly, how nice! Nothing like that had ever happened in the suburbs.

The houses around us, all as splendid as ours, removed their "For Sale" signs, one by one. Apparently our moving in had persuaded our neighbors that the block had not "gone." The owner of the house next door, a dowager in hat and gloves, paid a formal call. "I'm sure," she said, "your furniture will be arriving soon." Best not to tell her that it *had* arrived. It did look a bit lonely scattered around our enormous house.

July and August were spent, for the most part, in the Salvation Army, Goodwill, museums, and the zoo. The children romped as happily in the Salvation Army and other used-furniture shops as they did at the Franklin Institute. Store owners usually had boxes of mysterious junk for them to rummage through while I shopped to fill up our house.

At the museums I trained my eye while exploring Colonial rooms. At the junk shops I learned that reproductions were cheap —that *discarded* reproductions were just this side of free! Big, bulky furniture, too big for modern houses but perfect for mine, went for the proverbial song. Worn Oriental rugs were piled in careless heaps. They were no more worn than the rugs I had seen in the museum rooms, and the price was decidedly right. Soon our modern furniture was being moved to the second floor, then up to the third. From there, I teased George, I would simply heave it out the window to be hauled away. Meanwhile, my treasure hunts in junk shops were much more fun than buying new furniture could possibly be.

Between raids on the junk shops, the children and I made friends. With six-year-old Tige in charge, they could safely roam the wide sidewalks, walk to the candy store, visit a friendly car repairman, and even "help" the shoemaker as I had done. They returned from their expeditions with treats, smiles, and troops of other children.

My own first friend—and I suspected she would be my best friend—was Barbara Hamilton. A friend of Joan's, she had written me in Omaha with information and welcome. We had talked on the phone during my house-hunting trips. She was pleased we would live only three blocks apart, and now we would finally meet.

The look of surprise on her round, dark-brown face and then her unexpected reserve puzzled me. While her daughter, Paula, just Tina's age, melted happily into the backyard games, Barbara sat stiffly inside. At last she looked closely at her white-gloved hands and then directly at me. "I didn't know that you were white. Joan never explained."

By the end of our visit, Barbara had run the mysterious tests that I now knew black people ran on whites. I was glad I had passed whatever they were. We could talk like two women, two mothers, two friends. There was something about this quiet, contemplative woman that made me feel we would be friends for a long, long time.

My second-best friend lived conveniently next door. Sandra Kane's bright-red hair and translucent redhead's skin caught my eye as she came up the walk. Sandra, I learned, was a psychiatric social worker, and her husband, Dave, was a struggling attorney. They had bought and refurbished the carriage house of the big house next door.

"How did you know about our Mt. Airy section from way out in Omaha?" Sandra asked. "Realtors seldom show WASPs houses here. They save 'em for Chestnut Hill."

When I looked confused, Sandra explained. West Mt. Airy had once been an all-WASP section. "Then *my* people bought houses and most Gentiles fled. Then a whole lot later a Negro judge bought a house and the cycle *could* have continued." But the neighborhood, Sandra went on, had a lot of luck. The mayor's human relations director lived here too, and he had known how to quell a panic. "West Mt. Airy Neighbors, the school people, and a lot of others helped. Young professionals—both Negro and white —bought the small houses. We were worried about big houses like yours. You know, they could have become nursing homes or something like that."

I winced at the thought of our wonderful house being anything but a family home. Sandra continued: "I think *your* former owners decided to put a ridiculous price on the house and hope to attract some whites. Do you have any idea how many of the folks across the street were holding their breath until your blond kids trooped in?"

For just a moment I felt distressed. Would the price have been higher if we had not been white? I felt like the receiver of stolen goods.

Sandra read my face. "Don't be silly. It's good for the neighborhood having more WASPs move in."

Those were her comforting words. Her *discomforting* words involved Tige and the school. She had no children herself, but she

221

said, "It'll be interesting to see how a suburban kid adjusts. He'll probably have a Negro teacher and only about half the first grade is white. Let's hope Tige wasn't scarred by the Omaha experience. He may see Negroes as causing a family crisis and have some problems at school."

That night, with the children in bed, I sat in my luxurious sitting room off the master bedroom. The big sliding mahogany doors could be closed so that George could sleep while I sat on my chaise (slightly worn, but only $16) and read. But instead of reading, I held the book and worried.

I had been so pleased with the house and the neighborhood and with the children's future in school—and I had been terribly wrong before. Just as I had believed my Omaha neighbors could *not* be prejudiced, I believed my children would enjoy the mix of people in their new school. Sandra, with her professional knowledge, could be right. True, Tige seemed to like Barbara Hamilton. When he played with her son, Jimmy, at their house, he behaved well. But Sandra had said there were children at school from a much rougher section of Mt. Airy. How would Tige react to a *yardful* of children, at least half of them with brown skin that might mean "crisis" to him? Perhaps with my impulses in Omaha and here I had put my children into situations that might scar them for life.

Tige's first day of school came awfully quickly. Part of me was excited for him. "You'll learn to read, honey. And once you can read, there's nothing in the world you can't find out about. It's like having a special key that unlocks every door." Tige had to be restrained from leaving much too early for school.

At home, Josh and Tina played in their big, sunny playroom. Nursery school, for both of them, would start the following week. The frantic days had passed. Soon I would have five mornings a week actually to plan my time and have a fighting chance to carry plans out. If, of course, there were no severe problems at school. I watched the clock and straightened bureau drawers, something I did only under stress.

At lunchtime, a sober-faced Tige walked up the driveway. My heart took a lurch. No running and jumping as Tige usually did. I met him outside the door.

His blue eyes looked up at me seriously. What terrible things would he have to say? "Mom," he began, "I've been thinking about it all the way home. That school is just as nice as you are. They like everyone."

I hugged my son. Nobel Prizes, Academy Awards, or bulging bank accounts were nothing compared to Tige's compliment. What on earth could be more deeply prized than finding out that your child shares your values and likes you for them? All those chaotic preschool days paid off in a moment like this.

By Christmas, all my children were showing signs of their multi-cultural benefits. Tina, now three, had her first boyfriend. Leonard, a coffee-colored little boy, brought her candies, leaves, and abject adoration. His mother asked if Tina could come with them to Christmas Mass.

"Mommy," she reported excitedly, "there were ladies there dressed like penguins." Nuns, I explained. "There were candles, Mommy, and little boys in nightgowns, and it smelled so nice. Can I go again?"

I said of course, and thought of my father. At Tina's age I too had been enthralled by the smells, sights, and sounds of the Catholic church. I made the lump in my throat go away. Tina's father would never leave. I had chosen well.

Josh went to an African-Methodist-Episcopal church with a friend from nursery school. He returned with a bag full of Christmas candy and, as he munched away, the comment that "I didn't know some angels were brown."

Tige came home from school proudly bearing a Chanukah decoration. "I told the teacher I made Christmas stuff *last* year."

Our house, lovely all year long, was magnificent at Christmas. There was plenty of room for a ten-foot tree, for tinsel garlands laced through the stairway railings, for a gigantic wreath on the enormous front door—and three fireplaces, Josh reminded me. "No, dear, not stockings at each!"

On New Year's Eve, I began what I hoped to make a tradition, phoning people I had met and liked and asking if they were free that night. A grab bag of people like us—not night-club goers or the socially frantic—shared our celebration. With the worn Oriental rolled up in the center hall, we danced to records. When I danced with George, I did what I had done for years—blocked out the music and followed his lead. It was small payment for my reliable husband. In this house I loved, 1963, I felt, would be an incomparable year.

On a snowy night in January, I sat in the study, still filled with too much holiday joy to sleep. Only a year ago our family life had seemed to crash. And now, almost *because* of the error I had made, my children were growing up in a place so much better than the one we had been forced to leave . . . in a house that seemed to exude family warmth, in a neighborhood that reflected the world.

It would be a late Christmas card, but I wanted to thank the whole damned city for what we had found—truly peace in our home and, around us, good will toward man.

Silly, but harmless, I thought as I went to my typewriter. A letter to the editors of the *Philadelphia Bulletin* would drain off emotions so that I could sleep. I wrote of the benefits we had enjoyed since we left the suburbs for our integrated neighborhood. It worked; I went smilingly to bed and to sleep.

In the morning I briefly debated mailing the letter. It had accomplished its purpose the night before. But why not? A letter like that could never change anyone's life.

Chapter 17

THE LETTER WAS PUBLISHED the following Sunday—and our phone began to ring—neighbors who were delighted I had expressed their feelings exactly, dozens of voices all with nice things to say. I was glad I had mailed my impulsive letter. A few suburbanites had even asked if houses here were still available. Their children too, they felt, could benefit from our cultural mix.

For the next week, life went on as usual. In the mornings Tige went off to first grade, Josh and Tina to nursery school, and George to work. Sometimes as I watched him from the kitchen window, I wondered if I should remind him that he should be doing more to find a new job. I had reminded him quite a bit, and it was hard to understand why the usually pessimistic George felt, this time, that his Philadelphia-branch job would last. We had known it was scheduled to end in a year. But George had said that it might not end and that looking for jobs on a lunch hour or after work was "impossible."

For once, *I* was the pessimist. I had grabbed at Jane's offer to write Sieve and Knox, the ad agency people she had met at some utility convention. I was already writing television commercials for them while the children were in school, building our savings account and my relationship with Sieve and Knox against the day I might have to work full-time to feed my children and keep our house. Even thinking of leaving my children hurt. George would,

I told myself, do something serious about job contacts soon. Meanwhile, I did my commercials on pretzels, paint, and sausage while I tried to bolster George's ego and hoped he would act.

I had just come back with Josh and Tina from their cooperative nursery school. It had been my day to be "helping mother" and I had never realized how many children had *not* been taught to button their coats. They were, I reminded myself, the children of "involved" women—active in hordes of committees and projects. Rather grimly, I had zipped and buttoned nineteen coats while Josh and Tina smugly buttoned their own. Civic projects, I had mumbled, should—like charity—begin at home.

While the children ate their lunch, I checked the mail. Who was B. A. Bergman at the *Bulletin* and why was he writing to me?

I read the brief letter twice. He had read my letter in the Letters column and wondered if I would care to expand it into an article. He was editor of the *Bulletin*'s Sunday magazine.

Would I! A page, maybe two, on our wonderful neighborhood would be exciting to write. I could hardly believe his offer: all that space to tell our story—free.

While Josh and Tina napped, the words spilled out of my typewriter. I had never done "noncommercial" writing before, but I had believed in products and I believed in our neighborhood even more. Surely nothing written so quickly could be very good, but Mr. Bergman had asked me to come to see him and at least I would have a first draft to show.

With a bit of arranging, I made the appointment. I could take Josh and Tina to nursery school, catch the local to the *Bulletin,* and be back in time to pick them up. As I sat in Mr. Bergman's glassed-in cubicle amid the usual newspaper office chaos, I hoped his opinion of the article I handed him would be brief. A fast "Terrible!" would give me time to catch the train.

Mr. Bergman, a short, stout, gray-haired man, bent over my papers while I watched the clock. His phone rang. "No," he growled, "I *said* use Syd. And *you* use your head." He slammed down the phone. With his disposition, I wondered if he would do anything more than just tell me to go.

He finished reading, put my papers aside, and looked at me over his glasses. "Who wrote this for you?"

I fought a surge of indignation. It was, I decided, a compliment. It must be better than he thought someone like me could do. That made two of us. "I wrote it myself, of course. Why?"

"Well, I like it. I'm going to run it." He stood up in dismissal. "And send me anything else you write."

Fat chance, I thought, as I walked back to the train. I was a mother and housewife, not an aspiring writer. Whatever spare time I had was devoted to pretzel commercials to keep contacts open in case George lost his job. But, as I settled myself on the train for the ten-minute ride, I did feel rather pleased. A gruff big-city editor had liked what I wrote. If he ran it without too many changes, a whole city—millions in fact—would read about something that was important to me. And—I glanced at my watch —I could pick up the children in plenty of time.

Three days later, another *Bulletin* envelope came in the mail. Ah, Mr. Bergman had changed his mind. No! The envelope contained a check—for $100!

George was enthusiastic. This time I had cautiously asked whether writing the article could affect his job. It didn't seem likely to me. The corporation might care if I tried to integrate a neighborhood, but not if we chose one ourselves. George had agreed. Now he was pleased I had actually been paid. He held up the note that came with the check. "He says he wants you to write more." Well, I probably wouldn't, but the invitation was flattering.

The article ran on Mother's Day. That Sunday I paged through the magazine to find the story. It was hard to miss. My family looked out at me from a big color photo. I read the text. How great! They had not changed a word.

The phone rang all day. And all week long packets of letters arrived, forwarded by the paper. Of several hundred, only one was nasty: "May your daughter marry a big, fat nigger"—unsigned, of course, by the writer, who cared nothing for the marital future of my *sons*. Answering the letters took lots of time, but the chore was worth it. Almost two dozen white people had written to ask about houses for sale.

And then it seemed time for the excitement to be over, back, with a certain relief, to the daily routine. While the children were away in the mornings, I wrote commercials and, when I was through, found myself straightening my closets. Odd; neat closets had never been a hobby of mine; especially now that George and I had separate closets—his as neat as always, mine its usual mess. I untangled clothes from hooks, paired shoes I seldom wore. When this was done, I told myself, there were always the bureau drawers.

Then, holding a shoe in my hand and wondering if its mate still existed, I stopped. All right, I admitted, I was treading water. Mr. Bergman had said, "Send me anything else you write." This had lodged somewhere in my mind and I suppressed it, telling myself that the neighborhood article had been a fluke. *Real* writers wrote, were rejected, wrote, were rejected again. Sure, I loved writing, but it made demands that might interfere with my kids. I had much too carefully avoided outside work—even Sieve and Knox understood my *family* deadlines had to come first. If I avoided outside work that might take me away from the children physically, work at home might take some emotional toll. I crawled to the back of the closet to find the other shoe.

On my hands and knees, dodging dresses, I finally laughed at myself. I was fighting a conflict that did not exist. There was one easy way to resolve it: write another article for Mr. Bergman, get his polite "Sorry," and forget it all. Finding the other shoe could wait.

At the typewriter I plucked a subject from my head. Experts, these days, were writing about women: "unfulfilled," "confused in their role." Jolly well right! In my mind I went back to those days with small children. Any woman *not* confused and unfulfilled by diapers, Pablum, and chaos was either heavily into pills or had secretly had a lobotomy.

I didn't even retype the piece. I mailed it when I went to pick up Josh and Tina. So much for my early-aborted writing career. So much for experts on women.

A check came five days later along with Mr. Bergman's note: "Send more. I like it." This was ridiculous, I said to George.

"Well, Lois, as long as he keeps sending you money . . ."

In quick order, I typed out my opinions on watching baseball ("Take Me *Out* of the Ball Game"), on the advantages of marrying "old," and on my long-held distaste for exercise ("No, Thanks, I'll Just Sit Here"). Each time, a check came back. More flukes, I insisted. Those offbeat opinions had fermented in my mind for years. I would soon use them up.

Even George now seemed incredulous. Mr. Bergman had, without my asking, raised the price he paid—$100, $150, $200. George looked at a check. "Well," he said drily, "I wish someone paid *me* for expressing opinions."

It would stop, I was sure. But at least my morning writing hours didn't interfere with our family life. Family life actually helped the writing. I wrote one article about the frank, if embarrassing, things children say out loud: "Why is that lady fat? Why do nuns dress like penguins?" There are better answers, I wrote, than "Shh." A small religious magazine asked to reprint that piece; an author asked for permission to include my anti-exercise piece in his book. Nine o'clock until noon became hours I enjoyed, but if Tina felt ill at nursery school or Josh picked a fight or Tige's teacher felt pressed to complain about my son's inability to sit still in class, I found I could leave my work with no backward look and take it up the next day.

Often, working on an article in the room I had set up as my study, it seemed as if I had stumbled into the best of all possible worlds for a woman. I had work I loved and yet I was immediately available to my children. Sometimes I wondered what might have happened if writing were not my forte. Well, women painted, taught, sold real estate, or, according to articles in women's magazines, developed businesses they could run out of their homes. Meanwhile, I was having a marvelous time—and had earned enough money to send the children to summer day camp. While they learned swimming, baseball, and handicrafts, I could write all day.

In July, Sandra Kane waved a copy of *The Feminine Mystique* across the fence. "You've *got* to read it!" It was good to find out that women all over the country loathed housework as much as I, felt just as trapped through the preschool years. But other portions puzzled me. Why did women *allow* college officials, as Betty Friedan wrote, to steer them away from "male" courses? Or allow society—or their mothers—to push them into early marriages? Why didn't they simply change jobs if they weren't paid as much as men? If they were "exploited" by their husbands, why didn't they protest? (When George read the paper before a party, one "Hey, pal, it's your party too" had solved the problem forever.) Still, Friedan ended with a Life Plan for Women that I truly approved—early careers and late marriages. I returned Sandra's book. I would have Tina read it someday.

In late August, a newscast pushed books and writing out of my mind. While Barbara Hamilton and I sat in her kitchen and our children played outside, the radio reported "problems" in Folcroft. A black couple had bought a house. The all-white neighborhood was rioting.

Barbara's brown face creased with resignation and pain. "I'm afraid I know exactly what will happen."

Not here! Not five miles from our integrated neighborhood.

Barbara, unfortunately, was right. The neighbors threw rocks, ripped out utility lines to the house, set fires. At night the neighborhood men participated. During the day, the television cameras showed women, their hair in rollers, their faces contorted with hate. Nearby, children imitated their mothers, throwing rocks and hissing names. Not one generation but two were involved in this spasm of hate. The black couple had two small children.

I turned to Barbara. "What can we do?" She shook her head in resignation.

Two weeks later—four days after Josh began kindergarten and Tige began the second grade—a church was bombed in Birmingham, Alabama. Two small black girls were killed. In Folcroft, the young black family was still under siege. While my children played happily in their integrated school, others were willing to kill to prevent integration.

Over and over again, I said to Barbara, "There must be *something* we can do." Even Barbara's husband, Leland, an aggressive, dynamic minister, could make no suggestions. Leland, who knew of our Omaha experience, said kindly, "Don't feel guilty. You've paid your dues."

Guilt was not what I felt. Obligation was more like it. We had not merely survived the Omaha crisis, we had thrived. Our neighborhood, our house, the children's education—life was exactly as I had hoped it would be—*for us,* but not for the families in Birmingham, the Folcroft family, or their panicked white neighbors.

One fall day as Barbara's Paula and my Tina romped on our lawn, Barbara put down her coffee cup and looked out from our terrace at our two little girls. "You know what you *could* do, Lois," she said thoughtfully. "You could write about all you've learned as a WASP. The Omaha experience, living here—things like that."

"No, Barbara. I wish I could, but I can't. I've got too many strong feelings about it and I just can't write that well."

"You wrote the neighborhood story for the *Bulletin*."

Yes, but. "Well, I suppose I could try to rewrite it, make it good enough for a national magazine."

Barbara smiled.

But her mention of Omaha had tripped a switch in my mind. If four housewives from Kansas City had awakened *me,* perhaps a

Panel of American Women might work out here. I poured Barbara another cup of coffee and began to explain.

Months later, the Panel of Philadelphians was organized, functioning, and effective. The personal stories of the panel women did indeed move audiences to think—and often to act as the Omaha panel had done for me.

When Mr. Bergman phoned to complain he had "no Stalvey pieces to run," he .was willing to accept a piece on the panel. It was easy to write it—and to weave in the important things the panelists said. Letters poured in, requests to speak, but also "I never thought of that before." The panel women were having an undeniable impact on a big city.

Making time for panel appearances, some writing time, and commercials for Sieve and Knox called for the same organization I had learned in business days. But a big house really had proved easier to keep up—with so much room, nothing looked messy. Everything was scheduled around the children's school hours. Panel dates were mostly in the evening when George was home.

George, I decided one evening while putting leftovers away after dinner, was still—and would always be—George. He still bridled at any hint of criticism. I had tried at least a hundred ways to encourage him to find another job. No matter how I phrased it, George turned it into an accusation. "When do you expect me to job-hunt? On my lunch hour? After work? You're pushing me too hard."

Since it was well past the year after which his job was to have been eliminated, pushing was not inappropriate. It just didn't work. I took all the free-lance commercials Sieve and Knox assigned, hoping I would not have to use the money or the contact if George's job ended.

Still, when I thought of George upstairs in his den checking receipts or creating new files, I realized that things could be worse. He was good with the children. On weekends he made time to take them for hikes in the woods—always at the same time and on the same route, but they seemed to enjoy it. When Tina crawled up on his lap, I often got misty-eyed. My daughter, at least, had what I had wanted so much.

The success of the article on the Panel of Philadelphians reactivated Barbara's suggestion. Sitting in my study, *thinking* of redoing the neighborhood article—or the panel piece—for a national magazine made me realize why I had not. Tapping out articles for the *Bulletin* had been pleasant. I had felt successful. Writing for *Woman's Day, Family Circle,* or other magazines that reached across the country would not be so easy. And it would hurt like *hell* when, inevitably, my articles were rejected, at least at first.

That day I sat in front of my empty typewriter wondering how often people had to face the possibility of rejection in order to have a chance for success. It would be so much easier to keep things as they were. Mr. Bergman might be the only editor in the entire country who liked the way I wrote. Why find out I wasn't good enough for anyone else? I was no longer a fourteen-year-old, holding a sample column in a sweaty hand. I did not *need* to build a career. This time, I need not even think of walking away. I could simply sit there and do nothing.

And, again, never know. I put a sheet of paper into my type-writer. All right, at least I would find out. And no holding back so that I could reassure myself I might have succeeded if I had *really* tried.

The first rejection notice did hurt. *Good Housekeeping* felt my carefully rewritten article on our neighborhood "did not meet their needs." *McCall's* wrote that the panel piece was "nice, but not for us." While I was mailing and remailing the articles, I re-minded myself of the many best-selling books that (I read) had been turned down many times. Perhaps, I hoped, it was true of articles too. While waiting for the mail each day, I wrote other articles, most involving episodes with the children. If magazines liked these homey pieces, perhaps they would eventually buy the pieces on race. George raised his eyebrows over the postage. I was, I reminded him, making money for us by writing commercials. But even the life-with-children articles, like bottles tossed into the water, floated dismally back.

Still, although mail time, with its flock of "Not for us" and "Sorry" replies, was depressing, at least time with my children was not. It was rewarding to watch them grow, to see the development of qualities I had noticed long before. Tige had never stopped his mile-a-minute activity, maddening to teachers who valued immo-bility over innovative thought. But he read widely and well and, with his loving nature, made dozens of friends. Body-contact Josh sometimes got into trouble over kissing girls or wrestling with the boys. But he was beginning to understand that it paid to wait un-til each group was willing. Both boys had inherited my casual attitude toward grades. But not Tina. She had hit first grade determined to compete. Just as she had pulled herself up on her playpen bars until she conquered standing, so she now crumpled paper after paper, trying to achieve perfection. Within that blond, blue-eyed doll-like girl, a solid steel core lay hidden.

Tige quipped, "I think she'll be the first lady President—and then no more elections after that!"

Often, picking my children up from school, shopping with them, or exploring museums, I was struck by how much I *enjoyed* them. Older now, they were fun to be with. Their small heads were full of opinions, ideas, plans, and discoveries. Whatever else went right or wrong in my life, my interesting children were there. The frantic days of diapers and chaos had been simply a prepayment for now.

When, finally, the acceptances for my articles came, it seemed as if they came all at once. *Parent's* bought a humor piece, *Redbook* bought my story of the mischievous boy next door, and *McCall's* bought the article on the neighborhood—on its last time out, when I was planning to give up on it for good.

And in June, George lost his job.

When he announced, gray-faced, that his department, as planned, was indeed to be eliminated, there seemed no time for recriminations. I had only one question: How long would our savings support us? I had banked every penny I earned, used every meal-planning trick I had created against this day. George worked with the figures. Nine months.

Now writing résumés and letters for George became a part of my days while I counted off the months. Even the *thought* of leaving my children for a full-time job brought tears. The agency was willing to hire me—"Just let us know"—but, oh, how I hoped it need not be.

Friends I had made—both black and white—were helpful. Judge Raymond Pace Alexander, one of Philadelphia's first black judges, arranged interviews galore. In March, George went to Washington to see about a government job. I had little hope. The nine months had passed. I was steeling myself to call Sieve and Knox to say I would start the next week.

George came beaming into the study that afternoon. "I got a job!" For a moment I could hardly remember which interview he had had. All that mattered was that I would not have to leave my children—and they would eat.

"Believe it or not, I'll be working on school desegregation for the government. The director read that *Bulletin* article you wrote on the neighborhood. He said he'd rather have someone with a strong commitment than one with bureaucratic experience."

That night, after the celebration, after the relief, I sat up late. George had never really enjoyed the world of advertising. He might be much better suited to government work. In a round-about way, he might finally have found a job in which he would be happy.

Funny how small things worked out: that impulsive letter to the editor, the request to do the article—the article that George said had made the difference for his new job, the article that would let me stay home with my children *and* do the work I had come to love.

The day after the news about George's new job, another mother was murdered. Viola Liuzzo—white, just my age—died driving back from an Alabama civil rights rally. In May, death came closer to home. The father of one of Tina's playmates was beaten and died when white teen-agers attacked him for using "their" park. In August, I turned forty. If that "crucial" birthday might have had any effect on me, it was obliterated by the slaughter in Watts. Everything I knew about journalism was offended when I read through the long reports on property damage to the casual mention that thirty-three black Americans had been killed. In Philadelphia, the NAACP picketed Girard College trying to change its "whites-only" rules.

It was becoming harder and harder for me to understand why people had to picket and die for integration when our mixed school functioned so well. As my children progressed in school, their classes had become more predominantly black. Some white families, proud of having participated in *southern* integration marches, had fled to private schools. It was hard for me to understand why. On the playground and in the classroom, my children were doing well.

Yet outside our unusual neighborhood, 1966 and 1967 brought upheaval and death all across the country. Night after night the panel women spoke to different audiences. I wrote an article for the *Bulletin* on a panicked neighborhood nearby. *Woman's Day* bought my article on the panel. After it was published, women wrote from all over to ask how to organize a panel in their town. Women could have some effect on the terrible turmoil in America, and I was glad my writing had helped, but it did not seem enough. When black *children* were killed in Newark or Detroit, I agonized helplessly to Barbara.

"Someday," she said, "you'll write about everything you've learned and felt and feel. Not articles, but a book for whites."

The plaint that I knew nothing about writing a book died in my throat as I looked at Barbara's face. So often I had asked, "What can I do?" And she had been telling me for years. Maybe that was how enormous, impossible tasks got started—they became something one *had* to do.

All right, damn it, I would write a book. Other women with children had. Who? Well, Harriet Beecher Stowe, for one. I was not sure who else, but one was enough. If *any* mother had done it before, at least I stood a chance.

It would be about what I had learned in the past five years—my education—the education of a WASP.

Chapter 18

THAT FIRST MORNING, beginning the book, I decided it was best not to think about the enormity of the chore. Ordinary people did not write books; they were written by people with education (at least a college degree!) and years of training—not by housewives with three children, a once-a-week cleaning woman, and a frequently absent husband. Tightrope walkers, I had read, who thought about the height, the swaying rope, and their shaky feet were likely to plunge. Best to concentrate on some safe platform way up ahead and to think of how to get there.

How *did* one get there? Which publishers were likely to accept the kind of book I wanted—had—to write? I opened a book. How convenient! The publisher's address was printed inside.

Perhaps the way to start this outrageous task was to condense what I wanted to write—describe it in one paragraph—and send it to a list of publishers, one by one. Perhaps by the time I finished writing the book, one of them would have expressed an interest. I made the list and began the paragraph.

By lunchtime, when the children came home, part of my mind was still arranging words. No good. Josh told me a long, long story to which I replied, "Sorry, honey, my mind was wandering." He cheerfully began again, but as I served the hamburgers and poured the milk, I made my vow. For five hours a day, I could be a writer—nine to twelve and one to three. I was a mother for the rest of the time. My study door must be like Alice's looking glass. When I passed through it in either direction, my world changed.

George came home that weekend. "How will you find time to write a book?" Simple. No more articles for a while, and the panel could easily run without me. No need, now that George had a job, to keep writing commercials.

Sandra Kane was negative too. "Women with children don't write books. Sylvia Plath committed suicide, it's my opinion, when poetry and domesticity clashed." I clung desperately to Harriet Beecher Stowe. She had written while responsible for *seven* children and had published *Uncle Tom's Cabin* when she was almost the same age as I.

The same age as I. I looked in my mirror. Without noticing it much, I had reached forty-two—and didn't mind. My round, unlived-in face had changed. As the saying goes, "Everyone over forty is responsible for his own face." Lines, but laugh lines, were beginning to show. So was gray hair, but it gave a frosted look to my light hair. Forty-two. I tried to mourn a little for my retreating youth. My tennis game—if I played tennis—would slow up. My dancing career—if I had chosen one—would be over. No, getting old was not that bad. Sandra's mother had said, "I felt older at forty than at fifty and sixty." I hoped to find out. Harriet Beecher Stowe had made it to eighty-five. I was halfway there.

The reply from the first publisher on my list changed all my plans. "Interesting idea. Please send more." I had planned on months and months of "Sorry, not for us" as I outlined and wrote the book. Now I felt as if I had accidentally jumped into the deep end of the pool.

George said, "What are you going to do now?" All the authors' biographies I had read clicked into place. I would get an agent, someone who would know how to steer me through the pitfalls of contracts if they should occur. I would look up the names of literary agents in the library, write to them, and go to New York to choose the one who seemed right. It would not, I said to George's frowning face, cost very much. New York was only ninety miles away and I would eat lunch at some cheap counter. George finally agreed. Barbara smiled—"I told you so"—and agreed to watch my children.

Two weeks later I sat on the train. All five agents I had written to (chosen at random) had responded. My magazine credits and the expression of even mild interest from a publisher had made me, I found out, a fairly desirable client. Three agents followed up with phone calls. I eliminated the other two as less aggressive and made appointments with the three.

Strange, but as the train pulled out of Philadelphia and rolled past the New Jersey swamps, I felt as if I were leaving some other me behind. "She" had spent the last twelve years as a nurturing mother and supportive wife, had polished "nest-building" skills as much as possible. Through Camden, then Trenton, I could feel the change. Someone I had been a long time ago was emerging through the layers and layers I had covered her with. Could she handle the sophisticated business world that lay ahead, use the experience so firmly put aside so long ago?

The paperback I had planned to read lay closed on my lap. My reflection in the window looked different already—chin higher, a new kind of smile, and a sense of expectancy. The person I had abandoned twelve years ago was back, not weakened, not resentful of being abandoned, just glad to be out and—I grinned at the window—raring to go. I would leave her behind again on the train ride home, but how nice to know she was still around when needed.

Four hours later, in a New York coffee shop, I grinned again while sipping my coffee. It had indeed been a pleasurable day. I had left the train aware I was even walking differently. Like bicycle riding, moving through the New York crowds was a skill I still retained. I had talked with the agents—two women and one man. Each one was enthusiastic, informative, and helpful. Their payment, I knew, came from a percentage of whatever I made. My only problem was how to choose: toss a coin or simply pick Dee Peck, the small, high-energy woman who simply *felt* right? Sometimes, in the absence of facts, instinct had to do. Yes, Dee Peck. I paid for my coffee and left for the train.

One more striding walk before boarding the train and leaving the other me behind. I had a book to write and a family to care for.

On the first day back, sitting at my typewriter, I knew that what I was attempting demanded a much deeper commitment than writing articles. What I hoped to do was to take a reader with me through the naïveté, the surprises, the changes that had occurred. Was it possible to handle a deep commitment to this book as well as the deep commitment to my family? How would I feel if

I cheated either one? I picked up a pencil and reached for paper. Somewhere up ahead, I would find out.

A few weeks later, Dee Peck phoned to say she was negotiating a contract for the book. Soon I had an advance check—and mixed emotions. It was wonderful that the book would be published, but accepting the money meant there was no turning back.

In the months that followed, I asked questions often of the ghost of Harriet Beecher Stowe. All right, she had her *seven* children, but did she also have a hired girl? Did my washer, drier, and dishwasher even out the ancient wonders of inexpensive daily help? Probably a hired girl got sick approximately as often as appliances broke down. So much for that.

I wondered if Harriet's children volunteered her for school trips. There was apparently some status involved in having *your* mother help shepherd children through the Franklin Institute, the art museum, or the zoo. Since most of the other mothers who did not work were involved in back-to-college plans, I got to know the Institute, the museums, and the zoo very well. It was possible, I found, to keep track of children in the lion house while working out writing plans in my head.

However Harriet had handled the countless details of domestic life, I gradually tested and smoothed out my own system. I broke the habit of handling problems *now*. If the garbage disposal jammed after breakfast, calls to and from the repairman could cost an hour of distraction. Gradually, I learned there were very few things that couldn't wait until noon—a fire in the house, perhaps, or a call from school.

The pile of completed pages grew. Then flu hit the family. George, then Tina, then Tige and Josh groaned in their beds and took the liquids and aspirin I supplied, racing from kitchen to bedroom and back to the study. "How come," our family doctor asked, *"you're* on your feet when the bug flattened everyone else?" Probably because I was moving too fast for the bug to catch up.

Sometimes when I literally ran from typewriter to school to typewriter, I felt flashes of envy for writers who were men. Hemingway, John Steinbeck, Thomas Wolfe—all had, I had read, wives or mistresses who protected their time and ran the house. It would be awfully nice to *have*—instead of *be*—a wife. In moments of sanity I reminded myself that it would also be nice to have been born rich or with a beautiful singing voice or perfect teeth. Instead I had poor relations, a croaking voice, and a close relationship with my dentist. But I had surges of incomparable joy when a sentence, a phrase, an idea came out just right—plus the joy of watching my children grow that no male could feel in quite the same way.

It was I who looked into Josh's eyes when the mystery of Sandra Kane's "fried egg" car was solved. It had not, Josh said, wide-eyed and tremulous, been "black kids" who threw eggs on her car, as Sandra suspected. "It was me, Mom. I wanted to see if it really was hot enough today to fry an egg." Josh eagerly agreed to clean the car and to apologize. As I watched him walk resolutely up her walk, I could feel my special pride.

I could listen when Tige came home, distressed, from school. Twelve years old now, he was concerned that some teachers treated his black friends differently. "She sends *Gordie* to help the janitor, then scolds next day when he doesn't know the work. She calls on me, but she never calls on Donald no matter how hard he waves his hand. I told Donald to tell his mother." Tige noticed, acted, and cared.

Let Hemingway, Faulkner—and George—be somewhere else at moments like that. I might have the best of two worlds after all, two kinds of creative work to enjoy.

George, not really happier with his new job than with his jobs in the past, did seem to be "somewhere else" these days. Now that the children were older, his attitudes had changed. He didn't like them to disagree or discuss what he said.

"George, they *need* to disagree sometimes, kind of to test out their own ideas. It's part of growing up."

George tried clenched chin muscles and silence. I played go-between. So he was overcritical. Someone, sometime, had been that way with him. I had learned long ago, however, that George was not given to rehashing the past. Whatever quirks he had were likely to remain. And when the children needed praise, they could get it from me. That was, I decided, how families worked, why children needed two parents.

Months passed; the pages of the book came out of my typewriter. The first draft, the second, and into the third. Good friends knew not to phone during the hours I wrote. I told them all Jacqueline Susann's theory: you either write books or make luncheon dates—not both. Long, leisurely coffee chats with Barbara were, regrettably, out. So were treasure hunts in junk shops, naps, chats over the fence with neighbors, and letters to distant friends. But the book, miraculously, was taking shape.

And then it was done. Or as done as it was likely to be. Nearly every author, someone wrote, sent off the final manuscript convinced it was bad. Two years of writing, revising, and rethinking made, at the end, a mass of words too familiar to judge. I mailed it off to Dee Peck. She would pass it on to the publisher and my editor there, Andy Green.

Dee phoned. "I love it!" Well, we had become friends and she was probably biased. When Andy Green also phoned with praise, I was sure he was preparing me for the "minor rewrites" he referred to in passing.

While I waited for Andy's suggestions, George asked: "If they really don't like it, will we have to send the advance money back? Or maybe a publisher doesn't mind losing twenty-five hundred dollars." But Andy's revisions were indeed minor, and helpful too. His blue pencil across a page I had fought to write well stung—but, yes, I could see it detoured the story. And, yes, I had not explained *that* point well—and overexplained another.

I made the changes and waited. Books were not printed and bound overnight. Like a pregnancy, there was a wait—months, in fact, to fill with dreams. Surely no publisher would send a first-time author on a publicity tour. Still, in the moments before I fell asleep, I could fantasize. How *would* it feel to reply to Barbara Walters before an audience of millions? What would I say, in calm, well-chosen words, to questions that might be asked? It was silly to think about, but a good way to go to sleep.

During the days with no book to complete I was keeping a vow to myself. Back to a "normal" life—visits with friends, elaborate meals, sewing again, and, on an impulse, volunteering for a weekly stint at the school. Tige's eighth-grade class needed a volunteer mother to fill in during the teacher's union-required hour off.

Often, dragging back home on Tige's heels, I reflected that although my "teaching" time did make days pass, I was learning things I would rather not know. Tige's comments over the years had been more accurate than I had expected. Black classmates *were* close to graduation without being taught to read. I enjoyed my roomful of eager, curious young people but was appalled, even grieved, by what had *not* been done for them.

In January, Andy Green phoned. "I just got the first copies of *Education of a W.A.S.P.* Come up to New York for a celebration lunch." In his office, the book—a real book with covers and pages —was in my hands. It was a lot like holding my babies for the very first time, something Andy would not understand.

"What"—he grinned—"are you going to write *next?*"

Next! I had written this book only because there were things I urgently needed to say. No more books for me. Articles, perhaps, short sprints, but no more marathons, thanks.

Over lunch with Andy and "Missy" Pike, the tall, polished New Yorker who directed publicity, I talked about my volunteer teaching.

Andy said, "Why not write about that?"

I shook my head. There *was* something terribly wrong in big-city schools, but I had no qualifications at all to write about it.

Missy Pike reached into her stunning pigskin attaché case and, with a perfectly manicured hand, passed a paper across the table. "Oh, here's your schedule for the publicity tour."

Dragging myself back to the hotel in Cleveland (*probably* Cleveland), I thought wryly of the Chinese adage: Be careful what you wish for; it may come true. I had innocently daydreamed of all this—the interviews for the newspapers, on radio, on TV—the chance to let more people know what needed, I felt, to be said.

As I tried to focus my eyes to set my alarm on the bedside table and find my way to bed, I fumbled for the now-well-worn schedule again. Tomorrow, Chicago.

At least the "Today" show in New York was over. Missy Pike had said I had done "marvelously well." For all I knew, I had. With not one wink of sleep the night before, I had done the show in a strange state of shock, surprised only that Hugh Downs and Joe Garagiola had both treated me as if I were speaking coherently. They had kept me on, Missy said, "through two commercials—absolutely great!" Tige had tape-recorded the sound. When I got back home, I would learn what I had said.

If I got back home. The interviews now were easy. In Boston, Pittsburgh, Washington, New York, bright, attractive TV hosts and newspaper reporters usually asked questions I had answered before. But getting *to* the interviews was a draining chore composed of frantic dashes by cab from one place to another, long hikes at airports from Gate 1 to Gate 33, finding the next hotel in the next city, and, sometimes, finding a chance to eat. Then facing another bright, rested interviewer who didn't have to unpack, repack, and hike miles to a plane.

I was, however, learning—*never* to say, "It's good to be in Indianapolis" in case you were really in St. Louis, to *eat* any cookie, stale sandwich, or crust of bread in sight. And finally, in

Kansas City (if it was Kansas City), to phone Missy in New York and George in Philadelphia. "I can't *face* another airport until I get twelve hours' *sleep.*" Then to sleep and, at last, to make my way home.

Josh, Tina, and Tige met me at the door. It was good to be home. Only one more short trip to New York (I would take Tina with me) and a request to return to St. Louis (O.K., if they paid Josh's expenses, too). Tige could go with me to a local show. He was in love with a pretty blond and preferred to stay in town.

Life again returned to normal. *The Education of a WASP* was not outselling *Gone with the Wind,* but it was doing well. Most important to me were the letters. People who had read my words wrote to say they understood and that they would act. I had not changed the world as had Harriet Beecher Stowe, but I had made a small dent. I had discharged what I felt was an obligation. Now back to normal life.

In just a month, Tige would graduate from eighth grade and I would be done with my volunteer work at school. On graduation day I sat alone. George was out of town, but I watched my son, now nearly six feet tall, as he sat on the stage with his friends. He was prepared and eager for high school. Mixed with my pride was the wish that I didn't know how ill-prepared his friends were.

At the reception in the gym, I chatted with other mothers as the young people milled around, greeting relatives, saying good-by to teachers. Then, for a moment, I was standing alone. I felt a tap on my arm. A small brown face looked up at me. "I'm Cephas's brother—he's in that class you teach—and I know about you. You're the one who's on the side of the *kids.*" He grinned and moved away.

The catch in my throat told me that life was *not* going back to "normal." If an adult "on the side of the kids" was so rare, the climate at school was worse than I knew. I already knew too much. Not only Tige, but Josh and Tina too, had reported what went on in the classrooms. When only the children were present, teachers ignored, demeaned, and sometimes destroyed those they purported to teach. Now Cephas's brother had handed me another sense of obligation. I was "pregnant" again with another book.

A second book, I reasoned, would be quicker and easier than a first. After all, I had developed techniques—turning a marinating pot roast next to the typewriter, getting our phone unlisted to avoid unwelcome calls, training myself to push everything out of my mind when I passed through the study door. And the children were older—Tina almost eleven and Josh well past twelve.

Yes, older—and providing new material for the new book every day. Tina reported that her teacher had broken a window with a classmate's head. Impossible. Yet at school, there was the window and a fast-talking principal promising to transfer the man. Josh brought home his copy of *Huckleberry Finn* with Nigger in Nigger Jim carefully inked out. "That name hurts the black kids in class," he said. "I don't like to see it myself." Tige had insisted on our local, mostly black high school, and my idealism had bent. Writing this new book, I decided at last, was like describing the landscape while riding through it on horseback.

Although both the book and the children were growing well, such was not true of my relationship with George. He was still unhappy in his work, and I wished I knew how to help. Ideally, people should enjoy their work. George never had. Advertising, I had once believed, was probably wrong for George's orderly, tidy way of living. Yet his job in the government bureaucracy was not giving him satisfaction either. Were the people he worked with *truly* as "inefficient," "stubborn," and "self-promoting" as George complained they were? George asked for my opinions and advice, even when nothing I suggested seemed to work. His moods, never bright, got darker.

Sandra, who was now deeply involved with feminist groups, said, "Maybe he doesn't like a high-achieving wife."

"That's silly. He's always practically pushing my first book at people."

"I can see why. You've made him the hero."

Sandra, I decided, was reacting to her new beliefs too strongly. Suddenly, even her easygoing husband was "holding her back." Back, I never asked, from what? With no children, Sandra was free to conduct her career exactly as she pleased. Her husband, like George, seemed proud.

George's moods posed more serious problems, however, when directed against the children. Dinnertime often provided the opportunity for George to complain. Tige should study more. Tina's room was a mess, and Josh was playing his records too loud. And all three had table manners that needed improving. All true, I said over and over to George. "But a family mealtime is the wrong time for lectures. Please save the complaints for later. Let's just enjoy each other during meals."

George did try. I could see a certain hardening of his jaw muscles when Tige, still all arms and legs, knocked over a glass of milk while enthusiastically describing the new computer at his school, or when the children's music drifted (faintly, I thought) through our bedroom door.

He assigned—and inspected—the children's chores. That was good. Children should contribute to the running of a home. Yet when Tige or Josh or Tina spent hours carefully raking leaves, George invariably focused on the one or two they missed.

I was ashamed that, from small beginnings like this, I sometimes ended up screaming in frustration at George. My suggestion that the children deserved some praise resulted only in George's "You're saying I'm a bad father." Of course not; he was in most ways a good father, home on weekends and available to the children. Yet with George, it had always been impossible to focus on the point of a discussion. In sixteen years I should have learned how, but I still lost my temper and apologized later.

George's problems with Tina were, I felt, only natural for father and daughter. When Tina was invited to a boy-girl dance, I was amused and George was appalled.

"Good Lord, she's only eleven!"

"So are all the other kids. If we keep her home, she'll be the only one in her class who isn't there." Fathers, I decided, wanted little girls to stay little forever. "George, let's let her go. It's part of her growing up."

When I picked Tina up after the party, she was sparkle-eyed. It was indeed good to have a daughter. And she would have, if I did it right, the mother I wished I had had. I did not have to pretend interest in her excited report. All my old memories of parties returned.

At home, George quizzed her. "Did the boys behave?"

Tina looked puzzled. "Well, Barry did hide Kevin's hat—but otherwise they acted nice."

More memories. The puzzling questions my mother had asked me. So many years later, I understood. Tina, in her innocence, did not. It didn't matter. I tucked her in bed and listened, delighted, as she talked herself to sleep.

Later, reading in my dressing room after George was asleep, I remembered a long-ago lecture on child-rearing. The psychologist

245

had said that all parents have a time during their children's development when they are at their best. On the night of the lecture, Tina was six months old. I had sighed. The "best" time for me, I suspected, would be their teen-age years—then a long way off.

But the best time for George had been when they were small and dependent. I *liked* their growing up, but George did not. It would, I decided as I closed my book to get some sleep, even itself out.

The months sped by. In April 1972 Tige turned sixteen. In May Josh was fourteen, and by October Tina had her thirteenth birthday. They had, as I had hoped, grown up in the house we loved. Ten years now—and all my children were officially teenagers.

Tina had her first "real" date. Elliot, a high-school freshman she had adored from afar, finally asked her to go to the movies.

"Oh, Mom, I never thought he'd ask me. Oh, I'm so excited. Isn't it wonderful!"

As Tina radiated happiness, my own happiness was almost overwhelming. This was the kind of closeness I had always wanted. No questions from *me* about whether Elliot would "behave." Tony had. I had been only one year older than Tina when I was as thrilled as she at my "college man" date. Was I really going to live all my wonderful teen years over through my daughter? How great to love her, trust her, and simply enjoy her growing up.

More months passed. Nixon was reelected. Some burglary at a building called Watergate was ignored. Tige was in love again, this time with a black girl named Denise. He was bringing her home to meet me. I prepared to reassure some shy, nervous young girl. Denise appeared about as shy as Barbra Streisand. The romance ended when she took him to church.

"Mom, she wanted to 'testify' that God had brought her *me*." After that, Tige had no more time to walk her home. She finally stopped calling the house.

More time. To my relief, the Supreme Court legalized abortion. Women, all of us, should have a choice. A neighbor called to ask me to join the National Organization for Women.

"Oh, Lois, feminism is 'in' now. Civil rights is 'out.' "

In or out, I had a book to finish, I explained.

"Do it for your *daughter,* at least."

For Tina? Just the week before, she had held off a crowd of

male adults intent on moving a woman in a car accident. Josh had reported wide-eyed: "She stood there, Mom, just saying, 'You don't move injured people. We called the police.' And the men backed down." Tina needed "liberation" as much as Alaska needed snow.

In May 1973 the book was finally done (*Getting Ready,* Morrow, 1974). In June, Tina graduated from grade school—with two trophies and in a dress she had made herself. Once again George was out of town, and once again I watched my child with teary eyes. That pretty, smart, happy girl was my daughter. Life indeed had worked out fine.

So did the publicity tour. On the "Today" show, Barbara Walters, a mother concerned with her child's education as I was with mine, asked vital questions and let me speak. In Chicago I had arranged for a Saturday off. I would run up to Milwaukee for a day to visit with Mother and friends.

Martha, Jean, and Jenny arranged a party. Then, as we left for the airport, I saw a gray stone building and asked them to stop. The Llewellyn branch library was open. Inside, little had changed, except that on one shelf, just like the shelves from which I had taken books for so many years, were two books that I had written. There was no describing the feeling. I had found comfort among those shelves, grown up there, learned to think—and now . . . I wished that every child in the world could have this kind of happy ending.

The traveling part of the tour was finally over and I could go home. The children had alternated cooking dinner while I was gone. I arranged some small rewards—Tina could come with me to a newscast; the boys could come along to a popular local late-night talk show.

At the talk show, with no advance notice, the emcee put microphones in front of Tige and Josh. All right, I had written about *their* education. We all gulped and went ahead. My two young men handled themselves beautifully.

At breakfast the next morning, as they reported our adventure to their father and sister, I looked at my family. How nice that I really *liked* my children. I had not been as perfect a mother as I had hoped to be, but I must have done some things right.

I looked around the table. If I could freeze time at any point, this, I decided, would be it.

I wanted nothing—nothing at all—to change.

Chapter 19

DURING THE FIRST few weeks of spring 1974, it looked as if nothing *could* change. As I had every spring for twelve years, I watched the big azalea bushes in our yard show their buds, then their hint of color, and finally their spectacular bloom. My writing was now literally in demand. Magazine editors *asked* me for articles. I wrote them, but not at a frantic pace. I had more time for my friends. Barbara was facing a difficult time in her marriage. She was considering divorce. I could not encourage her, but I could listen while she talked, planned, and tried to decide.

I had more time to sit on the terrace, sometimes counting—like a child at Christmas—all the gifts in my life. After school the children came to look for me there. Tige would generally arrive first. After bumpy grade-school days, he had hit his stride. His lifetime of constant motion was finally diagnosed (largely through a women's magazine article I had read and forced on our pediatrician) as hyperkinesis. Medication—and Tige's determination—had ended years of study problems. Often, now, he would twine his long legs around the wicker chair and talk like the adult he had become. He and George were making his plans for college. Tige had received an invitation to apply to MIT. "Mom, I don't think I want to compete *that* hard. I'd rather take on Penn State for starters." George would be disappointed, but it was Tige's life and Tige's thoughtful decision.

Josh usually wandered in smelling like a barn. My city-bred son had chosen to attend the nearby agricultural school. He had also become the owner of a sheep that was kept at school. Her lamb—one of twins born almost dead—had been nursed to health in a pen Josh built in our basement. Josh's greeting was usually a perfunctory hello, before he went down to the basement to care for the lamb.

Tina's after-school moods concerned me a bit. She had earned her way into the highly competitive academic Girls' High. I shuddered to think how I would have done in such demanding conditions, but Tina was determined to excel. Some days she proudly displayed A papers; some days she merely walked past me on the way to her room.

I also had more time to spend with Ginny Arthur, an old friend from our school and the neighborhood, widowed now and back to a job as guidance counselor. Ginny had said, "Girls' High is rough. And so is being fourteen." Ginny and her daughter were veterans of both.

Then, one May afternoon, I sat in the auditorium of Germantown High School as Tige was admitted to the National Honor Society. Tige, now six foot three, loomed above his classmates on the stage. His grin sent a message. Yes, we had been through a lot together. When he walked across the stage to get his certificate, I felt we were both reaching the end of a long, hard journey.

In view of Tige's triumph, it was hard to understand the low spirits that attacked me the following day. They had no focus, just the feeling of darkness if I looked too quickly to either side. Better to look straight ahead—at my happy children, at the work I enjoyed, at our big old house that I had come to love more and more over the years. But the next day—and the next—I still had the uneasy feeling that something unpleasant was waiting just off-stage.

From babyhood Tina had always picked up my feelings no matter how hard I tried to hide them. Now, at fifteen, she not only picked them up but diagnosed them and handed her findings to me.

"Mom, I think you're sad because Tige's leaving in a few months for college."

To my surprise, I burst into tears. Tina put her arms around me and said what I had said so often to my children, "Just let it out, Mom. It's O.K." More tears, but at least some of them from feeling a closeness I had waited for all my life. Tina patted me. I tried to stop weeping. Tina crooned, "That's O.K., Mom. Mothers need comforting too."

Later, as I prepared dinner, I wondered why Tige's leaving hurt so much. I, of all women, should be able to handle the "empty nest." I had never filled my time doing things for my children that they could do themselves. I had my own very satisfying work to do. It would not only fill any empty time when the children were gone, but would help make money for their education. It was, I had occasionally realized, rather well timed, and I was proud I had planned for the empty-nest years this well. Then why did it hurt?

On a Sunday in June, it suddenly seemed as if everything— plans, relationships, the entire family—had come apart. George accused Tige of misplacing an important college form. Tige was losing the battle to speak. He walked to the table and picked up the form from a pile of George's papers. George changed the subject, postponed the work they were to do together, and went off in the car. A good idea, I decided. Let George cool off.

Then came George's phone call. He was parked outside the drugstore and the car refused to start. What was the name of our towing service? Half an hour later, George, his face muscles hard, drove into the yard, slammed the car door, and went up to his den without speaking. I followed him. "George, what was wrong with the car?"

"That crook you use charged me ten dollars to drive out and tell me the car was out of gas. You told me the tank was full."

I had not. He had not asked, or glanced at the gas gauge. But I avoided the argument. We might still have a pleasant Sunday afternoon. For a change, all the children were around the house. I decided to bake a cake.

All the way from the kitchen, even through the thick walls of the house, I could hear the quarrel taking place in the hallway outside Tina's room. "No child of mine will speak to me like that," George roared.

"Then don't say stupid things, Dad," Tina screamed in return. Then she was in the kitchen, her arms full of blue jeans and George on her heels. "Dad says I can't wear jeans anymore." George swept past both of us and out into the garden. He would, I knew, stay there, running the mower for the rest of the day. Again, just as well. The mower created a wall of sound that allowed George to be alone. I turned back to Tina.

Before I could say a word, I had inexplicably become her villain. The jeans were now thrown on the chair and, to Tina, I was "hopelessly blind" (about what?) , "needed a shrink" (I did?) , and "didn't know what was going on" (perhaps, but I knew hysterics when I saw them) .

Finally Tina switched moods again and let me hold her while she sobbed. She went off to walk in the woods with Tige. Josh joined them. I finished the cake. George continued mowing the lawn. I iced the cake, not quite understanding what had gone on. Whatever it was, I thought it had been resolved by dinnertime. I carried the conversation. Gradually George responded and the children too.

Still, my own spirits stayed in the strange state I had begun to call "navy blue," that darkening around the edges that threatened to come closer. All right. It was hurting more than I expected to have Tige leave. Every mother in the world survived children leaving. I would too.

Acknowledging what I thought was the source helped only a bit. In the midst of George's questions about hiring yet another new secretary, I burst into tears. I apologized. George liked to have me read the résumés and give my opinion. Surely one more résumé was no cause for tears.

George said, "What's the matter lately? Maybe it's 'that time of life.' You are forty-nine." He looked at me over the papers he was holding. "Women do . . . I mean, my mother had a bad time with menopause."

"George, I had a hysterectomy in 1966, remember? Eight years ago." Well, I had almost forgotten myself. My gynecologist had said, "Endometriosis. I'm afraid surgery is called for." She was surprised that I was delighted. No more worries about birth control; freedom from monthly inconvenience. "Some women," she had said, "feel a loss." Of what? Those female organs had done a marvelous job through three pregnancies. Let them retire with honor. Again, to her surprise, I had had no menopausal symptoms at all. The hot flashes and night sweats Mother complained of simply never appeared. I refused Dr. Bass's estrogen pills. With no symptoms, it would be like taking aspirin without a headache. No, there was nothing physical causing these moods. Perhaps menopausal women were themselves responding not to the loss of a period, but the loss of a child.

The summer was passing much too fast. Tige had always sought me out—in the kitchen, on the terrace, in my study—for his afterschool talks. He did the same now after his summer job. Tina, with her up-and-down moods, was agonizing through her teen-age rebellions. Tige, typically, met his head on.

In my study, he wrapped his legs around a chair and said with a smile, "Mom, I want you to know this. So far in my life, I've kind of absorbed your values—and Dad's. I think I agree with most of what you believe—maybe all of it. But now I've got to test stuff out for myself. So if I do things a little different from you, don't be hurt. O.K.?"

As I smiled back at my oldest son, I wondered if this could be the sweetest, easiest teen-age declaration of independence on record. Once I had experienced the miracle of walking through glass for this young man. With Tige, miracles seemed to abound. Now I told myself to enjoy his simple, clear, direct declaration and not to think of how I would miss him when he was no longer at home.

Home without Tige was hard to imagine. He had arrived nine months after the marriage. Don't think of it now. Work? Writing these days was like plodding through waist-deep water. In one more month, George and I would drive Tige up to State College. He would begin his new life at Penn State. Then I would do my weeping, my adjusting, my recovering. Then I would work again.

On September 3, 1974, Tige, George, and I left with a packed car for the three-hour drive to Penn State. The day before, we had put Josh and Tina on the bus for a visit to George's parents.

I tried to share Tige's enthusiasm for the mountains we were driving through, for the new dorm that would be his home. Tige directed George through the complex traffic pattern of arriving-student cars. Outside the big, new red-brick dorm, we all carried boxes up to a small, sterile-looking room. Some of his roommate's boxes were already there, still packed. Tige nudged me and pointed to the only thing his soon-to-be-met roommate had unpacked: a yachting trophy. Tige brushed his hands on his weathered jeans and pushed his long hair back. "This"—he grinned, looking at the trophy and the set of matched luggage—"could be an interesting year."

And then there was nothing more to carry or to joke about. George and I would be staying overnight at a nearby motel, but Tige had a dorm-orientation meeting that evening. I could feel he wanted to complete his good-byes.

At least I could concentrate every part of me on simply holding back tears. Tige didn't need them just then. He led me gently to the door of his new room, bent down to give me a kiss on my head, smiled the smile I would miss seeing each day, and said, "O.K., now. Turn around, Mom, and go. I love you and I'll see you at Thanksgiving." He gave me a gentle little push.

I made it to the elevator with George somewhere behind me. Then to the car. George asked what I wanted to do next. When I stopped weeping in the car, I answered George's questions. Walk, I guessed, eat, sleep maybe. George started the car, drove a few blocks, and argued with a campus policeman who said George had made an illegal turn. I sat through the confrontation as silently as if I were watching a movie. The movie continued as we walked around the campus, ate, walked again.

Then, at the hotel, with George instantly asleep beside me, the darkness that had been hiding just beyond my vision for weeks moved to center stage. Suddenly I was enveloped and suffocating. Something was terribly wrong. Taking my first child to college might involve some pain, but not a feeling like this. I was gasping for breath. I put on the light. George asked what was wrong. I could not answer his questions. "Lois, should I call a doctor?" I could only shake my head. Suddenly, he looked uproariously funny, standing naked with one hand on the phone. I buried my face in the pillow to stifle what I knew were hysterics. Odd, I could breathe into the pillow. I hung onto it, as if it were the edge of a precipice. And then I was finally calm enough to take a sleeping pill. George turned out the light.

As we drove home in the morning, I knew I would never remember the drive. Usually apprehensive when George was driving, I watched unfeelingly as he went through a stop sign. When we stopped for lunch, I pushed food around a plate. Something totally out of my control was happening to me, and it was way beyond anything that could be termed "normal." Waves of blinding, ear-shattering fear rolled over me, then a calm, frightening too because of its inexplicable suddenness.

George wanted to know if I wanted to go home or drive with him to the bus station to get Josh and Tina.

"George, I want to go home. And I think that tomorrow I ought to call a psychiatrist."

George nodded. "Whatever you want."

It was not what I *wanted,* but whatever was happening was nothing I could handle alone.

That evening, Josh and Tina came into the house and went almost immediately to bed. Yes, they had had a nice time with

Grandma and Grandpa. The bus trip was tiring. I sat up while the family slept. The decision to call the short, stocky, kind-faced psychiatrist I had once met at a party had, I noticed, pushed the fear farther away. I would call Dr. Roberts in the morning. Tina's outburst had had some truth to it after all. I did "need a shrink." Long ago, in Chicago, I had felt just a bit disdainful of people I knew who were "on the couch." Most of them, in my opinion, were avoiding making choices on their own—never my problem. But now, where else was I to go? If a tooth hurt, you went to a dentist. If your emotions hurt and there was no explanation, you went to a "shrink." Cavities got worse. I had the feeling that this would too, unless I got help.

Dr. Clinton Roberts's reception room was quiet and comfortable, but I realized I had arrived nearly an hour early. No matter. I could read. No? Well, look at *New Yorker* cartoons then. At least I didn't have to worry about the expense. I had checked George's government Blue Cross policy when he questioned the cost. It paid 80 percent of Dr. Roberts's $35 fee. George wanted me to ask how long I might have to see Dr. Roberts. Perhaps he could tell on this first visit. By now the fear of that horrible night and the drive back home had abated. Perhaps, as George said, I had overreacted. Perhaps I should just tell Dr. Roberts it had been a mistake and go back home. As if to remind me it was still alive, the navy-blue dragon of fear flicked its tail. Yes, I had better keep this appointment.

Dr. Roberts, when he opened the door to his office, looked as I remembered him. He listened while I struggled to be clear. Only to psychiatrists, I decided, could one safely describe navy-blue dragons. "But"—I smiled—"navy-blue dragons and your first kid leaving home might go together like circuses and elephants?" Dr. Roberts nodded. "Do you think I'm overreacting, as my husband feels?" Dr. Roberts moved his shoulders and asked if *I* thought I was.

Abruptly, I felt as if George were right. This feeling would pass. It was only because Tige had left for school. I thanked Dr. Roberts. He said, "Please feel free to call me, though, at any time." That was kind, but I was sure now that I would not.

I was home a short time before Tina arrived—and went straight to her room. No comments about her visit or the trip on the bus? I started dinner. Josh came home and, atypically, folded me in a hug. My nose barely reached his collar. Yes, he was assuming the position of oldest son. Then, again untypically, he went up to *his* room. When I carried a load of sheets from the drier up to *my* room, I heard the sobs through Tina's door. I knocked. "Mom, go away." I sounded like Dr. Roberts when I said, "Just call if you need me."

When I turned, Josh was behind me. He led me downstairs. Unlike Tige, Josh always sat still and touched. Now he sat on the kitchen counter and looked down at the floor. "Mom, I wasn't going to tell you, but—well, I think you've got to know. Grandma said some awfully funny things about you when we were there. Mean things that weren't true. It upset Tina."

From the look in Josh's long-lashed blue eyes it had upset Josh too—unless they had both misunderstood Alice Stalvey's teasing. And it must have been teasing. We had what I had always felt was an affectionate relationship. Not as open and warm as with my father-in-law, but certainly a friendship.

"Oh, Josh, she was teasing, playing a joke."

"No, Mom. I don't know why she did it. I didn't even know what to say. She said you thought you were better than others because you wrote books—that Dad could have written books too. She said you didn't know as much about cooking either as you thought you did. Silly things like that. But she wasn't teasing, and it upset Tina. Tina didn't talk at all, all the way home."

This was, I felt, some kind of nightmarish misunderstanding. It had to be. My mother-in-law had never said one unpleasant word to me. I had often thought that Dad Stalvey laid on his praise for my cooking a little bit thick, but I always asked for her recipes, praised them, and used them. No matter how sure Josh was, he must have misunderstood.

George came through the door. Josh repeated what he had just said.

"George, I'm sure the children got things confused. But I think it would be a good idea to phone your mother and clear it up."

George said, "No."

"Honey, we can't let something like this just sit there. Tina's crying in her room." I began to dial. "I know your mother wouldn't say things like that. Get on the extension. We'll straighten it out." I was astonished that George had balked at my calling. It was so easy to clear up this misunderstanding.

Ten minutes later, I held the phone, unable to speak anymore.

"You *do* think you're better than others," Alice Stalvey had said.

On the extension phone George was silent.

"You've always exchanged all the presents we sent the children." I appealed to George now. "Honey, tell her that's not true."

George did not reply, but my father-in-law on *his* extension did. "Lois, you're upsetting Mother. You'd better hang up." Spouses were supposed to support each other, and I understood Dad Stalvey's stand. But where was George?

I was sobbing in surprise, pain, frustration, still holding the kitchen phone. George was not coming downstairs. I found him in our bedroom, arranging his briefcase.

In the morning George left for a two-day trip to Washington. Josh and Tina left for school. I sat in my robe among the breakfast dishes. At that moment it seemed beyond my strength to straighten the kitchen or even to get dressed. Yet I had to. As I scraped egg off plates and hid them in the dishwasher, I gradually persuaded myself that I was vastly overreacting. All right, I had never realized that my mother-in-law saw my achievements as being in competition with her son's. I might have the same mixed feelings for a wife of Tige or Josh. Tige or Josh might someday choose to support me instead of their wives. I hoped not, but they might. Those were all quite human family relations. I firmly closed the dishwasher door.

I would, I decided, visit Barbara. No. How could I have forgotten? She was at work. Why this fuzzy-mindedness? My best friend had separated from her husband and I had hardly thought of her for weeks. All right. I could not visit Barbara. I would work in my study, straightening my desk. I abandoned that quickly enough when I found myself standing, papers in hand, absolutely unable to decide which ones to throw away. Closets then. There, too, the impossibility of deciding what to keep, what to throw away. Somewhere I had read—heard?—of a woman who crouched in her closet, refusing to come out. The memory made my neck prickle; then cause the breathlessness and the fear that had no face.

At four o'clock, when Josh and Tina came home, it was hard to remember how I had spent the day. Not, I noticed when I passed the center-hall mirror, putting on make-up or combing my hair. Yet the children's homecoming appeared to lift my mood. At least, with George out of town, I could cook their favorite foods. Lemon chicken for Josh, peppers and corn for Tina, and Tige's favorite dessert. Tears welled again. Tige was far away.

Tina, at least, had embraced me before she went to her room. Someday we would have to talk about her visit. But her swift retreat made it clear that this would not be the time.

Josh had anxiously studied my face. I forced a smile and some questions about his new ewe's pregnancy. We talked about missing the lamb in the basement now that she was back with her "family." After one more searching look, Josh relaxed and went outside to rake leaves.

At dinner with Josh and Tina, I pretended I had "done too much tasting" while I cooked. Josh happily accepted most of the meal I couldn't touch. Tina said, "I guess you won't let us stay up to watch *Dracula* on the late show." She knew better—not on a school night and especially not this night. I was feeling more and more like a suitcase that had been overstuffed, hinges ready to give, the sides strained to bursting. I prayed I wouldn't "burst" before the children were in bed.

By ten o'clock they seemed to be settled in. I had taken one sleeping pill after they came to my bedroom to say good night. At eleven I tried a second pill to tame the anxiety that made me unable even to sit. I walked down the long hall from my bedroom, past the children's doors, to my study. Then downstairs, through the kitchen, the dining room, the center hall, Up the stairs. Was this going to be like the night we left Tige? That damned dragon flicked its tail. Was it to be worse? Up the stairs, past the second floor, to the third.

A gleam of light showed under the third-floor playroom door, and there were faint sounds. Perhaps, for once, my terror had a cause. When, trembling, I opened the door and looked inside, I saw Josh, Tina, and the blue glow of the small TV.

Someone who was not me lunged across the room, picked up the TV, and hurled it down the stairs. Someone who *was* me looked at my children's terrified faces, reached for them, and saw them recoil. I sank to the playroom floor, sobbing apologies. Josh and Tina led me to bed.

But when they left, I knew I had to make a call. Whatever was happening to me was much more serious than I knew. Until I understood, it was not safe for me to be at home with my children. There were hospitals for times like this, and Dr. Roberts must be used to midnight calls. For a moment I hesitated with my hand on the phone. Checking into a psychiatric hospital was a serious step, a mark—even today—on some records for life. But I was, after all, not going to run for political office or apply for a gun. I thought of

Josh's and Tina's horrified faces and the flying TV. Going voluntarily to a hospital now would be better for them than waiting until I *had* to go. I dialed Dr. Roberts's number. "I'm afraid I'm much sicker than we thought. I think I ought to be hospitalized." Yes, he would arrange for me to be admitted to Philadelphia Psychiatric in the morning—as soon as my children left for school.

Sandra Kane had taken charge in the morning with her psychiatric social worker's expertise. Sure, she would gladly keep an eye on the children, but she would also drive me to the hospital, find George in Washington, and let him know. At the hospital she sat with me while a woman took information—and *removed items from my handbag.* No matches, no mirror, no sharp objects at all. Incredibly, I felt interested and amused. But at least I knew why. Details were all arranged and taken care of at home. I was where some part of me knew I should be, under the care of a doctor I liked and trusted. I could now almost gaily enter into an interesting adventure. "Don't be scared. This is a good hospital. You did the right thing," Sandra assured me as an attendant came to take me to my ward.

Following along, I was far more curious than frightened. This, as far as I could see, was no "snake pit." The halls were quiet and clean. The attendant carried my suitcase as if he were a bellhop. At the nurses' station on the floor where I would have my room, I was welcomed as if to a hotel—except my suitcase was taken away, to be searched, I assumed. No point then in going to my room. Open doors showed they all looked alike—small, bright, and empty. The patients must be the women in street clothes, walking mostly to or from a big room at the end of the hall. There, other women sat on sofas, chairs, or around tables, playing cards. A nurse sat in a corner chair. I chose a sofa and leafed through a magazine. Dr. Roberts had said he would be in to see me at four o'clock.

Between glances at the magazine, I looked around. Several women were reading. There were two enthusiastic card games going on. Another woman sat staring bleakly at the wall. One woman was quietly weeping while another sat close and patted her hand. Except for the weeping woman, this could have been an all-female resort. Beyond the big window, I could see well-kept, nicely landscaped grounds: a shuffleboard court no one was using, people—men and women—walking outside or sitting on benches.

I took out a cigarette and looked for my matches. Oops. What now? I saw my suitcase being carried to a room. All right. I would unpack. Perhaps take a nap.

Unpacking, I giggled to find I had taken a blouse printed with pecans, walnuts, and almonds—appropriate for this place. Cardboard hangers—plastic or wire could, I supposed, be used by someone terribly bent on mayhem or suicide. I stretched out on the bed and closed my eyes.

A voice boomed, "You *know* you're not allowed to be in here sleeping. Get up!"

I opened my eyes to a white-clad, red-faced nurse—and my own surge of adrenaline. I did not *know* a goddamned thing—not where to get matches and certainly not this embargo on sleep. The look on the nurse's face convinced me that this was not the moment to fight for my rights. She was already scribbling something on a chart. Maybe "Patient hostile—consider restraints."

Back in the lounge. A nurse called out, "Medicine time." Women lined up. I sat. No medicine for me that I knew of. Another nurse stood over me. "On your feet and in the line."

A mental hospital, I decided, was no place for unstable people with fragile egos. The medication nurse dismissed me with a wave of her hand and "Nothing for you." Back to my magazine—one I had written for. Suddenly I remembered that one of my articles was due out this week. Did mental hospitals have magazine stands?

An ear-splitting bell rang. The women began to move out a door. To where? Shock treatments, for all I knew. The red-faced nurse nudged me as I sat. "Dearie, it's another mark against you if you don't eat." Eat! I was famished. Where? Concern crossed her face. "Why, dearie, where you always go." I explained I had just checked in. It might be best to get that straight rather than be marked as someone who was slipping additional cogs.

The food, eaten with knives and forks of plastic (more suicide prevention, no doubt), was good. There were both men and women in the cafeteria—some obviously more agitated than others. I noticed that some groups were being marched to another building next door and then inside. I walked outdoors, waiting for someone to stop me. No one did. I saw other patients going in and out of a long, low building. It seemed safe to explore but all those unknown rules and unknown buildings could get hard on one's nerves—that, plus the awareness that mental patients' actions were clearly vulnerable to misinterpretation. Too many wrong steps and I might not be *able* to get out of here! I was already down for "illegal sleeping" and losing the cafeteria.

At least I had found the rec hall. I sat at a table, watching the Ping-Pong players, more card players, a sobbing woman being led away, and a shouting man ("I *am* Lyndon Johnson") hustled out by two big attendants. A red-haired woman in a pastel uniform with a name tag (Occupational Therapist) sat down next to me. Did I want to learn to weave "a simply beautiful rug"? No, thank you, I certainly did not plan to be here that long. Her face was sympathetic. Perhaps even the folks locked up in that other building thought they were going home soon.

She said again, gently, "What is your occupation? Housewife?"

"Yes, that—and I also write books and magazine articles."

A wary expression came over her face. They had just removed "Lyndon Johson." Now she had one who thought she was Gloria Steinem—or maybe even Norman Mailer. She moved back ever so subtly in her seat.

Laughter felt good and, anyway, it was unavoidable. I managed, "Honestly, I really do write books." Of course, dear. She left. A slim, blond woman patient had joined us moments before. "I'm Dorothy Sanchez. I noticed you in the lounge. I didn't think you were really a patient. Are you writing about us from inside?"

My inner laughter met head on with the vulnerable look on her face. "Oh, no. I *am* a patient. I wouldn't . . . look, my name is Lois Stalvey. Who lights cigarettes around this place?" From Dorothy I learned about cigarette lighting (ask a nurse or light from a patient's butt), naps (get your doctor's permission), weeping (not to be done openly: "If I cry too hard, I'll get sent back to Winkleman"), Winkleman (the building for disturbed patients; Radbill, ours, was for the more controlled).

Dorothy told me she had attempted suicide four times—with aspirin twice and twice by cutting her wrists. I could see the crosswise scars. I didn't think it appropriate to mention that she'd stood no chance with the aspirin and that I had read wrists were best slashed lengthwise. Her husband had not been willing to give her a divorce. Now, with her hospitalization, he was quite willing, but demanded custody of her children. She struggled to hold back the forbidden tears. "Looks like I've painted myself into a corner. My new doctor—the one Joe found—is starting me on shock therapy tomorrow."

It did also not seem appropriate to plead with her not to take shock, but I made a mental note to ask Dr. Roberts where he stood on this controversial and irreversible technique, to drop him if he used it, and to warn George not to sign anything that even looked like permission.

At four o'clock, Dr. Roberts's short, stocky figure came down the long hall. I had been chatting with a tiny, cheerful nurse. "Here comes my doctor."

"Oh, Roberts! You're lucky. He's a great doctor—*and* a good man."

Dr. Roberts looked genuinely appalled at my question about electroshock therapy. "No, no. Never use it. But *if you are willing,* I'd like to try what some call 'truth serum'—sodium amytal. We can work without it, but it could speed up our work."

In that instant, the idea of submitting to "truth serum" seemed like jumping off a cliff. Could I allow this man—anyone—to learn everything there was to know about me, some things I might not even know myself? Or want to know?

But people did jump off cliffs—if the fears behind them were worse than gambling on the jump. To find out what was causing my terrors, I would have to talk more openly with this man than I had ever talked before. It made sense that once I had talked under sodium amytal, there would be no urge to hold anything back. There on the bedside table was the cliff—the hypodermic. I rolled up my sleeve to jump.

Lying on the bed, I could hear my voice, talking, talking, talking, as if a tight, hardened cork had suddenly been removed. Somehow I knew that this fresh, open-air freedom was not going to last, but for the present, it was as delicious as if I were drinking it. I had always believed—and been told—that I was an "open" person, but this was like having every part of me spread on a hill, exposed to a healing sun.

Eventually, I realized that the medication was wearing off. I was conscious of Dr. Roberts sitting beside my bed. He now knew as much about me as I did myself. As we worked together to get me well, there would be no point to my evasions, embarrassment, pretense.

He knew *more* about me than I knew about myself. I had believed I was totally conscious under the serum. Now he asked, "Do you know what you meant when you said, 'If my mother and father had not married each other, I would not be wishing I were dead?'"

I said that? Dr. Roberts nodded. Then, as if to himself, "The trauma was not in adolescence. It was much further back." What trauma? And why was it affecting me *now?*

That, Dr. Roberts said almost wistfully, was what we had to work on. How long? Perhaps a few months—but not, he added hastily, in the hospital. He would, however, be back at the same time tomorrow. Still soaringly groggy, I asked him to sign permission for me to nap.

For an hour I lay, not quite dozing. What on earth did my parents have to do with the navy-blue dragon stalking me now? Yes, of course I wished my mother had been different and that my father had not abandoned me all those years. But, damn it, I had managed a productive life.

The hunger pangs struck suddenly and pulled me out of bed. The other patients were already lined up at the cafeteria door. I looked for Dorothy Sanchez. Nowhere around. Two patients introduced themselves. I ate dinner with Theresa, a bright, pretty woman in her early forties, and Karen, fiftyish, who had spaniel eyes. Confidences came easily, I learned, in a mental hospital. Each of the other two women had been there several times. Like a litany, Theresa kept repeating, "My mother says . . ." With Karen it was what her grown children believed. From the scraps of conversation, Theresa's dominant mother and Karen's selfish kids sounded like monsters. Yet both women contended it was *their* fault they could not function. That was not my impression. Yet it was sadly apparent that they had stopped fighting their fate—if, in fact, they had ever fought it at all.

After dinner I strolled around the grounds alone. I had asked George to bring the children at visiting hours. George wondered "if they should see you there." That was the point. This attractive setting with its majority of quiet, calm patients could put their imaginations to rest. They needed to see me comfortable, even cheerful.

Tina and Josh hugged me. They were "fine" and I should "get a real good rest—and then come home." George looked strained. He had been having, he said, a lot of trouble with the car. I explained once again how to unscrew the carburetor cover and unstick the butterfly valve. Also, George said, the dishwasher wasn't acting "right." For that I suggested he call the repairman. Tina told me proudly about being put in an advanced algebra class. Josh told me funny stories about his day in school—a cow had "escaped."

At the end of the visit, when George herded the children out the visitors' door, I held my smile until they were gone. I wanted to be with Tina and Josh so much. Why, then, was I terrified at the thought of going home?

Back to the lounge—and there was Dorothy Sanchez, with a small, faint smile, playing solitaire. I had looked for her all day. I sat down next to her with a feeling of relief. "Dorothy, I'm so glad I found you. Where have you been?"

She raised her small blond head to look at me. "Oh, if I know you, I'm so sorry. They say most of my memory will come back. I think I slept all day after the shock therapy. Please don't be offended, but what is your name?" Her eyes were serene and very, very blank.

That night I lay in my hospital bed knowing that the sleeping pill was not going to work. Too many disorganized images were playing some game in my mind. Theresa, Karen, Dorothy, weighed against the unexpected pleasures of custodial care. So good to be in the hospital where all problems, all decisions, were made easy. Navy-blue dragons were not admitted. They were asked to wait outside. What was so wrong with a few more days, a week, a month of feeling safe? I felt as if I had been fighting one thing or another all my life—fighting to grow up, to test my abilities, to be a good mother, to build a good life. In this hospital I could float for a while. No cooking, no need even to decide when to eat, no fixing the car or diagnosing the dishwasher. Everyone else here floated, accepted rules and directions and the decisions of others.

Like Dorothy and Karen and Theresa. Theresa and Karen going in and out—and Dorothy now going nowhere at all.

I did not like the decision I knew I was making. That navy-blue dragon, I *knew*, was waiting outside, probably stronger now. Did I really, as I had said under amytal, "wish I were dead"? If I harbored feelings like that without knowing it, there must be other things in me that I had shoved aside.

I turned over in bed, burying my face in the pillow. Whatever I had shoved aside, I suspected, would be excruciating to remember. Perhaps *by* shoving memories and feelings aside, I had given that navy-blue dragon its strength. It would not be easy to take on that dragon, fight it, and win.

Or I could stop fighting it—and with Dorothy, Karen, and Theresa make an eternal fourth for bridge.

I turned on my back. Now, oddly, I thought of the physical pain of that long-ago abortion. Who said pain could not be remembered? I could recall it well, as the worst pain one could possibly survive. That thought had always comforted me, as a kind of plateau impossible to duplicate. I wondered why I recalled it now. To reassure—or to prepare—myself?

Then I could sleep. I knew what I was going to say to Dr. Roberts when I saw him the next day.

His lightly lined face looked across at me as we sat on chairs in my room. "Dr. Roberts, I want to go home. I mean, I know I must go home."

He said, "Ah. Good."

Chapter 20

THE FIRST FEW MONTHS of psychoanalysis, I had read,
were called the "honeymoon period." While I waited in Dr. Roberts's outer office, I could not imagine why. Behind the blank,
dark-walnut door, I sensed danger. Or perhaps it was just my conscience punishing me for the disdain I had always felt for the
process. Once I had seen analysis as a self-indulgent, sophisticated
fad, a way of blaming parents or spouses for choices we had made
or refused to make. Even George had said, "I never felt you re-
pressed very much." No, indeed, in my opinion, I never had. People had talked of "the unconscious," the "superego," and, of course,
Freud's famous "penis envy." The only time I had ever wished for
a penis was in an unclean rest room where I had to urinate. My
brother's "dangling parts" and George's otherwise seemed like
rather vulnerable and inconvenient organs to carry around.

I was surprised, however, at how hard I fought for psychoanalysis. At our first session after my hospitalization, Dr. Roberts had
said, "It's very painful probing. Plain psychotherapy is less painful." Yet Dr. Roberts was an analyst, which meant he had been
through a complete analysis himself.

"It doesn't work for everyone," he had said. Well, it *had* to work
for me. The night before, something had led me to a book I had
not even thought of for years, *The Way of All Women* (Longman,
1933) . A woman analyst, M. Esther Harding, had written that

mothers must keep themselves not only physically clean to protect their children from disease, but *emotionally* clean as well. Children could be "infected" by their mother's neuroses more harmfully than by the germs of flu. Being "germ-free" for Tige, Josh, and Tina was as important to me as being free of this frightening condition myself.

If indeed I had talked of death under amytal, I told Dr. Roberts, if I could not understand the strange reference I had made to my parents, if I did not know why a happily married, work-fulfilled woman like me could throw television sets, then analysis—the surgery, not the Band-Aid—was necessary.

When he had finally said, "All right, let's try it. There's the couch," I had flounced and stretched out. Driving home later, I grinned. "Why, that son of a bitch! He *wanted* me to fight."

Honeymoon, indeed. For weeks I felt as if the talking I did only confused me more. My thoughts were like dull or vivid strands of yarn, all so tangled with each other that it was hard to know where any one of them began. Sometimes I raged at Dr. Roberts sitting silently behind me at his desk while I started, interrupted sentences, tried to decipher indecipherable dreams. "You know more than I do what's bothering me and you won't help."

Dr. Roberts's soft voice floated from over my head. "It doesn't work that way. *You* have to know."

"People," he said, "sometimes sweep things under rugs. Sometimes for a long, long time. Sounds as if you tripped on a big bump in that rug. The job is to find out what it is."

Four times a week I tried to find out. Because I had been hospitalized, George's government Blue Cross covered nearly all the costs. Yet I knew he was concerned, not so much for the small amount of money ($7 a session) but because, as my husband, he felt pushed aside by this doctor who was probing my life. I tried to share what was happening. George believed all therapists were charlatans. I told him of M. Esther Harding's belief about children suffering for their mother's emotional "germs." George responded strongly. Was I saying it applied to fathers too? *His* emotions were perfectly fine, he said angrily. I explained I was talking only of myself.

Tina's emotions were, however, worrying me. Her moods were up one day, down the next. And she was seeing a lot of Joe, a young man George called "a Black Panther if ever I saw one." To me, Joe was more a Black Pussycat. He acted as if he would gladly jump through fire at the snap of Tina's fingers. Her schoolwork, I suspected, was suffering, but she had always slaved for A's. A few C's for a while would hardly be tragic.

At Thanksgiving, finally, Tige came home. A lot had happened in the two months he had been gone, and it was so good to see his long, lean frame again draped over chairs, sofas, doorways. It was good too to hear George and Tige discussing college. I could not reminisce about courses and majors and professors, but George, with his master's degree, could. There was, I felt, a new closeness between father and son as they talked behind closed doors in George's den. A few times I had seen Tige's face look troubled and George's face look hard—disagreements about pocket money or the phone bill, no doubt.

Then, one evening during dinner, Tige put down his knife and fork and looked soberly at George. "Dad, I've been doing a lot of thinking since I've been gone and there's something I need to tell you. Do you realize you don't listen when people talk and that you interrupt? I don't—"

George interrupted. "Certainly I listen."

Tige held up his hand. "Dad, *please* hear me out. I always thought it was my fault, that I talked too much or wasn't clear. But I don't have that problem with other people. Only with you. It's—"

George was angry. "I don't interrupt. *You* interrupt."

Tige sighed and resumed eating. Josh and Tina were silent. George reminded Tige that he had promised to clean out his closet. Josh and Tina volunteered to help. I listened wih mixed emotions, proud of Tige for his calm, careful, and—if George could have seen it—loving statement. I was used to George's interrupting and his not really hearing what people said. I felt sad that George had missed Tige's tender, sincere attempt to communicate and possibly to help.

Again, the months moved on. Sandra Kane had said, "In *successful* psychoanalyses—and there really are few—people say that at the end it's like looking at the answers to last week's crossword puzzle. It's all so obvious, they can't believe it took them so long."

My crossword puzzle was far from filled in. I was, I mourned to Dr. Roberts, a straight-C student in Dreams. Occasionally I could figure one out. The dream about standing at one opaque window through which Dr. Roberts could see but I could not was obvious, and I had awakened crying. The silly dream about Tina saying, "We all used Mom's bicycle until she threw it in the river," made no sense. If dreams were the solution to "last week's crossword," I was inept.

Then, one afternoon, a phone call came from Western Union. An impersonal voice repeated words I could not believe. It was from my brother, Bobby. "Mother died in sleep last night. As per her request, body given to medical school. No funeral. Nothing you need do." I mumbled a request for a copy and looked for a chair.

Nothing I "need" do—nothing I *could* do. My relationship with Bobby had not been good for years. My "little brother" had published an unsuccessful novel before my books came out. He had been "Lois's brother" much too often, and his hostile attitude had made me sad. But a telegram instead of a phone call? And Mother had talked of her funeral for years. Someone—Bobby? Aunt May? —had, as always, overridden her decision. No funeral, no grave to visit. I caught my breath. People might forget that she had ever lived at all.

I sat down on the chair near the kitchen phone, next to the refrigerator. I looked at its whiteness and waited for a reaction. Sandra had once said, "You had better come to some comfortable feelings toward your mother before she dies. If you don't—as we were taught over and over in social-work classes—you'll carry a lifetime of guilt." I had never managed comfortable feelings toward Mother. I waited for the guilt to hit, something engraved perhaps on the refrigerator, something horrible in large letters. My mother was dead and I had never been able to love her.

But the feeling that began to grow inside me had nothing to do with guilt. There was instead a sadness followed by a sense of defeat—and then by resignation that felt inexplicably good. The ball game was over and I had lost—but at least and at last, the ball game was over. The tears that came then were not happy or sad, but they were immensely cleansing.

An hour later, at Dr. Roberts's office, I could finally go back to memories that had seemed beyond reach. A cobblestone street, a black shining car fender, hiding beneath a table, stair railings that bumped my head. That navy-blue dragon was now sitting on my chest. Who said that abortion was the greatest pain possible to survive? The greatest pain was remembering—lying on cobblestones at the age of three, aware my mother had said it was safe to cross and I had learned it was not. No safety with Mother. And then an uncle I hated hitting Father, carrying me away—to wait and wait and wait and wait for the father who never came, never wrote, never sent Christmas gifts—who would have "if he loved you." Tears actually filled my ears as I lay on my back. The couch was a brown-tweed torture rack.

Then the crazy crossword puzzle was filled in. No wonder Christmas was an agonizing time for me! But how silly, as an adult, to wait for gifts from a father long dead. Yes, I had lost all faith in my mother at the age of three. I had grown up rejecting all "experts," and it had not been bad. I had never listened to what people said I could *not* do. Yes, I had wept out all the terror I felt as a child, knowing I had to grow up on my own, but I had grown up —I would be fifty years old in August. I could now tell that terrified child inside me it had all turned out all right.

Dr. Roberts was talking in his end-of-the-session tone of voice. I sat up and looked at him triumphantly. Perhaps the analysis, after these short months, was at an end.

"Are we finished?"

"Perhaps. But are you aware that there is one area of your life you never talk about? Over the weekend you might try to think of what it is. But be glad you made a wonderful breakthrough today."

The weekend didn't allow much time for reflection. George came back from a trip that night. I was so very glad to see him. Josh chuckled as I fussed affectionately. I had not, as many women did, married a man like my father. George would never leave his children to grow up alone. He had stayed—reliable, predictable, dependable—over the soon-to-be twenty years. I had run to meet him when he came up the path. Who cared what the neighbors thought! Tina watched us as I threw my arms around him, something in her face. Oh, Tina, I thought, the rivalry is natural, but I will always let you win. I stepped back and let Tina hug her father as I wished I had been able to hug mine.

After dinner, Tina went off to a special overnight baby-sitting job. The parents were out of the country. Tina would entertain the children, but an aunt would be there too.

At six o'clock on Saturday morning, the aunt phoned. "I'm terribly sorry to break this news, but Tina appears to be gone. She didn't sleep in her bed last night. I felt you should know right away. Do you want me to call the police?"

Yes. No. I would be right over and call them from there. I threw on clothes, waked George, and asked him to meet me at the

DeBrills' with the car. For me it would be faster to cut through several yards to reach the DeBrills' back door. I ran through the kitchen, grabbing a photo of Tina. Oh, Lord, the police would need it to find her. I plunged through bushes, fences, and finally the DeBrills' high hedge.

And saw Tina, walking calmly up their driveway. She pushed away from my embrace. "Tina, are you all right?"

Her small chin went up. "Of course I am. I went to a party with Joe. He just brought me back." She looked over my shoulder with an oddly triumphant expression. "Oh, there's Dad, always a little behind." George had come crashing through the bushes, explaining at length that he couldn't start the car. Then he looked at Tina —and then at me. "Where was she? What are you going to do?"

Some instinct told me to do nothing for the moment. Mr. De-Brills' sister was coming outside. "You did a terrible thing, young lady. I found the basement door you left unlocked. I'm afraid you're fired." She turned and left. For conscientious, proud Tina, that humiliation seemed punishment enough for now. I was prepared simply to be silent until I could put the incredible pieces together. George raged. Joe was "no good"; Tina was "acting like a fifteen-year-old tramp"; she had "not gone to a party—had probably been laying up somewhere with Joe instead."

George's words got harsher. I took a breath to counter them— and, inexplicably, Tina turned on me. "I hate you. You're ruining my life. Who wants a sick mother like you?" Sobbing and red-faced, she turned and ran ahead to the house. George began to run after her. "That girl needs a good whipping." I grabbed his arm. A whipping would resolve none of the confusion I felt, that I suspected Tina felt too.

I was back at the house. Tina heard me on the stairs and called, "Mother," from her room. Suddenly, she was holding onto me and sobbing. "I'm sorry. I don't know why I did it. Mama, I love you. I don't want you to be unhappy." I held her while she sobbed. Then, finally, "Mom, I know it won't make up for what I did, but let me make dinner for you. And the cake you like. And I'll clean the kitchen. You relax and read and think." Tina's tear-racked face was now smiling. "Think deep thoughts while I cook, O.K.?" It had been our private, loving joke.

George said, "You mean you're going to let her get away with this?" He had already laid down "no allowance, no dates, no phone calls." Punishments, I reflected, bridged generation gaps; those

270

were the same punishments Mother had given me—and infrequently enforced. "George, shall I *not* let her try to earn forgiveness?" George went to work in the yard. I went up to the sewing room. Tina brought me a cup of tea. "Can you think deep thoughts while you sew?" I'd been doing it for years!

As I stitched on a dress, Tina's words triggered Dr. Roberts's comment. I could try "deep thoughts" about what he felt I had avoided discussing. Darts got pinned and stitched, sleeves set in place. What area of life had I not explored? One could not, I decided, think "deep" thoughts while putting in a zipper. And dinner was ready, Tina called up.

On Sunday, as usual, George finished the paper and spent the day in the yard with occasional visits inside to be sure Tina was not on the phone. She was accepting her punishments gracefully, doing schoolwork, cleaning her room.

On Monday I tried for more "deep thoughts" as I drove to my appointment with Dr. Roberts. Driving there had become automatic. I thought of some still-undecipherable dreams—Mother and George, hand in hand, walking through a bleak landscape; an Oriental archer with three arrows threatening someone I loved. I would never be good at interpreting my dreams. My car suddenly skidded on a patch of leftover March ice. Better concentrate on my driving, then concentrate on finding a parking spot that didn't require a skidding walk through the lot.

No luck with the parking spot. I inched my way through the other cars, my hands clutching at fenders for support. Then with a quick clarity that made me stop, I *knew* what Dr. Roberts had meant. It was March. I had been in deep analysis for six months and had not once discussed my marriage. Standing in the parking lot between a Plymouth and a Buick, I caught my breath. There was no denying that it was decidedly odd. Yet my marriage was fine. When others around us got divorces, I had clung to that. My children would never feel the confusion of so many of their classmates. Their parents' marriage was "till death do us part." I inched away from the Plymouth and Buick, took two steps, and fell.

Irritably I brushed at my coat and my ripped stockings. My knee hurt. Then, when I reached the building door, it did not. But my stomach lurched. Good marriages survived discussion, yet I had been silent. Why? I walked through the building lobby and up the familiar carpeted steps to Dr. Roberts's office. This "good marriage" of mine had to be looked at. I opened the second-floor door. At the end of the hallway I would enter the room where for six months I had avoided the subject. The walls of the hall looked like a tunnel leading to danger.

On the couch I took a breath. "I'm ready to talk about my marriage."

Dr. Roberts said, "Ah."

For the next three weeks I felt like a traitor when I was with George. I had never criticized him to friends, never—as some women did—rebuked him in public. I had, I was learning, seldom criticized him to myself.

It was my fault, I told Dr. Roberts, that our sex life was almost nonexistent. I forced myself when I could, felt guilty in between. Dr. Roberts made a rare, soft comment: "It is the husband's responsibility to arouse his wife." What an unusual thought! George's procedure was to look at me accusingly when I stayed up to read. I had felt it was my responsibility to feel aroused.

George had acted admirably, I said, when I had lost him his Omaha job. "But it was through your article that he got another," Dr. Roberts said. "And you've glorified him in your books. Do you feel a debt that's unpaid still?" Yes. No. You did not pay debts in a marriage. George had been faithful, reliable, and conscientious.

Dr. Roberts said, "Somewhat like your mother." From calm, unemotional conversation, I burst into sobs. Oh, yes, of course there were many times when I ached for George simply to *understand,* to help with all those decisions about the children, to make decisions himself, on his own, to hold me just once and say, "Don't worry. It will be all right," to talk intimately with him without watching my words, afraid to imply any criticism at all, to feel—as I sobbingly realized I never had—close to the man I loved.

All right. I could accept the fact that my marriage was not "perfect." What marriage was? But now that I had finally faced its flaws, stopped assuming all the flaws were mine, George and I could work it out. I had been wrong to withhold my criticisms— from George and from myself. George would understand why we had to talk.

Yet I put off the discussion. Other events interfered. Tige came home for a weekend to say that he was no longer sure that engineering was for him, that next semester he wanted to work for a while and think. I felt it was a mature decision. George was enraged. "Lois, you have to change his mind." I didn't want to.

"George, if he works for a while, he may find out what he *does* want." "He won't like working the kind of job he can get." Then, it seemed to me, he would go back to college with new motivation.

George switched his anger to Josh. "I'm tired of having my basement cluttered up with your junk." Josh readily agreed to dismantle the lamb pen. "Dad, is it O.K. if I move your pile of scrap lumber at the bottom of the stairs? It's hard to step over." George's voice suddenly went high in an angry recital of every mistake Josh had made in the past year. Josh, shoulders drooping, moved the lamb's pen—and George's scrap lumber.

It was time to drive Tige to the bus. George was silent. Tige and I chatted. It still hurt each time he left. Heading home, I was as silent as George. I noticed a red light ahead. George did not. In the intersection a car barely missed us. I gasped. "Lois, I can't drive if you distract me." George's driving had never been good, but it was getting worse. "George, if you're tired, I'll drive." "No, I'm fine." An argument now would only make him worse. I hung onto my seat belt, counting the minutes to home.

We would, I decided, simply have to talk soon. The following weekend Josh and Tina were going up to visit Tige. George and I would have quiet, privacy, and no interruptions. It could wait until then. But no longer. I was now too clearly aware of the cost to the children. George and I had problems we had to work out—and we would.

On Saturday morning we drove Josh and Tina to the bus. On the way home I said, "There are some serious things I'd like to talk about today."

"Some things that shrink planted in your mind?"

I looked over at George. Which one of us had changed—or was it both? Ever since I had begun discussing my marriage with Dr. Roberts, George had become more silent and sullen. Perhaps he felt our marriage was threatened, but really it was not. I had no problem admitting my mistakes. George would admit his. People who loved each other worked things out.

At home George went out to the garden. Some spring inside me got tighter as the hours passed. "George, please. We have to talk." "As soon as I get the lawn seed spread." Then the fertilizer, then clearing out last year's vegetable garden. He would have to come in when it got dark. I waited.

Finally: "George, we *have* to talk. Problems are building up and—"

"There are no problems. Shrinks always want their patients to get divorced. Well, you can forget about that."

Tige had been absolutely right—George did interrupt; he did not hear what people said, but this time, I believed, he *had* to hear me. The rupture was getting wider. I was being swept away by a feeling of suffocating frustration.

"George, I'm not even thinking of a divorce. I only want to—"

"Forget divorce. I can't support two families . . . even now that you've talked Tige out of college."

Several times I thought it might be best simply to walk away from this fruitless nightmare. I took a tranquilizer, a sleeping pill. No, I could not abandon the hope of some understanding.

"George, can't we each just admit we've made mistakes and—"

"Ah, easy blaming me, isn't it?"

I tried admitting every mistake I could think of. Yes, I had probably neglected the children when writing my books; yes, I should have been stronger in controlling my depressions.

"Good. Now maybe we can get back to a normal life—as soon as you stop wasting money with that shrink."

Something inside me had begun to scream. I took another sleeping pill. "George, we're both tired. Let's—"

"Go to bed if you want. I feel like reading."

All right, I could sleep with the light on. Just as I was feeling the three—four?—sleeping pills, George said, "I wish you'd decide if we should spend more money on this car or get a new one."

Suddenly I felt as if I had wandered into a maze from which I could not possibly escape. Hopelessness descended like a blanket. I stumbled out of bed. George, incredibly, took off his robe, turned off the light, and got into bed. I closed the door and groped to the study. Now I knew why I had put off discussing our problems so long. I had always known how it would end. And this was an ending. There was no place to go from here. It was all over. I could stop sobbing because I knew the only thing left to do. In thirty minutes George would be sound asleep. I forced my eyes to focus on my watch. The children could no longer live with this tension, and I could not take them from their father. What I was about to do was the last act of a desperate person, of a failed person—but there was nothing else left. Tomorrow was a day I could not bear to see. It all ended here.

Then it was safe to creep down the back stairs. From the back closet I took a coat. Odd to think of comfort now. The garage door was heavy but silent. When I closed it again, I was glad the heaviness made a good seal. In the car I started the motor, then held the steering wheel as I had done so often before. The children no longer needed me to drive them to school, to doctors, to the homes of friends. They would survive; I could not. Going back to the pain and failure in that house where George was, was simply beyond me. In a little while I would sleep and I would end. I put my head back. The motor sounded loud in the small space. Sleep was coming. It would soon be over.

I felt a hand on my shoulder, shaking me. Whoever it was, I wished he'd stop; I had just gone to sleep. The shaking continued. I opened my eyes and saw George's face. From some deep, enormous well of anger, I thought, "Damn you, George. You even screw up my suicide."

"Lois, what are you doing?" What did he *think* I was doing—trying to save wear and tear on the tires?

He began to pull me from the car. "I got up to go to the bathroom, Lois. The light in the study was out. I couldn't imagine where you were." He sounded accusing, as if I had carelessly misplaced myself.

"Lois, should I call Dr. Roberts? How many pills did you take? Should I take you to the hospital?" I felt too groggy—and defeated —to answer questions. I just shook my head. I had apparently not been in our large garage long enough for the carbon monoxide to affect me at all. George pulled at my arm and I found I could walk, out into the clear midnight air I had never expected to breathe again.

That escape had been thwarted. I had been pulled back forcibly from where I wanted so badly to go. We were in the driveway now. I looked yearningly back at the garage. George continued his questions: "What do you want to do?"

"Just want to go to sleep now." I would sort it out tomorrow.

George led me toward the back door. I steadied myself on the porch post. "George, go back and turn off the motor."

I woke Sunday morning in a silent house. From the bedroom window I saw George working in the yard. At lunchtime he did not bring up the past night's event. Josh and Tina came home. While they reported on their weekend, I cooked a dinner I had not expected to cook, an elaborate one to keep me busy. I looked at my children. How *could* I have attempted something that would have hurt them forever?

The attempt, however, had shaken me—enough to have produced a dream I finally understood. Tomorrow I would see Dr. Roberts.

At bedtime George reminded me that I was to drive him to the train in the morning for his week-long meeting in Washington.

At our session on Monday, Dr. Roberts said, with atypical surprise, "George *left for the week?*"

Uh-huh.

I told him of my dream: I was sitting in my car—in the garage—aware of a monster behind me. It crawled over the seat from behind and I saw that it was George. Then, in the quick scene change of dreams, a small girl was chained to our house. The children and I cut the chains. Tina led her to the car and we all drove off.

Dr. Roberts's voice came from his desk behind the couch where I lay. "And what does that mean to you?"

This time I knew. "I've been living a *monstrous* lie for too long in my marriage. That little girl is me—chained to the marriage because it hurt so much when my mother left my father. I think I tried to die because I saw no way out. But my children helped me free her."

Tige's leaving for college had shaken a careful but fragile construction, a fragility I was then not ready to face. I *had* given my children a father who was always there as they grew up. Now that they were almost grown, the price I had paid came due.

Dr. Roberts said, "And?"

I took a deep, relaxing breath. "As soon as I can, I am leaving George. In five years Tina will be twenty-one. By then I can be self-supporting. Not by writing alone—that's too insecure; but I think I can also *teach* writing. And then, Dr. Roberts, I am leaving George." Just saying the words felt like the sodium amytal was again in my veins.

Dr. Roberts said, "Ah."

The following week I composed letters I would send to the area's colleges. Suddenly there was so much to put into a writing course—things I wished I had known.

George said, "They won't let you teach without a degree." Possibly not, but it was worth a try. If, somehow, things improved between George and me, it would still be a new career for when all the children left. I had, I believed, five years to get ready.

Then, abruptly, years, months, even days meant nothing. The following Saturday, Tina hugged me good-by to leave for a girl friend's house. At dinnertime she had not returned. There was no answer at the girl friend's house when I phoned. This was not like Tina at all. An hour passed. Josh took the car to search for her. I stayed by the phone. Then Josh returned with two neighborhood youths, all three white-faced and sober.

George said, "This is no time for visitors." Josh said, "They've got something important to say."

The tallest boy spoke. "We feel bad telling on Tina, but Josh says we have to now. Tina and Joe are running away."

I felt relief. Tina was, at least, not lying dead in some ditch. She was, at least, with Joe.

George exploded. "See! I told you that Black Panther was up to no good." While he raved on, I sorted facts. Joe, of course, was no Black Panther, but he was certainly black. He was also tall, strong, street-wise, and protective of Tina. He and blond, petite Tina would make a noticeable pair. I prepared to dial the police.

The other young man spoke. "They've got some wheels. Joe's friend used to work for a Chinese laundry. He gave Tina the keys to the truck."

Again, that deep relief. Tina and Joe in a Chinese laundry truck! Nothing but a brass band alongside could make them much easier to spot. I dialed the police.

George outlined all of Joe's character flaws to the two policemen who responded. I explained that Joe was very black, Tina very blond, and they were in a Chinese laundry truck. One of the policemen made valiant attempts to hide a grin. I said they were headed for California. They would not, the policeman said, smiling, even make the state line.

Joe's mother called. Was Joe there? I broke the news. "Your daughter talked him into this. My Joe would never do this. Tina's bad. I knew it." I made a mental note to keep George and Joe's mother apart.

And walked the floor with Josh. "Mom, at least he's big. She's safe, but why did she go? Why didn't she tell me? But she'll be all right." I had to believe she would. Why *did* she go? There had

277

been no quarrel, no note—she had hugged me when she left the house.

During the hours that passed like slow drips from a faucet, I reassured myself. Instinctively, I agreed with Joe's mother. It had been Tina's idea. Adoring Joe turned cartwheels at Tina's request. At least she had chosen her running mate wisely—he was husky, easily directed, and fiercely loyal. With that in mind, I managed to sleep.

The phone call woke me at seven. A bored, official voice said that my daughter and "her companion" had been picked up when their truck broke down on the highway. They had spent the night in a small town jail. They were now back in Philadelphia, where Tina could be released to my custody if I picked her up.

The other parents who waited in the grimy, scarred building outside a door marked "Juvenile Division" looked as dazed as I felt. Other children—not ours—were in places like this. It was a tawdry dream that was sure to end.

Finally, George and I were admitted to a room where Tina sat slumped in a chair, a policewoman next to her, typing a form. Tina saw me and sat up straight. "Mom, you have to do something about conditions in that jail! The food was awful and there were cockroaches."

I let the policewoman tell Tina how to avoid "the conditions." George had begun to shout. I simply looked at Tina, trying to understand this defiant young woman.

In the week that followed, my confusion and concern got a great deal worse. In the mornings she left for school. In the afternoons, as I counted the minutes, she returned—some days to tell me she "loved me so much," others to say I was a "blind, stupid fool," that she would "shake me up—no matter *what*." I was beyond anger at her behavior, only stunned.

Dr. Roberts said during one of our sessions, which now centered solely on my anguish for Tina, "I think her behavior is a bit beyond normal. Dr. Apmann is good with teen-age problems. Do you think she'd talk with him?"

To my surprise, Tina agreed. "I'll talk to anyone. I sure can't get through to you."

Dr. Apmann was a gray-haired, gray-bearded man with a jaunty air. He talked alone with Tina, once, twice, three times, and then requested that George and I participate in a joint session.

George balked. This time, I vowed, he would come if I had to buy a gun. "George, it's our daughter. You must." The look on my face must have persuaded him.

In Dr. Apmann's office, Tina sat across from us, looking down at the floor. George asked Dr. Apmann what was wrong with Tina. Dr. Apmann waved his question aside and said to Tina, "Remember, we agreed that you would talk about your true feelings toward your parents."

I tried to brace myself. Whatever I had done wrong, I hoped it came out. There was nothing I could not stand if it would take the strain from that troubled, beloved face.

Tina looked up at Dr. Apmann and nodded, and I held my breath. But she turned to George and said, quietly, calmly, "Dad, I've always seen you as a weak person. You could never let Mom leave you. You're too dependent to stand on your own."

In horror, I watched George's face for the pain I was sure he felt. Involuntarily, I reached out to touch his arm. But his face showed nothing at all. He said simply, "What does she mean?" looking first at Dr. Apmann, then at me.

Tina screamed, "You see!" and ran from the room. Dr. Apmann looked at me. I looked at the floor. My daughter had indeed seen what I had avoided so long, and it was apparently hurting her badly. I could, however, tell Dr. Apmann there was some hope. I asked George if he minded my talking with Dr. Apmann alone. "About what?" "Oh, female things." A low, unlikely trick, but it worked.

The door closed behind George. "Dr. Apmann, I *am* planning to leave Tina's father as soon as I can."

Dr. Apmann toyed with some objects on his desk. He looked up finally with sad gray eyes. "Mrs. Stalvey, the marriage has been tearing that young lady apart for a long, long time. If you are leaving, the sooner the better."

My mind had never functioned so fast as it did during those seconds—minutes—I looked back at Dr. Apmann. If the marriage was hurting Tina, it would not last one more day than it had to. I had no source of income. At the age of fifty, could I find a job? But I had long ago sent a royalty check to Switzerland to buy silver bars. It was, I told George, something for a very, very rainy day. That very rainy day was *now*. There was—there had to be—enough to live on for a while. If not, I would leave anyway. My daughter's health was the rainiest day there could be.

"Dr. Apmann, I plan to be gone in ten days; if possible, less."

"Is there any place Tina can be out of the home until it's over?" he asked. "She's going to feel a lot of guilt as well as relief."

Again, my mind functioned fast. George's younger brother and his family lived in Illinois. George's brother was like my father-in-law—easy going, kind, understanding. After the academically demanding high school she attended in Philadelphia, Tina could easily adapt to her cousins' small-town school, even finish the semester there. Somehow I knew she would be willing to go.

Dr. Apmann said, "That sounds best." He rose to shake my hand. It was trembling, but then my chin went up. I took a deep breath.

As I drove George and Tina home in silence, Tina's body moved closer to mine. I was surprised to find that outdoors it was raining too. It was indeed a very rainy day. I reached to squeeze Tina's hand and then to advance the speed of the wipers. Now, much better, I could see ahead.

Chapter 21

TINA WAS WILLING, even eager, to go to Illinois. As I helped her pack, I wondered why walking through glass to reach Tige had once seemed such a miracle. What was happening now demanded much more than a few barefooted steps through shattered glass.

It was time to say good-by. "Tina, things will be different when you get back." A look in her green eyes made me feel she knew how. "I hope so, Mom." Her slim figure looked small but straight as she walked to the plane.

Driving back from the airport, I reviewed the events that had whizzed by in the last few days—whizzed inside and around me. It was as if I had made my first step into a long chute down which I now sped with no possibility of stopping. Barbara Hamilton had recommended her lawyer. Best, I had decided, to do that first. The morning after my promise to Dr. Apmann, someone who did not seem to be me dialed the phone, made an appointment, and sat across the desk from a *lawyer*.

Attorney Richard Diedrich had been involved in the dismantling of possibly hundreds of marriages. What was office routine for him was a state of shock for me. Surely I could not be sitting here discussing the end of a twenty-year marriage with this gray-suited stranger.

"Mrs. Stalvey, it sounds as if you have unquestionable grounds for mental cruelty. Now, I suggest that you *gradually* introduce the subject of divorce. We need to find out how cooperative he's likely to be."

Not very. During our last bitter quarrel, I had suggested a temporary separation. George had said, "I can't afford to support two households and *I'm* not living in some hovel."

"What your husband doesn't know, apparently, is that you can get an order to remove him from the house. A court would also order him to pay your expenses and those of the minor children."

Weary defeat settled over me. I could leave my children's father, but I could not have them see George hauled away from the house. Nor could we withstand the legal battle George was sure to mount over child support. On the other hand, I could not support Josh and Tina even for the short time they would still be in school. Tige already had a job and a place of his own. Josh would graduate high school in five months and wanted to work before college. Tina would be in Illinois, at least for a time. Dr. Apmann had said it was the tension of the marriage itself that had upset her. If she had to live with George for a while when she returned, she could handle it. If, by then, she wanted to live with me, I would find a way.

"Mr. Diedrich, what are the legal problems if *I* leave the house?" From the beginning I had somehow known that this was what had to be. "I think I have some money."

First, Mr. Diedrich expressed professional incredulity that I had put all my writing earnings into joint accounts. "An obviously intelligent woman like you—you ran a business!" Yes, but I had also committed my life to a marriage. What kind of woman, intelligent or not, allowed herself to *prepare* for an ending?

I could, Mr. Diedrich said, "clean out all the bank accounts. Many women do." Not if I left my children as hostages to George's good will.

"No, I just want to take half of what my silver bullion is worth." There at least my luck had held. I had never made a penny before without working for it, but Harry Browne's book on financial crisis had been on a table next to me as I autographed my own book in Kansas City. What he wrote made sense. George had protested, but now the silver I bought had quadrupled in value. Even half—$10,000—would last me until I found a job.

"If I were you," Mr. Diedrich said, "I'd take *all* the money and run—but you know your husband better than I. But do get a safe-deposit box of your own and a mailing address. And then prepare him . . . and let me know."

First I had to prepare myself. As I should have expected, my friendship with Barbara had survived my neglect during her divorce. As I cried out my pain at Tina's leaving, at the leaving I would have to do, Barbara gave me tea and forgiveness. "I knew exactly why you stayed away during my divorce, Lois. It's pretty standard even with the closest friends. Your marriage was too shaky to watch me get out of mine." Barbara had been making her plans for a year, had gotten her degree, and now she had a job she loved with a counseling center. "I'm glad," she said, "that Tina pulled the plug. It happens more often than most people know. A child acts up just to get all the crap to the surface. At last!" She poured more tea. "You know, I never could figure out why you were so smart about most things and so dumb about your marriage."

"You knew?"

"So did most of your friends. Wait and see."

"Why didn't you say something?"

"Would you have listened?"

I listened now as Barbara prepared me from her experience and the cases she handled at work. "Initially children side with the weaker parent. Be ready for their anger at you. It will pass. Be prepared for George's anger too—and to feel scared out of your wits at times."

I already was. The only comfort I could derive from leaving my marriage at the age of fifty was in knowing that it was easier than leaving it at fifty-five. There had, as yet, been no answers to the letters I had written to colleges. There might never be. But that old image I had had before, of people lost in jungles or stranded in snow, came back again. You stayed where you were and perished—or pushed on ahead. I left Barbara's apartment and went home to write a letter that would instruct the bank in Switzerland to sell the silver.

Barbara had been right about my other friends. Sally Chapman, happily married, had hoped I could work things out. Now she said, "The day George came into your house and said, 'The lawn mower's on fire. What should I do?'—well, I don't blame you a bit. How can I help?" Ginny Arthur, with her school counseling work, felt I was doing the best thing for the children by not making the divorce "as messy as some." Eve Chisholm, divorced herself, said, "Use my mailing address for the silver check. How much do you need for an apartment deposit till then?"

It was hard to keep my balance when time was moving so fast—and so slowly. I was forced to pretend while I waited for that check. Attorney Diedrich had told me to "prepare" George only after I had my money. "He could do to you what you refused to do to him." George—and Josh—must sense something different in me, I felt. Tige came to dinner. He liked his restaurant job: "Gives me a free mind to write poetry, Mom, while I'm slinging the hash—and a good way for starving poets to eat." Then Tige's words came out strong: "Mom can do *anything*. She always could." A loving look at me. Somehow Tige knew too.

And, I decided later, so did George. Dr. Roberts had given me a startling description of a particular form of behavior termed *passive-aggressive*. "It is what these people do *not* do—or do very subtly—that hurts. 'Forgetting' something important, being 'unable' to do a task, saying the wrong thing 'innocently.' " George had "forgotten" to mention he had talked with Tina from his office phone, "couldn't remember" anything "important" she had said. A crystal decanter I had bought in my single days "fell" from his hands. Later, "Tige quit college because *you* never went. I hope that doesn't make you feel guilty." Not anymore. Twenty years of unexplainable surges of pain had now become clear—along with a present awareness that an undeclared war was escalating. I could remain calm now as George increased his subtle bombardments. "Lois, I think Tina's problems came from your going to the hospital." I could now shrug at what once would have torn me to bits.

Finally Eve called on Saturday. "I have a houseguest from Switzerland I want you to meet." I raced right over. The check was there. I could now begin preparing George. It was still possible that the reality of my wanting a divorce might cut through to him as I had never been able to do. What if he said he needed me, asked me to stay?

George was in the kitchen, drinking coffee, when I got back. I took a breath. It was going to hurt to inflict this pain. "George, I have been thinking that I might want a divorce. It might—"

George's face turned red. He slammed down his coffee mug. His voice held a whine of irritation. "Think all you want, but there'll be no divorce. I won't be at the mercy of your whims. I'm not leaving this house. You can if you want to, but not with a penny of mine." George was standing now, glowering down at me. He turned and stomped up to his den.

Was this how the marriage would end—with George's *irritation?* I followed him up the stairs. "Lois, I don't want to talk about it now." When could we? "I'll let you know, Lois. *I'm* busy."

Josh was spending the weekend with Tige, had spent many weekends with Tige lately. Perhaps that was his way of handling what he must have known was awry. If George was willing to talk, I hoped it would be before Josh came home on Sunday. I went to the sewing room, then made dinner. George ate in silence except for a brief "I am not ready to discuss your crazy ideas." He returned to his den. When I passed his open door, I saw he was making new file folders. Yes, if the Russians took New Jersey, George would note it, file it, and ask me later where it was. Or expect to ask me where it was. "George, not talking about it won't make it go away." He did not look up.

At ten o'clock George walked into the dressing room where I was trying to read. His face had a strange smile. "Lois, remember how pleased you were that Tina packed the skirt you made her? She didn't really want to take it. I told her she must."

I didn't even glance at the wedding ring on my finger. After twenty years, I knew it was there and how to remove it. I placed it gently on the bedside table, took my pillow, and went into Tina's room. And, without a sleeping pill, to sleep.

In the morning I noticed that George had gone through my handbag and removed my checkbook and credit cards.

The manager at the apartment building was a woman. Yes, the apartment could be ready immediately. I wrote a check from my new account. She looked at my trembling fingers. "Leaving your husband? I've been there myself. Good luck."

I had broken the news to Josh the night before. At first he had been calm. "I'm leaving your father, honey, but I'm not leaving you. I'll be living just up on City Line. You can be with me as much as you want. The bus from school takes you right past." Josh nodded. "It's O.K." Later he came, red-faced and teary-eyed, to accuse me of breaking up the family. Let him shout out his hurt. At dinner, when George came home, Josh said, "Dad, I'm sorry." George said, "I don't need sympathy from you."

Before Josh left for school, I told him I thought it would be best if I left that day; there was no point prolonging what I felt I had to do. Josh said, "Mom, it's O.K. Actually, now that I think of it, I don't know how you stayed this long."

All my careful thinking collapsed. "Josh, if you want to come with me, we'll find some way to manage."

"It's O.K., Mom. I'll be leaving here soon anyway."

We both worked very hard on smiles. "Mom, can I see your new apartment tonight?" Sure thing.

I cleaned up the breakfast dishes for the last time, glad I had taught my sons to cook. It was a crazy thought for now, but I felt like the patient set for surgery—not a time to think too far ahead, just to do what must be done. Sally would be there at noon with her station wagon to help me move clothes and the furniture from my single days that had somehow survived. Before that, a quick trip to the bedding store and to the Salvation Army, for pots, pans, dishes—then back to pack my clothes.

At noon Sally and I loaded her car. We managed miraculously to wrestle with the big overstuffed chair I had curled up in as a child. In the parking lot of my new apartment building, we carried the lightest cartons across pebbled ground. I stepped on a rock I could not see. A flame of pain shot through my ankle. This, I told my body firmly, was simply not the day for a sprain. I consigned the pain to some other part of my mind and walked on.

The apartment looked incredibly bare, but the bed had been delivered. Sally and I again wrestled the overstuffed chair from the elevator down the hall. From somewhere behind the chair Sally said, "Poor old George. I wonder how he's going to make it on his own?"

Suddenly I knew. "Sally, he'll be married again within a year."

"How does that make you feel?"

I slowed a bit to give it full emotional consideration. George and some other woman—"I only hope she's not someone I like and that she knows what she's getting."

Finally the furniture—such as it was—was in place. Sally had to get home and I had to pick up one more carton of books. My car, by lucky fate, was in my name alone. I had bought it (used) with a small royalty check and there had been no time to get George's signature for the title. I drove it back to the house.

The anesthetic wore off as I carried the carton down the broad center stairway—the stairway I once expected that Tina would walk down as a bride. This big, warm house was nothing but wood and stone and layers of paint, but my children had grown up here. I knew and loved every inch of it . . . the basement where we had raised the lamb, the corner were the Christmas tree had stood, the study where my writing dreams had come true and where Tige and I had held so many after-school talks, Tina's room with the rainbow she had painted over her bed. How on earth could I leave this house—and those memories?

I got into my car and forced myself to drive down the driveway, carefully, as if breaking a beautiful, iridescent web that had to be broken. This was also the house Tina had fled in agony. This was the velvety lawn on which George had never allowed the children to play. In this garage I had tried to die.

As the car passed the kitchen window where I had watched so often for my children returning from school, I did feel as if something had torn. At the end of the driveway I had to wipe my tears to see. For a moment it was hard to remember where I was going.

Both Josh and Tige visited that evening. When I broke the news to Tige, he had said, "It figures" and "It's not as if I were still at home myself." Now he was planning to build a bookcase for me—and to give me advice on the classes he was sure I would teach. "You don't know how lousy some of those college instructors are. The colleges will fight over you." None had yet, but I let Tige talk enthusiastically on. "I can give you some tips, Mom, on how a class *should* be run."

Finally, at the door, my two tall young men gave me tender hugs. Then I was in my new bed, feeling both free and frightened. Somewhere out there beyond the roofs, lights, and stars Tina was asleep by now. Her response to my news on the phone had been monosyllabic: "Good." She had not prolonged the conversation.

I turned in the unfamiliar bed and looked out the window at the stars. Now I knew how acrobats feel—free in the air, but hoping they can catch the swinging trapeze. Right now, tonight, it was best to forget there was no net down there. Suddenly the ankle I had hurt so badly early in the day began to throb. I truly had banished it until this crucial day was over. I gave it permission to swell now and to hurt a bit, but I went to sleep.

Josh brought me the mail. It seemed that my luck was holding up after all. Three colleges wanted to talk to me, one as soon as possible. Would they want to see me if I had mentioned I had no degree? That, I decided, was something we would have to find out.

"As soon as possible" for the Community College of Philadelphia was at noon the following Monday. At eleven o'clock I got off a bus on Chestnut Street, a block from the college. Instinctively, old techniques had returned. I had always planned a thirty-minute preappointment coffee break—to sip up confidence, to think, to prepare. As I looked for a coffee shop, I saw my reflection in the windows. This was no fourteen-year-old approaching a department store, no seventeen-year-old applying for a sign-writing job at Gimbel's, and no advertising woman in her twenties approaching an important client with a new idea. This time I was fifty years old, after a twenty-year layoff, applying for a job for which, on paper, I had no qualifications and no experience at all. I slunk into a coffee shop. I had had crazy ideas before, but I had finally reached the point of idiocy. I would have a cup of coffee, make a call of apology, and head back home.

How had I gotten into this in the first place? I thought as I stirred black coffee. There must be other, more reasonable jobs I could try for—salesperson, waitress. What on earth had made me think that I could . . . ?

Well, the volunteer teaching at the children's elementary school for one. I had enjoyed those wild but enthusiastic eighth-graders. Rita McNeil, a senior at Tige's college, had described what was *not* being taught her in journalism. I took a sip of coffee. Darn it, I *knew* how journalism and creative writing could be taught. I had learned it on my own and enjoyed passing the tricks and techniques on to others. I could do it now.

Once more I felt ready to grab at scraps of confidence and wrap them around me. This was how one kept appointments: leave the doubts behind with the crumpled napkin.

Tom Spivak, head of the Humanities Division at the college, looked like Mark Twain. Clay Barrett, chairman of the English Department, looked like the models in expensive liquor ads. "Mark Twain" and the "Meyer's Rum" man looked out of place in this remodeled-department-store college whose students looked like Tige's former classmates in his mostly black high school.

"Mark Twain" smiled benignly. The "Meyer's Rum" man told me how much he admired my books. Would their favorite small French restaurant be all right for lunch?

Over Quiche Lorraine, I realized I was being courted. By the time the scampi was served, I understood why.

"Other colleges," Clay Barrett, the "Meyer's" man, said, "can offer you a pretty campus and well-prepared students. We can offer you a challenge."

I wondered, for a moment, if I had one more challenge left in me just then. Yet, as I walked into the school, I had felt a familiarity—these were the kids from our neighborhood, grown-up now, full of a desperate purpose—the kind of young people I had written about in *Getting Ready*.

Clay was talking. "You can teach creative writing or reporting or whatever you want. Morning, evening, or afternoon." The interview was not going at all as I had expected. Then: "Just as a formality, there are forms to fill out. Just put down your highest degree."

Ah, well, it had been a delicious lunch.

I grinned cheerfully at Clay. "I have *no* degree. High school was about all the formal education I could handle."

Clay casually waved aside someone else's years of college work. "Oh, well, then just list your books."

A memory of the halls of Barker High superimposed itself on this elegant French restaurant. So that old insight still held true! If people think you're good enough at something, rules are conveniently ignored.

Over coffee and chocolate mousse, I promised Clay I would let him know after I talked with the other two colleges. But I knew—and I think he did too—where I wanted to be.

The other colleges did indeed have tree-shaded campuses, well-dressed and, probably, well-prepared students. In contrast to the downtown clatter, the graffiti-filled walls, and the incredible mix of students at the Community College, the other schools looked awfully dull. I called Clay Barrett. If I had my classes in the early morning, I could write in the afternoon. The semester, Clay said, would start in two weeks.

I now curled up in the overstuffed chair to work out what to teach about writing in thirteen weeks. Clay had introduced me to the other creative-writing teacher, a man with darting eyes who asked *me* how I planned to structure *my* course. No help there. But, gradually, by simple logic, a structure was emerging on the pad in my lap.

The phone rang. I hoped it was not George again. I had never realized before how many things George lost, broke, or insisted I misplaced. Or how frequently he now fought with Josh. George had announced he was selling the house. There was nothing I could do about that, but I could enjoy the luxury of answering his questions and accusations with a simple, glorious "Umm."

It was Ginny on the phone. Her aunt had called from New York. The guest speaker for their church program had canceled. Would I, for expenses and an honorarium, fill in on short notice? Why not? No more complex arrangements. I was free to take a train and go.

At Mrs. Pierce's church, I enjoyed the give-and-take of the questions after my speech. An attractive gray-haired man in the audience asked some of the best. He was, it developed, Dr. Henry Putnam, a friend of Ginny's aunt, and he would join us for lunch.

During lunch I learned that Hank Putnam was a professor at Columbia and was busy checking out my left hand for a ring. He had been divorced, he volunteered, for many years. I admitted I was in the process of mine—and about to start teaching soon at a Philadelphia college.

Two days later, a note from Hank arrived. He would very much like to see me again. Could I come to New York for dinner or would I prefer having him come to Philadelphia?

I held the note for a long time in my hand. Funny, but dating had never entered my mind. I had not had a "date" in twenty years. The word itself sounded like something I had left behind along with Glenn Miller records and menstrual cramps. Still, Hank was an attractive, intelligent man and he wanted to see me. "Dating," I supposed, had to start sometime. At the least, I could pick up some tips on "professoring" from him. Hank phoned. I recommended a good hotel nearby where he could stay and we could meet for dinner. The restaurant, I knew, had a dance floor. Was Hank a good dancer? Too much to hope.

As I dressed to meet him that evening, I felt like an overaged actress assigned to play the ingenue. Could I—did I want to—carry this off? Fate was funny. If Hank had been a doctor or a lawyer, I would probably have said no. But a college professor from whom I could learn something useful—all right, eye shadow on the rather crepy lids, make-up on the slightly sagging chin, and off I would go.

Hank, standing in the lobby, looked eager and attractive. He held the door to the dining room, looking hesitant. Ah, yes, the feminist movement had made men unsure. I thanked him and breezed through.

Thirty minutes later, I was smiling secretly to myself. Some things never changed. Twenty years had fallen away and I was enjoying a date again. This man, flattering, attentive, and fun to be with, had gray in his hair and veins on his hands, but everything else seemed the same. The rapt attention I had once had to pretend was now completely sincere. I listened to his teaching advice. "Establish a close relationship with your classes, but not with any individual student." "Stay out of college politics—just teach your best." Hank, I found, had two master's degrees and one Ph.D.

Hank said, "Where did you get your degree?"

"Barker High School, '43."

Hank slapped the table in laughing delight. "Good. They're finally hiring people who have done what they teach."

Now I could ask him questions that *really* worried me: Do you take attendance in a college class? (Yes.) What happens if I can't get to class? (Cancel by calling the school.)

"Hank, my first *day* in a college classroom will be next week. And I'll be the instructor."

Hank's square face grinned. "Don't worry. You'll do fine. Do you want to dance?"

Did I! It was astonishing to find that Hank actually followed the music. No more blocking out music to follow George's steps. It felt unbelievably wonderful to let the music flow through my body as Hank and I moved around the floor.

The first day of my improbable teaching career began. As I watched an astonishing mix of students enter my (my!) classroom, I reviewed Hank's—and Tige's—suggestions. Hank had said, "Try to spot the different personalities." Tige had said, "Find out which ones are serious and which are taking the course only for the credit." I could then, Tige said, spend more time on the serious ones. It had seemed a good idea to hand out mimeographed questionnaires that asked directly if they were serious about creative writing and to ask that they tell something about themselves. And —another of Hank's suggestions—to let them ask questions about me. ("Students respond better to a *person* than to an impersonal instructor.")

Twenty assorted bodies now filled the room—a slim, lithe black woman, a middle-aged white man in a fireman's uniform, a tall, thin, blond boy, a group of swaggering black youths—and one giant with corn rows in his hair. Neophyte that I was, I still felt a wave of happy excitement. In plotting my syllabus (See! I had learned the new college language!), I had found I had more theories on teaching than I dreamed—from my own school days, from my children's. We would now see which ones worked.

I passed out the questionnaires. "Just tell me about yourself. Don't worry about spelling and punctuation. This is creative writing, not English grammar." I could feel bodies relax. As I moved among the students, I invited questions about myself. Only fair. Yes, I had three children, twenty, eighteen, and seventeen, was separated, and wrote books. I did not volunteer that this was my first day in college. We all needed confidence in me.

Nineteen heads bent over papers, but the "giant" rose from the back of the class and lumbered toward me, his questionnaire in a hand the size of a car battery. His ebony face loomed somewhere way above me, and it frowned. "I ain't answering no questions, lady. None of your business."

Well, my first crisis in the classroom! But as I craned my neck to look up at him, I could not help smiling. "Listen," I said, "I'm five feet five. You're at least six six. There is no way I can make you do *anything*."

The giant looked surprised. Few people, I suspected, had ever smiled at him before. Close-up, I saw scars on his arms, forehead, and chin.

I took the questionnaire he had thrust at me. "But if you don't fill this out, I can't teach you as well as the rest. You paid your money. It's your choice."

Nineteen pencils had stopped moving. The giant still looked down. "You don't take off for bad spelling?" No, this was a writing class. He would have to learn his spelling from the dictionary. But, I asked, "could we please sit down? My neck hurts."

The giant's scarred face split with a laugh. "O.K., my *choice* is to fill out the paper."

Two weeks later I felt as if I had known these students for years. My ideas about teaching had worked. Finding something in each paper to praise had been like water on flowers. They had even taught themselves to spell.

By now I had met other college instructors. Some obviously loved teaching as much as I. Others made scathing remarks about "teaching these cretins until I can move on" or "How was your animal-training act today?"

On weekends Hank came down from New York or I went there. "Hank, they're not cretins and they're not animals. They're determined—and talented—people. And they work so damned hard."

Hank said, "They work for people who respect them. It's as simple as that."

Of course I respected them. Those questionnaires had told me what their lives were like—the menial jobs, the family and health problems, the failures. Each student was trying to improve his or her lot, and they were doing it. Their papers were not on their "summer vacations" or "the country in spring." The question-naires had opened them up. These students wrote about Vietnam, about fighting drugs, of humiliations at the welfare office, and they wrote well. On the days when papers were read aloud for class evaluation, hardened classmates wiped moist eyes. So did I. I had climbed up my sturdy WASP middle-class ladder, but they had had to grab rotting ropes and rusting beams, and they had survived. Just the fact that some of them were sitting in a class-room now was close to incredible.

Near the end of the semester, I announced to the class that their work was so very good that it was a pity not to give more people a chance to read it. If they wanted to take on some extra-hard work, I would see about having the college print shop mimeo-graph and bind it. They must be their own editorial board, type, correct, and prepare the work for print. The "giant," Elroy Zigg, roared "Yes!" Nineteen others asked when they could start.

Clay Barrett agreed to "find" English Department funds. "I expect you'll clean up their language, Lois." I heard myself say-ing, "No." A sergeant in Vietnam was unlikely to say, "Oh, fudge," and the language of Janice Sanchez's social worker made a point in itself. "Cleaning up the language," I knew, would be an artistic and psychological betrayal. "Our readers will be college students, not grade-school kids."

Clay shrugged. "Well, you lived dangerously in Omaha, but you don't know Dean Morgan. Lots of luck."

All right, my college teaching career might be very short—but it was very sweet. At least this time I was risking my own job.

The magazine, *Expressions,* came out the last day of classes, complete with *fuck* and *shit* and *cocksucking bastard.* Complete too with Elroy's Tolkien-like fantasy and Melissa Gavodny's gos-samer verse.

Dean Morgan's secretary was waiting outside my classroom to say he wanted to see me immediately. Would he strip me of my record book and escort me out the door?

Handsome, silver-haired Kevin Morgan stood up behind his desk, reached out his hand, and—smilingly!—shook mine. He held up the yellow-covered *Expressions*. "This is the finest publication this college has ever put out. I'm wondering if you'd consider being adviser to the college paper. Now that's a *real* challenge, but I hope you'll try."

Would I! Was it twenty-five or thirty years ago that I had told Marquette University a college newspaper should be used as a lab for journalism students? I had always regretted not having the time. Now, when I wanted it—needed it—I was being handed a second chance.

"Yes, if Clay will let me teach news reporting and copy editing —starting with the summer semester."

Dean Morgan picked up his phone, talked with Clay, then turned to me. "All set. By the way, the job pays a fairly good amount."

Money? Like the day J.D. O.K.'d my writing the column, I had forgotten to ask.

That month—June 1976—Josh would be graduating from high school and Tina was coming home. Her letters had been infrequent; my calls to her met with a cool response. Barbara had said, "She wants to test the waters. Also, pet, she has a healthy need to compete with a strong, accomplished mama. She may need time to figure out how. It will be a while before things are smooth."

I had finished my therapy with Dr. Roberts the previous month, but not without some startling new insights about my mother, my daughter, and myself. Now I could see that I had tried to be for Tina—and for myself—the kind of mother *I* had wanted so much, not necessarily the mother *Tina* wanted. Unconsciously, I had hoped, through Tina, to heal old hurts. If I could not *have* the mother I wanted, I would *be* that mother. And, of course, it could not work. Tina was not a second-chance Lois. Tina was—and had to be—herself. Now my daughter was coming home. Could I show her how much had changed?

Tina and I would meet at Josh's graduation. George had phoned to say he had gotten her from the airport that morning. I walked across the parking lot, seeing my tall, robed son and the slim blond figure of my daughter up ahead. Her first hug was tentative, but as she sat between George and me during the ceremony, she took my hand. When we parted, Josh said balefully that his father was taking *them* to dinner. I held my smile. Tina said, "I hear your new apartment has a pool. Can we swim tomorrow?" My smile was now sincere.

The next day as Tina splashed in the pool, she talked about Illinois. "Uncle Wayne absolutely rules that family. Aunt Sue does whatever he says. Very funny. I can't imagine why." My daughter had learned the important lesson that marriages were different. She could make her choice someday. Now Tina wanted "all the details of how you're teaching college," the "giant," the magazine, my new advising job.

Then, impishly, "Mom, you need a rest. You and your daughter should take a trip. You've always talked about Aunt Josey in Indiana. Let's just get into the car and visit her."

Tina's tanned, water-splashed face waited for my answer. Driving to visit my father's sister somehow seemed just right. I had not seen Aunt Josey since my father died, but all the years of my childhood she had kept in touch. It would be nice to see her. I said to Tina, "Good idea."

We shared the driving. I was proud of Tina's capable yet cautious handling of the wheel. When the highway took us past the town where she had spent the night in jail, she slumped in the passenger seat, silent. I wondered when, if ever, she would be able to talk about those days. Then she brightened and asked about Aunt Josey. I realized that, like the observation of my sister-in-law, Aunt Josey would provide another feminine life-style for Tina to see.

Aunt Josey had never married. She had, single-handedly, run her farm, plowing, planting, and, according to my father's teasing, selling her crops for "a pirate's price." She had raised my cousin Ruth when Ruth's mother died and Ruth's father, my Uncle Bob, had remarried and moved away. Ruth, a bit older than I, now raised her own family next door, giving Aunt Josey the love and loyalty of a daughter.

We drove into the quaint farmyard, incongruous but refreshing among the Holiday Inns, McDonald's, and Marriotts that almost engulfed it. Ruth, white-haired now, heard our horn and started out her door. Aunt Josey, well over seventy, beat her to our car. She looked closely at Tina. "Not much meat on those bones, but you'll do. Want to go pick blueberries?" Tina hurried off, trying to keep up with Aunt Josey. They returned in an hour,

Tina's face glowing with awe and adoration. "Mom," she whispered, "I didn't know you had relatives like *this!*"

Dinner over, dishes done, we sat in Ruth's living room to talk. Finally Ruth said wistfully, "I can now confess how I used to envy you, wished my father loved me as yours loved you. He used to take me with him when he bought your presents. Gee, he never missed a holiday—Easter, Valentine's Day—always a special present." Then, "Lois, what's the matter?"

"Ruth, I never got those presents."

"But you must have. I was with him when he mailed them. Don't you remember the little gray fur hat and muff? And the toy stove? That cost him every cent he had that day."

Yes, I remembered them all—they had been given me as presents from Mother . . . along with "If your father loved you, he'd at least send a card."

Aunt Josey's gravelly voice responded: "Ruthie, that explains why the checks were never cashed."

Ruth said, "Oh, Lois, I'm so sorry I brought it up." Tina reached for my hand.

I could hardly speak. "Ruth, don't be sorry. You've just given me . . ." I took a breath to absorb this joy. Ruth had just given me the most wonderful gift of my life: proof that my father had loved me all those years.

Ruth said, "Don't be bitter toward your mother. I'm sure she felt she was right."

The thought had not even occurred to me. What did it matter? The only important thing was that he had never forgotten me, had always cared, had sent gift after gift with no reply. I hugged the knowledge around me like a sable coat, warm and priceless and new.

I could not wait to put other facts together. "Aunt Josey, his car accident. When did it happen?" The night my mother had left him. He was in the hospital for over a year, in a wheelchair for months after that—and on crutches for most of the rest of his life. "He couldn't come to see you," Aunt Josey said, "after the time your mother had him arrested for alimony arrears."

Of course! In the depths of the Depression, even able-bodied men were out of work. My crippled father had not had a chance. Yet he had sent what he could. Checks to Mother, I learned, were cashed. Checks to Bobby and me were not.

"But when I never wrote to thank him for his gifts . . ."

Aunt Josey lowered her eyes. "Yes, it hurt him bad. I told him to stop, but he never did. Until he sent you that watch for your high school graduation. He figured maybe you wanted to forget by then."

The watch! I thought it had come from Mother. I had lost it long ago. Father's last gift—until an ungrateful daughter had finally sought him out; then he had mortgaged all he had to put her in business. How could I not have known!

Ruth said again, "Don't be angry at your mother."

I found I could not be, even if I tried. A lifetime of hurt and loss and yearning had just been swept away, replaced by breathtaking tremors of joy. There was no room for any other feeling. The truth I had learned was too big and too precious. My father had loved me deeply after all.

That night in the guest room, I lay in the dark next to Tina, trying to silence tears of cleansing rapture. Aunt Josey believed my father, from his assured place in Heaven, knew what I felt. I chose to believe she was right.

Tina heard my breathing and read my thoughts. She snuggled close. "Mom, it's all right to cry. It's all over now and it's gonna be good up ahead."

Two well-loved daughters finally went to sleep.

Chapter 22

THE NEW COLLEGE SEMESTER began, giving me more satisfaction than I could have imagined. The "newspaper-as-laboratory" plan I had conceived thirty years before worked perfectly. In my news-reporting and copy-editing classes, one mention of extra credit for newspaper work had students packing the newspaper office. Art Conner, the student editor who, the previous semester, had somehow managed to get out skeleton editions with a staff of two, now looked thunderstruck by his staff of thirty-three.

I sat at the back of the newspaper office, smiling at the administrative experience Art would get and at how well old bits and pieces of experience had come together for me—from my own school newspaper days, the southern paper I had worked on when I was married to Tony, even my experience with the ill-trained college graduates I had hired at my agency. Maybe all women had mental attics where their skills gathered dust until needed.

One month into the semester I realized that my life was falling into place much more easily than I could have hoped. The only part that was not yet working well was finding time for my writing. After a morning of teaching and newspaper work, I always vowed I would go home and write. My resolve lasted until I sat down in the overstuffed chair. I usually woke up for dinner.

Weekends were devoted to Josh and Tina. George, to my astonishment, had bought a house in all WASP Chestnut Hill. Now I picked Tina up outside that unfamiliar house, sometimes to visit

Josh at his new apartment or Tige at his. Josh, like Tige, wanted to work instead of going straight to college. He too had gotten a job and was supporting himself. "Anyway, Mom," he'd said, "I couldn't stand it in that all-white neighborhood. I wanted to move back here." "Here" was six blocks from the house we all had loved—a house I avoided passing whenever I could.

At least one of my predictions had come true, however. "Dad has a girl friend," Tina announced one day. I was, I realized, happy for George—and for myself. Until recently he had been phoning me often—after quarrels with the children, to get the names of workmen—and then to complain that they were "high-priced and sloppy." His calls had fallen off. A new girl friend might take pressure off me.

"She's older than Dad, she says. A widow. She says she 'set her cap' for Dad the minute she saw him. Ugh! She treats him as if he can't do a *thing* for himself. And she gushes at me about how *much* she loves him. Yuck!" Still, sorting through Tina's naturally negative comments, Nancy, the "girl friend," sounded all right.

I hoped George would not move *too* fast. Of course, we were still not divorced, a safety measure I was happy to have. Hank Putnam had proposed and so had Max Brace, another professor whom I had been dating for the past two months. It was handy to be able to say I was separated, not divorced. I liked them both, but marriage seemed like a jail term I had recently served. I might feel different later, but for now I was enjoying my parole.

There had been moments, I had to admit, when—in silly ways—I felt torn from my comfortable married state. A trip to Lord & Taylor to buy a lipstick had depressed me the first month on my own. No little green plastic card with *Mrs.* embossed on it to give me legitimacy. I had crept in, paid cash, and fled.

Now, in spite of Sandra Kane's predictions, I had my own plastic cards. I had simply opened charges with small merchants who had known me for years and used them as references at the most expensive stores in town. A few promptly paid bills established my reliability, a kind of prestige—and had given me access to whatever new credit cards I wanted.

But a wallet full of credit cards had not eased those first weeks of coming home to a silent apartment. Many days hurt. It helped to remember that being Mama in the house I had loved would soon have ended anyway. With Tige gone, and now Josh and Tina leaving soon, I would have been coming home to silence. This line of reasoning invariably brought on the merry thought, as I dropped my briefcase on the overstuffed chair, that at least I would not be coming home to George. There were, indeed, worse things than being alone.

At the college, the sheer joy of teaching increased. Theories I had always held were working. My class assignments involved news stories, features, editorials about real events in college life. Copy-editing students corrected, condensed, and criticized material for print. Marginal students somehow taught themselves to spell when it came time for their own stories to appear in the paper their friends would read. The newspaper expanded. My students were getting experience rather than busywork, learning to be aggressive and inquisitive, to get quotes right or to suffer the rage of the misquoted, to meet real deadlines.

Hank and Max Brace were fun to share teaching experiences with—and dinners and dancing. They both continued to propose. My mirror told me that I had *not* become Helen of Troy. These nice men wanted wives. Having been one, I could understand why. Having been one, I was not eager to resume the responsibilities. The first year after divorce, I had read, was dangerous anyway. People "fell in love" with opposites of the spouses who had hurt them—or twins, "to make it come out right *this* time."

George, it appeared, was feeling no such caution. Suddenly his phone calls were very, very friendly. Did I still want the painting we had quarreled over when the house was sold? (Damn right; I had owned it before marriage.) George asked "casually" when I was going ahead with the divorce. (When I could afford it.)

According to the children, George planned to remarry as soon as possible. I reminded myself that I was no longer responsible for George. He had met Nancy in July. It was now late August. Still, everything I had heard about her sounded good. She was obviously the kind of woman who enjoyed taking care of her man.

Eve said drily, "Sounds like a marriage made in Heaven—with God's usual sense of humor. And do you realize that you finally have some leverage to get a decent financial settlement?" No, I had not. But it was certainly a happy thought.

Nancy would have no real effect on my grown-up children, and I sincerely hoped the marriage would be as lucky for her as it seemed to be for me.

At school, the enormous satisfactions of teaching continued. Second semester, it was a special delight to see brand-new faces in class, to know that behind each face was a personality I would watch emerge, to try to guess which one would be the natural class leader or the student needing special encouragement.

I delighted in teaching my students about the power of the press. A course was announced as canceled. "Interview students," I suggested, "then write about how they feel." The course was reinstated. When the escalators went unrepaired for a week, student reporters "investigated" maintenance and the steps again rolled.

Tina asked to visit my classes. "Hey," she said, "you're interesting in class. Maybe I'll go into teaching. No. Psychology, maybe. Maybe work with runaway kids." She grinned. "I do have experience." Her small joke lifted my heart. Tina was well into growing up.

The semester, then another, passed. Much as I loved teaching, I was becoming more and more concerned that I had not written in almost a year. I was still coming home too tired to work. Max said, "You give too much to your students—try giving less. Pull in your antennas." I tried. For a day. Squelching the natural creativity of teaching made it into something as dull as putting bolts into slots. Sure, I could walk briskly out of class, avoiding the usual knot of students who followed me to chat or to draw me aside for some special concern. But then I missed that exciting feedback that let me know I had reached a mind. Trying to stay awake on the bus ride home, collapsing in a chair with one apologetic glance at my typewriter, I could only hope I would somehow develop the emotional muscles to teach *and* have some strength left to write.

At least my personal life was running smoothly. George had indeed married Nancy after giving me the settlement he had refused before. Sandra Kane said, "You could have gotten much, much more." Foolish, I felt, to spend time in court as some women did, "making a career of divorce." Tina had started at a local junior college—not my choice, but it did have dorms where she could live instead of in Nancy's enormous house. Tige had developed an unexpected talent for cooking, creating new dishes at his job by day—and writing his poems by night. Josh had been promoted often at the department store where he worked, and now he talked of a retailing career.

Max and Hank had agreed, rather reluctantly, that we could be "friends." I enjoyed them both—dancing with Hank and meeting his friends, having Max cook dinners for *me* in his bachelor apartment. (I had announced to both quite pointedly that *I* was taking a long sabbatical from cooking.) Hank was sure I would return to my writing "when teaching becomes routine." Max had asked, "Is there something you really feel *pressed* to write?" Well, truthfully, no. The excitement of teaching had not only exhausted me but blanked my writing mind as well. Still, damn it, other people wrote and taught. What was wrong with me?

Cy Pasnow entered the newspaper office. I had the immediate impression that, had there been no door, this husky, gray-haired man with the good-humored smile might simply have walked through the wall.

I was alone in the office. He sat down on the chair near my desk. "I need directions to the comptroller's office, but frankly I'd rather you didn't give them to me too quickly."

In fifteen miuntes Cy knew what I did and how I felt about it and had a capsule history of my life. I knew he manufactured paper supplies, had lost his wife to leukemia the year before, and was concerned about his son's early marriage. He also learned that I had not yet had lunch. After lunch, he found out that my classes were over for the day and that I had no plans for dinner.

"Cy, how respectable is it to be picked up in a college?"

"It's respectable and it's Fate. You looked hungry. We'll drive to New Jersey, meet my aunt, and she'll formally introduce us. She's a very nice lady." She was. By coincidence, she had read one of my books—and liked it.

Within two weeks, Cy had literally taken charge of my life. I was driven home, told to rest or to write if I could while he cooked dinner. "You have a precious talent. Not like me. It's going to be my job to see you have the time to write."

It was delightful, for a while. I could remember no one so completely dedicated to my comfort. This was, I suspected, how a good parent cosseted and supported a child. Inappropriate, perhaps, now that I was fifty-two, but delightful nonetheless.

Cy said, "I lost one wonderful woman to death. I have no intention of losing you."

Soon Cy's suggestion that I try to write while he cooked dinner began to work. Pieces I had promised to magazines long before the divorce (good heavens, how had eighteen months passed so fast!) began to come together in my mind. With the aroma of a good dinner wafting through my bedroom door, I began to outline articles again. Some days, at dinner time, Cy looked in, saw I was involved, and announced that dinner could wait. He spent the time rewiring a lamp that had always flickered, or even picking up my cleaning or returning my library books.

One day I stopped in the middle of writing my agent. Good heavens, this was exactly like having a *wife*. As I had done for twenty years, Cy was now handling domestic details so that I could work. Cy was supporting *my* ego. When I protested that he was doing too much, he held my hand and said, "If I help you write something important, that reflects on me too." Through great good fortune, I had found what I had once, jokingly, decided I needed: a kind of wife. I continued the letter. I should be totally happy.

Even the children responded to Cy. Josh discussed a new job offer in upstate New York. I flinched at the thought of his being so far away. Tige talked about traveling across the country. Poets, he said, needed experience, and cooking jobs were easy to get. Cy calmly discussed the pros and cons with both boys and later reminded me that children *had* to leave to grow.

Then I learned that George was being transferred to Atlanta. Fine. But George would not pay out-of-state fees for Tina's college. She would have to go to school in Georgia next fall.

That night I sobbed in Cy's arms. Of course children had to leave to grow, and I had gritted my teeth to keep from making the departures difficult for them. I had promised to drive Tina to her plane, promised Josh we would help him move his things. Tige planned to hitchhike. "Mom, just wave good-by at the turnpike." But that evening my control collapsed and I sobbed out pain.

Cy held me, then stroked my head. "There, there, honey. It will be all right."

Suddenly, I was four years old again, waiting, hoping that someone, anyone, would hold and reassure me. No one ever had. I had grown up believing no one ever would. And now, at last, someone was holding me and saying the simple words I had waited a lifetime to hear.

Strangely, my sobs stopped immediately. It was as if I had always longed to visit a special place, to know that it existed. Now I knew. It was not a place where I wanted to live; just to know that I had seen it was enough. I said, "Thank you, Cy." And, inexplicably, almost added: "I'll never forget you."

For reasons that seemed almost—but not quite—clear, I woke the next morning with a new kind of energy. My classes were more stimulating than ever. At lunchtime I wondered at the striding, head-up figure I saw reflected in windows and wearing my clothes. At the newspaper meeting I looked with excitement at all the student reporters gathering for the first session with our new editor, Jenny Gates.

Jenny had been surprised when the students elected her. I had not. Jenny had been an associate editor the previous semester. It was not a popularity contest; she was elected because of her unquestionably excellent work.

Which was being displayed, I observed, right now. The belligerence this brown-haired young lady had shown when she joined the paper had gradually disappeared, to be replaced by strong but affable command. She still wore her feminist T-shirts ("A Woman's Place Is in the House—or Senate"), but I noticed that she worked well with David, the previous editor, thinking of him more and more not as the enemy but as a colleague.

Jenny had quizzed me about my career. When I told her about opening my own advertising company, she had said, wide-eyed, "Wow! That took balls!" "No, Jenny, that took *ovaries.*" Jenny had grinned. "Touché."

Now she was conducting the meeting skillfully, finishing it up, and, with a surprisingly bleak face, asking if I had time for coffee. Of course I did. Sometimes a table in the corner of the noisy cafeteria was the place where the most important work with students took place.

Amid the din, we had to sit close to hear each other, and I could see unshed tears in Jenny's eyes. "What's the matter?"

"Ms. Stalvey, you'll think I'm silly, worrying so far ahead, but I love newspaper work *so much,* and I don't know if I have the balls —O.K., ovaries—to fight that hard for jobs on the outside. *You* know what it's like for women . . . and I don't want to fight all my life." Two large tears rolled from two brown eyes and splashed unnoticed on Jenny's copy of Germaine Greer's *The Female Eunuch.*

At that moment I realized that the feminist movement had completely passed me by. I had been too busy with civil rights, my children, my writing, the divorce, and reestablishing my life. Sandra Kane had once insisted I read Greer and Kate Millett. I had, glad I had not read them in my youth, aware that I had somehow grown up believing that women had the edge. A handy concept. I had had no idea that what I was doing was anything but ordinary. I still believed it was.

But Jenny did not. And with all her feminist reading, I found, she knew nothing of Jenny Churchill, Ida Tarbell, Dorothy Thompson. "Jenny Churchill founded a magazine back in the days when women couldn't even vote. Ida Tarbell, a reporter, took on—and beat—Standard Oil. Dorothy Thompson, back in the thirties, was the most widely quoted political columnist in the *world*. If they could do it then, think of what you can do now."

Jenny dried her eyes. "But didn't *you* have to fight male chauvinism every step of the way?"

I thought of J.D., who had pushed a teen-ager through doors instead of closing them; of all my male clients; even of George, who *too often* deferred to my judgment; of the men right now, at the college, who had hired a woman without a degree. Certainly there were places where women were underpaid and passed over for promotions. My friend and employee, Jane, had been one. But she had quit and found another job. I thought of Lovett and Wynn in Milwaukee, where I had earned more than all the men and still kept their friendship. Male chauvinism surely existed, but if I had met it, I must have rushed right by.

"But you're different," Jenny offered tentatively.

"No, Jenny, I am *not*. Maybe having a passive mother was an advantage. Being an older sister might have been too, but otherwise, Jenny, I'm about as ordinary as anyone can be."

Dry-eyed now and chin up, Jenny grinned. "About as ordinary as Scarlett O'Hara, but I see what you mean."

We talked on. Thoughts I never realized I had came out. "One thing we women have is choices. A lot more than men. My girl friends in high school *chose* marriage as a career. I guess I was lucky that I had both. But men can't choose. Noncompetitive men, untalented men, can't gracefully stay home. They have to stay out there all their lives. *They* get passed over for promotions, *they* get paid less than their colleagues." I remembered Billy, another copywriter at McCann. Billy's slum background, I felt, kept him so amazed he *had* a job that he never asked for the raises he deserved.

Jenny said, "And men can't blame their failures on being men. At least until *female* chauvinism comes along."

A possible point. White Protestant men, I said, had no place to put the blame. Then, in the noisy, crowded cafeteria, another thought surged up. I was, I realized, a little irritated these days at women being seen as a faceless group along with "all blacks," "all Jews," "all Catholics." "All blacks," as I very well knew from the mostly black students in my classes, were not lazy, stupid, and violent. "All Jews," I had learned from having David and Murray as agency partners, were not "clever" at business. Women too could be either passive or assertive, ambitious or lazy, supportive or domineering. Some, like Rachel Carson, were capable of creating the ecology movement, or, like Golda Meir, Indira Gandhi, and Margaret Thatcher, of running countries. Others genuinely prized their prerogatives to stay at home and bake apple pies. Making a woman like that feel guilty that she was not out running a corporation was like telling a flower it should be a potato. Potatoes and flowers were both important, but women—ideally, men too—should be free to choose.

Jenny's brown eyes were twinkling now. "O.K., coach, I'll go out there and win." Then, more soberly, "You helped. A lot. It *is* better to know you have a chance than to think it's an uphill fight." A bell clanged. Jenny swooped up books and ran for a class.

I stayed in the cafeteria, thinking—perhaps more than Jenny— about what I had said. Women did have choices that men never had to make. Perhaps those choices were what caused the agony and anger.

It was time to leave. Cy would be parked outside. At that moment he represented some choices too. It had been good to have him in my life. He was talking more and more of "after we get married." I made evasive replies, but perhaps it could work. I sometimes felt selfish taking all Cy gave, allowing him to smooth out my life so that I could write. But he clearly enjoyed what he was doing, had apparently done it all his married life. He and Laura had married young, built a business together, and then she had died. Now, as Tony had, he put my growth, my comfort, first.

In front of the building, there was Cy's worried face looking out from his car. "Sorry, Cy honey, a student had a problem." At home, I looked at my typewriter with its page of a half-finished article. I looked at the bed. Cy pushed me toward it and went back to the kitchen. Two hours later, his voice and the smell of steak woke me up.

Over dinner Cy said, "I *should* go up to Princeton to settle an order. Would it help you to have me out of the way for the weekend? Could you finish the article then?"

I could try. On weekends we did things I thought Cy would like —going to movies or visiting friends. With a long, quiet weekend, perhaps I could get the article done. I was doing very little on it after school.

By Saturday evening I knew, sadly, that Cy had made a mistake. It should not feel this good to be alone. I had finished the article and, dismayingly, was looking forward to a lazy Sunday. I had worked, snacked, walked through the apartment grounds to clear my head, worked, napped, and worked again. From the window I had watched a cloud and leisurely worked out parts of the article as it moved by. No one—bless them—had phoned. Tina was with her father in Atlanta, looking over the college she would attend; Josh was apartment-hunting in Ithaca, and Tige was, no doubt, involved in arrangements for his upcoming trip. Stretched luxuriously on the sofa, the article done, I realized that for the first time in more than twenty years, I was absolutely free. Even the silence in my apartment sounded thunderously pleasant.

Was there, however, something wrong with me? A loving, helpful, understanding man wanted to marry me. Yet I was ecstatic at being alone. Marrying Cy would mean an end to counting pennies, to wondering what might happen if I got sick. I thought of Sandra, of her words at my divorce: "I'd like to leave Dave too, but he's better than nothing if I get sick—or old." At the time I had thought of George. If *he* had gotten ill, I could never have left. Why did we think only of *being* taken care of when we might as easily be the ones giving the care?

Cy was much easier to love than George had been, but as I lay on the sofa, I knew I liked, admired, appreciated, and enjoyed Cy —and that that was not love. Love was what I felt for my children and for my work—the fierce, passionate protectiveness, the walking through glass without a thought; not, sadly, what I felt for Cy.

Without thinking of the pennies I had to count, I dialed Eve's new number in the small Arizona town where she had moved to be near her ninety-year-old mother. I missed the insightful conversations we had had during the chaos of the divorce. Eve too had chosen not to remarry. Perhaps she now regretted it; perhaps she would point out something I was ignoring.

Never subtle, Eve's words came over the wire. "I don't think you want to marry Cy. I think you want to write. Personally, I'll be quite relieved when you quit teaching and write your book."

What book? "The book you want to write." I could chuckle at

Eve's impractical view of my future, but I knew she was right about Cy. And Cy was too good, too loving a man to let time slip by with me. I could be friends with Max and Hank. Cy should not be "friends" with me. There was another woman somewhere for him.

On Sunday night, Cy heard what I had to say. Yes, he understood. He had hoped, but, yes, he understood. Then he cocked the square, familiar head I would miss and said, "You are the only person I've ever known who has truly conquered loneliness. Perhaps I'll learn. That may be my priceless gift from you."

At that moment, I was glad that Cy had found anything he felt repaid his kindness to me. I wished I had felt more pain when he walked out my door.

Later, his words returned. And, abruptly, my oldest memory did too. *Loneliness* was not the word. *Aloneness* was. That little girl lying on the cobblestone street after her mother had said she would be safe had learned what aloneness meant, had grown up believing that she alone would be responsible for her own survival. Odd how that memory now lifted my heart. A very early lesson that had served me all my life was serving me now. It was possible, of course, that I would love some man again as I had loved Tony and had tried to love George. But the greatest love in the world did not guarantee being together at those times when we needed our hand held most. How much better, then, to know you could— had—survived alone. And how good to have learned it so early.

I did not expect to use these skills so thoroughly so soon. But all too quickly, Tige began his cross-country trip. I waved him good-by on the turnpike as promised and even managed to smile.

Josh was leaving the following week, over the long Thanksgiving weekend. He had arranged to rent a truck to get his furniture to Ithaca. I helped him pack. My twenty-year-old looked older, competent, fully in charge. His two years of independence had made him ready to take on his world. "One last favor, Mom. Could you drive me to the Ryder place to pick up the truck?"

The truck was larger than Josh needed but all they had left. Josh signed some papers and the manager said, "You are, of course, over twenty-one."

Fifteen minutes later, I was driving a fourteen-foot truck out into the traffic. My past came back, once more, to reassure me. Driving coast to coast, at age eighteen, two days after learning to drive, had to be riskier than driving a truck at age fifty-three. I repeated this like a litany, as I followed Josh, who was driving my car, through mountains and a blizzard. In Ithaca, another parting. I saw the homesickness behind Josh's eyes, reassured him, and did not shed my tears until I had driven away.

Then, the last few months with Tina, enjoying her calls to come out to the dorm for dinner, to meet her friends, or to talk in her room; relishing our weekends at my apartment and knowing the quiet delight every mother must feel when she hears her own long-held values espoused by a daughter. And, finally, driving Tina to the airport, where she would board her plane to start college in Georgia. One last hug and I walked back to the parking lot alone, sat in the car, and waited until I could drive back to the city where my children no longer lived and wonder how to fill the weeks until my own semester started.

Back in my apartment, missing Tina dreadfully, I dusted bookshelves. I had said good-by to each of my children, but at least I had managed to let them feel comfortable about going away—the last chapter, perhaps, in the education of a mother.

Tears streaming, I dusted the books I had written. More dusting, and then I remembered the old list of goals I had set in my twenties: to have a baby, to write a book, to go abroad. I wiped my eyes. Two out of three was not bad. The last I would accomplish someday.

Why not now?

Don't be silly, I could not afford it. My savings were again for a rainy day. I could not simply put down a dustcloth and head for, say, Cairo.

Yet I had acted quickly once before, on another "rainy day." And with the weeks stretching blankly in front of me, with my daughter newly gone, it seemed pretty rainy just then. I put down the dustcloth and picked up the phone.

I continued to tell myself it was a thoroughly crazy impulse— during my call to a travel agent, while I arranged for a passport, while I planned what to pack. When my agent phoned to say she had sold an article outline for *exactly* what my trip to Egypt was going to cost, the craziness seemed like fate.

The woman travel agent had asked, "Are you going alone?" She acted surprised. I had driven a truck through mountains in a snowstorm; I hardly needed a companion on a package tour— hardly needed the tour except for room reservations.

On the plane my sense of craziness turned into a sense of unfettered delight. At my Cairo hotel I opened the blinds. There, as if I could touch them, were the Pyramids. I was surprised by my gasp; surprised, the next day, to find that a camel provided an unexpectedly comfortable ride; that the people in the countryside I toured still looked exactly like the illustrations in Grandfather's Bible.

In Cairo, Idfu, and Aswan I chatted with bearded merchants in galibiyehs. In spite of some language problems, they were as friendly as the neighborhood merchants I had known as a child.

In Luxor, at the Temple of Karnak, my mind wandered as the guide droned on. People, thousands of years ago, had spent life-times building those pillars, statues, and burial crypts in a fruitless attempt to drive *death* away. I hoped they had taken some time to enjoy *life* too. Even today, I reflected, some people did not.

Then, at the scene of such elaborate and futile preparations for eternity, I sat up straight. Soon I would be heading back to the teaching I *enjoyed*—and the struggle to do the writing I *loved*. Like those ancient people, I had believed there would always be time for what I wanted most.

On the plane ride home, when the end of my life seemed closer than I dreamed, it was simple to make the decision.

On a sunny day in Philadelphia, I packed the last cartons into my car. The moving van was already on the highway somewhere ahead.

One more crazy gamble—I grinned at my reflection in the car window—might be all I had left in me, but I did have one more. I had found a fine teacher to take over my classes and the paper. The transition would be smooth. I had enjoyed my teaching ca-reer, and if I stayed in town, its pull would always be there. Now I was taking my rainy-day savings to buy some sunny days to write. Eve had found an inexpensive house for me to rent in her small Arizona town. With the belt-tightening habits I had practiced so often before, I could survive while I wrote a book for Tina, for Jenny, and for myself.

The early-morning sunlight gleamed on my car as I got behind the wheel. The small child hit by a car at three was now, at fifty-five, able to drive one with confidence. It was only a matter—as perhaps it had always been—of turning the key and moving ahead.

Epilogue

IDEALLY, an education has no end. One new piece of knowledge came only as I wrote this book. All those years, marching along to my own drums and trumpets, I seem not to have heard the voices of those women with scars different from mine who fought—and conquered—the discrimination on which I had never even stubbed my toe.

One part of me wishes now that I had known those other women. Another part of me is selfishly glad I did not. The expectation of victory is a wonderful armor. And, because of those women who met locked doors and forced them open, it is now an even more realistic one.

But I still think of the choices my daughter must make for herself, and of the contradicting voices she will hear. Women truly content with traditional roles are urged to "achieve." Potential achievers, still trapped by tradition, exhaust themselves in dual roles. It may take several swings of the pendulum, and greater male-female understanding, before all women feel free to listen to the only voice that counts: the voice inside themselves.

As they hear it, I hope they will hear too the echoes of Albert Einstein's reply to a student who apologized to him for being female: "*I* do not mind . . . but the main thing is that you yourself do not mind. There is no reason for it."